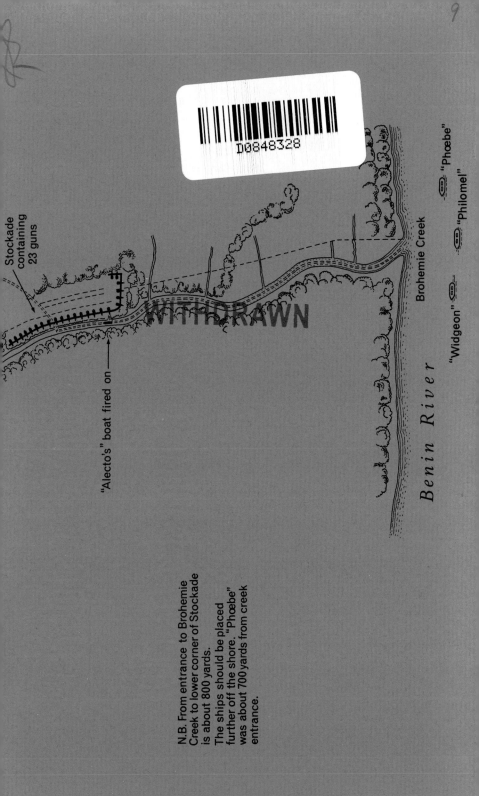

Stockade containing 23 guns

"Alecto's" boat fired on

WITHDRAWN

Brohemie Creek

Benin River

"Widgeon"

"Philomel"

"Phœbe"

N.B. From entrance to Brohemie Creek to lower corner of Stockade is about 800 yards.

The ships should be placed further off the shore. "Phœbe" was about 700 yards from creek entrance.

Merchant Prince
of the Niger Delta

Merchant Prince
of the Niger Delta

THE RISE & FALL OF NANA OLOMU
LAST GOVERNOR OF THE BENIN RIVER

OBARO IKIME
Lecturer in History
University of Ibadan

AFRICANA PUBLISHING CORPORATION · NEW YORK
An affiliate of International University Booksellers, Inc.

Published
in the United States of America 1969
by Africana Publishing Corporation
101 Fifth Avenue
New York, N.Y. 10003

Library of Congress catalog card no. 72–80852

Printed in Great Britain by Butler & Tanner Ltd
Frome and London

This is but a little book.
It is as a little token of my unutterable gratitude
to one whose love and sacrifice have made me what I am
that I dedicate it to my brother Isaac.

Preface

A great deal of work has been done in recent years on the history of West Africa in the nineteenth and twentieth centuries. An aspect of this work which has received a great deal of attention is the reaction of African peoples to the coming of European powers into their respective territories. It is now generally recognised that the beginnings of nationalist struggles in Africa date back to the nineteenth century when various African leaders spearheaded the resistance movement against European economic exploitation and political domination. In the context of Nigerian history, certain names spring readily to mind— Bishops Crowther and Johnson, Kosoko, Jaja, Ovonramwen (Overami) and Nana, the subject of this study, to mention but a few.

Although the names of these and other leading Nigerians of the nineteenth century are freely mentioned in history circles, it is a fact, at the time of writing, that on none of them is there any detailed study. The reason usually advanced for the absence of detailed studies is the lack of the kind of material required for biographical surveys. This is largely true. But the absence of detailed studies has meant that even such material as does exist has not been fully used in existing works. This book seeks to utilise existing material to present a fuller account of one of Nigeria's historical figures than is at present available.

Let me point out that I have not set out to write a biography, in the technical sense, of Nana Olomu (or Nana the Itsekiri, as most schoolboys know him). What is here attempted is a detailed study of the life of Nana Olomu in the period beginning in 1884, the year he was appointed 'Governor of the River' by the Itsekiri elders, and ending with his death in 1916, ten years after his return from the exile to which the British condemned him in 1894. The year 1884 is also important for this study because in that year Itsekiriland became British 'protected' territory as a consequence of the 'protection' treaty signed by the Itsekiri in July. A study of Nana's career during this period therefore entails an examination of his relations with the British administration.

But his relations with the British were, to some extent, conditioned by his position in Itsekiriland and his relations with the neighbouring peoples. Consequently one chapter is devoted specifically to this aspect of Nana's life. In addition, throughout the work attention is constantly drawn to how the internal Itsekiri situation affected Nana's relations with the British.

There is not, at present, a great deal written about Nana. I have therefore not used published works to any great extent. I must, however, acknowledge my debt to Dr P. C. Lloyd whose article, 'The Itsekiri in the Nineteenth Century' in *The Journal of African History* Vol. IV No. 2 1963, I have frequently cited in this work. Most of the material for this study has come from administrative records. These records have, however, been reassessed and interpreted in the light of information collected from my field investigations over a period totalling six months. Indeed it would have been impossible to produce the work in its present form without using oral traditions. In making use of this type of material, I have been constantly aware of the problems of assessing oral traditions—problems which, it is now increasingly recognised, are not far different from those involved in evaluating and using written sources.

In connection with my field investigations, I wish to put on record my gratitude to Chief Newton Celleone Nana, aged about seventy-eight, Nana's oldest surviving son, who was always pleased to discuss his father's life with me. I am also grateful to him for permission to make copies of some of the pictures in the family album. I am grateful to the elders of Abraka, Agbarho, Agbon, and Udu clans whose names appear in footnotes in the body of the work. Their accounts of Itsekiri-Urhobo trade and other relations have been extremely valuable in filling some of the gaps in the administrative records. I wish to thank my friends—G. E. Umukoro, J. Esiri, J. A. Ekpere, and W. Oshevire—who accompanied me on some of my fact-finding tours.

Some of my appendixes deserve comment. Appendix III, a 'General Memorandum' on the Ebrohimi war, the expedition mounted by the British against Nana, has been included in order to demonstrate that the British did not, after the initial stages, regard lightly the impending encounter with Nana. Appendix IV, a list of munitions of war captured in Ebrohimi, has been included to give the reader some idea of Nana's wealth and power in terms of armaments. Appendixes V (*a*) and (*b*) are two letters written to Nana by two consular officers which were submitted as Exhibits I and J at Nana's trial. They are given in full for comparison with the summaries of Ralph Moor at Nana's trial. I think that Appendix VI—minutes by Foreign Office officials on Nana's trial—is important as demonstrating what in fact the Foreign Office did think about Nana's trial and sentence.

I am grateful to the Institute of African Studies, University of Ibadan, for a grant towards the writing of this work.

My thanks are due to the respective staffs of the Public Records Office, London, and the Nigerian National Archives, Ibadan. I am also grateful to the Librarian, Royal Commonwealth Society Library, London, for permission to make copies of some of the photographs and diagrams, which appear in this study, from works deposited in that library. I thank my friend and colleague, R. A. Adeleye, not just for reading sections of this work in manuscript and making valuable suggestions, but even more for the general interest he took in it. I owe immense gratitude to Rev. Father J. O'Connell, Associate Professor in the Department of Political Science, formerly University of Ibadan who, despite his heavy load of work, read through the entire manuscript and made very useful suggestions about style and presentation. Finally I thank my wife without whose encouragement and cooperation this work would have been unnecessarily delayed.

O. I.

Department of History
University of Ibadan
Ibadan, Nigeria
July 1967

Contents

List of Illustrations

(*Note*—Nos. 4 and 5 have been copied from an Article by Lieutenant J. D. Hickley in *Royal United Services Journal*, Vol. 39, by courtesy of the Librarian, Royal Commonwealth Society Library, London.)

List of Abbreviations

Cal. Prov.	Calabar Provincial Papers.
C.M.S.	Church Missionary Society.
C.O.	Colonial Office (British).
C.S.O.	Chief Secretary's Office (Nigeria).
F.O.	Foreign Office (British).
H.M.S.	His/Her Majesty's Ship.
J.H.S.N.	Journal of the Historical Society of Nigeria.
N.C.N.C.	National Council of Nigerian Citizens.
N.C.P.	Niger Coast Protectorate.
R.N.C.	Royal Niger Company.

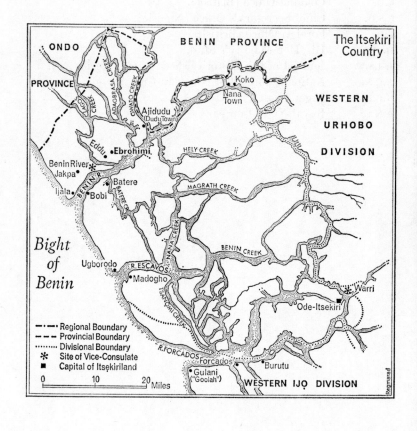

ONDO PROVINCE

BENIN PROVINCE

The Itsekiri Country

Koko

Nana Town

Ajidudu
(Dudu Town)

WESTERN

URHOBO

DIVISION

LAGOS CREEK

ADAGBASA CREEK

OWATO CREEK

HELY CREEK

Eddu

Ebrohimi

Benin River
Jakpa

BENIN R.

Batere

BATERE CREEK

Ijala

Bobi

MAGRATH CREEK

Bight
of
Benin

Ugborodo

R.ESCAVOS

Madogho

NANA CREEK

BENIN CREEK

Warri

Ode-Itsekiri

TSANOMI CREEK

R.FORCADOS

Forcados

Burutu

Gulani
("Goolah")

WESTERN IJQ DIVISION

—·—·— Regional Boundary
— — — Provincial Boundary
·········· Divisional Boundary
*   Site of Vice-Consulate
■   Capital of Itsekiriland

0   10   20 Miles

Regmarad

CHAPTER I

Introduction: Trade and Politics in Itsekiriland, 1850-84

NANA OLOMU, the last great middleman trader of the Niger Delta in the nineteenth century, was born about 1852 into the Itsekiri* community of Jakpa.[1] The town of Jakpa is situated on the right bank of the famous Benin River. The Itsekiri inhabit the north-western extremity of the Niger Delta in an area bounded approximately by latitudes 5° 20' and 6°N and longitudes 5° 5' and 5° 40' East. Their neighbours are the Bini to the north, the Ijo* to the south; the Urhobo to the east and the Yoruba of Ondo province to the northwest. Most of the area lies within the deltaic belt of mangrove swamps. Only on the eastern fringes is there some firm land. Ode-Itsekiri, the capital of the Itsekiri kingdom, which stands on part of this firm land is, in fact, only some twenty feet above sea level.[2] It is not surprising therefore that the dominant feature of the vegetation is the white and red mangrove. Itsekiriland is watered by three large rivers, the Benin, the Escravos and the Forcados. They are connected by a dense network of creeks, most of which are navigable only by small craft.

The mode of life of the Itsekiri people has been determined by their environment. The Itsekiri are primarily fishermen and, like their Ijo neighbours, are known as suppliers of fish and

* The name 'Ijọ' should be rendered thus with a dot underneath. The author has rejected the more common form of 'Ijaw' because this leads to mispronunciation by English speakers. Other names which occur throughout the text without dots are—Itsẹkiri, Ologbotsẹrẹ, Uwanguẹ, Iyatsẹrẹ, Eyinminsarẹn, Batẹrẹ, Ẹku, Ẹvhrọ, Ubviẹ, Okpẹ Kwalẹ, Orit-sẹmonẹ, Ọtọn, Dọghọ, Tsanọmi and Agbọn

[1] Neville, G. W. 'Nana Oloma of Benin' *Journal of the Royal African Society* Vol. XIV 1915 p. 162. Nana's real name was Eriomala. The name Nana was a pet or 'play name' which, as sometimes happens, virtually superseded the proper name. I have decided to stick to the name Nana as it is obviously the more widely known.

[2] Ikime, O. *Itsekiri-Urhobo Relations And The Establishment of British Rule, 1884–1936* Ph.D. Thesis University of Ibadan 1965 p. 41.

1

'crayfish' to the peoples of the hinterland. From an early date
the Itsekiri also engaged in the manufacture of salt. One process
was by evaporation of sea water. But the more widespread method
was to get it by burning the shoots, roots and leaves of the mangrove tree; a solution of the ashes was filtered and then evapor-
ated. Salt was an extremely valuable article of trade in the period
before its importation, and even today local salt is preferred to
imported salt for the preparation of certain dishes. A third industry in which the Itsekiri engaged was pottery. Salt-making
and pottery were essentially the concern of the womenfolk; the
bulk of the men were engaged in the fishing industry. The
Itsekiri have never been farmers to any great extent, their land
being little suited to agriculture. They have therefore been dependent for their agricultural products on the farming folks to
the hinterland, especially the Urhobo.

It is not, however, as fishermen or manufacturers of salt or
earthenware that the Itsekiri have made their name in history.
Their location by the sea coast enabled them to develop into
middlemen traders at an early date. Accounts by Portuguese and
other travellers indicate that the Rivers Forcados and Benin were
highways of trade from an early period. The Itsekiri took advantage of this fact and their contact with European traders dates
back to about the fifteenth century.[3] From that time till the
opening years of the present century, the Itsekiri remained the
great middlemen traders of this part of the delta. But it should
be stressed that at all times only a relatively small proportion of
the population was engaged in trade. This was because trade
required capital in cash and kind. Indeed large scale trade tended
to be the preserve of the more wealthy members of the community who, naturally, employed others not in a position to trade
by or for themselves. There thus grew up around each great
middleman trader a body of people involved in his commercial
enterprise. Some of these people would be the traders' kith and
kin; others would be non-relatives eager to make a living; yet
others would be slaves.

[3] Ryder, A. F. C., 'An Early Portuguese Voyage to the Forcados
River' *Journal of the Historical Society of Nigeria*, Vol. 1 No. 3,
1958

Although the term 'house' does appear in administrative records to describe these Itsekiri trading establishments, they themselves scarcely used the word. Perhaps the most significant thing about Itsekiri society in the nineteenth century was the tendency for each wealthy trader to found a village of his own from whence to organise his commercial ventures.[4] To such a village moved the founder's brothers and sisters, more distant relatives, close friends and slaves. All these people then constituted themselves into a corporate trading concern. At the head of this concern was the founder of the village. Authority within the village was vested in the founder and the elders who acted as a consultative council. It was unusual for the founder or head of the village to take decisions entirely on his own. All the villagers had a common interest in promoting the trade of their settlement and defending it against the encroachments of rival villages or traders. While there was a certain amount of central control over the trade of the village a great deal of freedom was left to individuals. The founder or his descendant remained, however, the leading trader of the settlement and to him everyone else looked for leadership both in time of peace and unrest. The really important point that must be stressed, however, is that because nineteenth-century Itsekiri society was dominated by these trading concerns, trade and politics became intertwined, since trade was the source of wealth and thus of power and influence. Hence it is impossible to understand the story of the rise and fall of Nana Olomu, except within the context of the trade and politics of the Itsekiriland of his age.

Nana was born at a time when important developments were taking place in the Itsekiri kingdom, for its history in the second half of the nineteenth century was markedly different from the first. Two major factors help to explain this difference. The first is that Itsekiriland seemed to have been little involved in the struggle between African slave-dealers and British naval authorities engaged in the task of suppressing the slave trade. There were few instances of visitations by the British naval squadron to this part of the Niger delta at a time when they were causing an

[4] Lloyd, P. C. 'The Itsekiri in the Nineteenth Century' *Journal of African History* Vol. IV No. 2 1963 p. 217

B

upheaval in the political and economic life of the Eastern Delta.[5]
Indeed the only recorded instance was in 1837 when a Portuguese
slaver was forced to discharge its human cargo and was itself
eventually seized by a British schooner, the *Fair Rosamund*.[6]
We look in vain for any 'slave trade treaties' negotiated with the
rulers of the Itsekiri country—the type of treaties described by
K. O. Dike for the Eastern Delta.[7] It would appear that in this
part of the delta, unlike Brass and Bonny, the trade in slaves was
negligible during most of the period after 1807. P. C. Lloyd has
stated that British admiralty records of slave ships seized and
taken to Freetown in the 1830's indicate that few ships took on
slaves in the Benin River.[8] Captain John Adams reported on the
decline in the trade of this part of the delta in the 1820's.[9]
Captain Owen confirmed Adams' view.[10] Because of the absence
of slave trading on a large scale and the general decline in trade
the British, the leading European power in the Niger delta at that
time, took little interest in the Itsekiri country in the first half of
the nineteenth century. In the second half of the century, however, the British took a great deal more interest—a fact of importance in the life of Nana Olomu.

If the overseas trade in slaves had virtually ceased in this area
by the 1830's, what was happening in the realm of 'legitimate'
trade? The palm oil trade which eventually replaced the trade in
slaves took some time to develop. By the 1820's it was reported
by Adams and others that there were large quantities of oil in
the Benin River area.[11] Owing to the lack of the type of competition which existed between the various (mainly British) firms
in the Eastern Delta, the price of oil in this area was reported to
be low.[12] By the 1840's there were two important Liverpool firms
established on the banks of the Benin River; Horsfall were near

[5] Dike, K. O. *Trade and Politics in the Niger Delta* chapters IV & V,
Oxford 1956

[6] Lloyd p. 214   [7] Dike p. 83   [8] Lloyd p. 214

[9] Adams, Captain John *Remarks on the Country Extending from Cape
Palmas to the Congo* pp. 115–16 London 1823

[10] Captain W. F. W. Owen, *Narrative of Voyages to explore the shores
of Africa, Arabia and Madagascar* Vol. II p. 357 London 1833

[11] Adams p. 117

[12] Lloyd p. 214

Bobi, and Harrison & Co near Jakpa creek. Other firms like Douglas Stewart, Miller Brothers and James Pinnock were to follow in the years after 1850.[13]

The palm oil trade which replaced that in slaves posed its own problems for the Itsekiri as for other West African middlemen traders. It called for infinitely greater organisation and resource than did the trade of the earlier period. The 'trust' system now became a more general feature of trade than it had been earlier. Not only did the white traders have to entrust goods to their Itsekiri customers, but the latter had to entrust goods in their turn to the producers of the palm oil, in this case the Urhobo (and also some Kwale) to the hinterland of the Itsekiri country. In these circumstances, it became necessary for any Itsekiri who aspired to be a great trader to be seen to be credit worthy. This in turn had its various ramifications. First, it meant for the successful trader an ostentatious display of wealth in the form of dress, house furniture, the quality and quantity of food and drink. Secondly, the trader had to possess a large fleet of trading canoes which could collect the palm oil from the various Urhobo settlements. Throughout the greater part of the nineteenth century these trade canoes were manned by slaves[14] of which, consequently, the successful trader had to own a large number. Indeed the wealth of the trader was often measured in terms of canoes and slaves, so that the internal slave trade continued for most of the nineteenth century. This explains why Nana, the greatest Itsekiri trader of his day, owned such a large number of slaves.[15]

These features of the palm oil trade led to great rivalry between the leading Itsekiri traders—rivalry in the display of opulence to justify continued trust being given, and rivalry in securing oil from the Urhobo producers. This rivalry was serious enough to lead in a few cases to war and lasting family feuds as can be seen in Chapter II. The possibility of war was only one reason why the Itsekiri trading canoes were armed, and why special canoes capable of carrying forty paddlers and a hundred fighting men were designed primarily for war. There were two other reasons: the need to strike terror, when the occasion so demanded, into the Urhobo oil producers and force them to meet the obligations

[13] Lloyd p. 214   [14] Lloyd p. 219   [15] See pp. 36 & 44

into which they had entered with the Itsekiri, and defence against Ijo attacks. The Ijo seem to have been a terror to canoes in this area. In 1856 and again in 1857, the British Consul had to take out warships against the Ijo because they had 'ventured in great force to within sight of the English factories and committed great depredations, capturing several canoes with cargoes of palm oil, making captives of their crews'. In 1863 R. Burton referred to the Ijo as a large and influential tribe who were 'almost always at war with the Jakri men, because like these they traded for oil to the Sobo country'.[16] Herein lies the explanation for the fact that the trade in arms and ammunition continued to be one of the most profitable throughout the nineteenth century. This, rather than Ralph Moor's argument that he had been deliberately building up armaments for the purpose of trying conclusions with the British authorities of the Niger Coast Protectorate, explains why Nana was so heavily armed by 1894. J. C. Anene gives the impression that Nana suddenly woke up in 1894 to the need to arm himself at a time when the British offensive against him had all but started. Apparently he did not study closely the list of arms and ammunition captured in Ebrohimi, Nana's town, after the British took it, for if he did he would have realised that it was impossible for Nana to have accumulated that quantity of arms (see Appendix IV) within a few months in 1894.[17]

The trade in palm oil also affected relations between the Itsekiri middlemen and the Urhobo oil producers. The Urhobo were not always able to meet the obligations they undertook with their Itsekiri customers. Some of them were apt to grow idle in the enjoyment of goods entrusted to them by the Itsekiri and so fail to produce the agreed quantity of oil. It was in this kind of situation that the giving of children and slaves as pledges became strongly entrenched in the commercial code observed between the Itsekiri and the Urhobo. In strict law the children thus given out as pawns were not slaves. They could be redeemed at any

---

[16] F.O. 84/1002 Campbell to F.O. No. 9, 24 March 1856. Also F.O. 84/1031 Campbell to F.O. No. 3 Feb. 1857; R. Burton, 'My Wanderings in West Africa' *Fraser's Magazine* Vol. LXXIII 1863 pp. 145–6

[17] Anene, J. C. *Southern Nigeria in Transition* p. 153 Cambridge 1966

time on payment of the outstanding debt. Similarly when slaves were given out as pledges, they reverted to their original owners as soon as the debt for which they had been pledged was paid. If, however, the debt was never paid, these pawns continued to serve the creditor and over the years the legal distinction between them and the ordinary slaves was lost as they became to all intents and purposes slaves of their new master.[18] It is here necessary to stress the point that the giving of pledges was sanctioned by local usage in view of the great emphasis which the British were to place on the issue of local slavery, whose complications and practices they did not fully comprehend. A great trader like Nana was thus clearly in a position to receive a fairly large number of children and slaves as pledges for outstanding debt. There can be little doubt that some of the slaves found in Nana's town after it was captured by the British were originally pawns.

The development of the palm oil trade had another effect on Itsekiri–Urhobo relations. Although through the system of pledges and 'diplomatic marriages' it was often possible to maintain friendly relations between the middlemen and the producers, disputes between the Urhobo and the Itsekiri were not always resolved peacefully. Sometimes the Itsekiri traders, offended by the non-fulfilment of promises made by their Urhobo customers, sent their slaves, usually described as their 'boys', to raid the villages of the offenders concerned; the idea was that slaves taken during such a raid would, by working for the Itsekiri, eventually make good the loss sustained by the non-fulfilment of the obligations previously agreed on.[19] Once under way such raids tended to become indiscriminate, since the 'boys' did not always confine their depredations to specific individuals or villages. This practice usually referred to as 'chopping'[20] was to be frowned upon by the British administration in the years after 1891. Once again it was regarded as perfectly normal by the Nigerian peoples concerned,

---

[18] Ikime chapter II
[19] Ikime chapter II
[20] The origin of the word is not clear. It would appear to have been first applied to the seizure of oil by European supercargoes in lieu of debt owed them by African middlemen.

so much so that Nana had no hesitation in admitting, during his trial by the British in 1894, that some of his slaves were obtained as a result of such raids.[21]

The second factor which made Itsekiri history in the second half of the nineteenth century different from that of the first was the interregnum which was ushered in by the death of Olu Akeng-buwa I in 1848.[22] Akengbuwa's two princes, and most likely successors, followed him to the grave with an astounding rapidity which one source has attributed to a curse by the Oba of Benin.[23] The death of the two princes was followed by a civil disturbance organised, it would appear, by the slaves of the late Olu and princes. Backed by Iye,[24] they were determined that no other prince of Akengbuwa or any other eligible candidate[25] should occupy the throne. William Moore states that the slaves planned 'a wholesale massacre of the adult princes of Olu Akengbuwa'.[26] It is not clear, however, whether they carried this out. What is definite is that the slaves were so powerful that no one succeeded in seizing control of the capital from them. Thus Iye and Ebri-moni, one of the head slaves, became for a while the only people who could exercise a measure of political control over the capital and its immediate environs. Efforts made in 1851 to elect a new Olu proved futile as will be seen later.[27] To the problems arising from the palm oil trade was thus added a new problem of a

---

[21] F.O. 2/64. Evidence of Nana at his trial

[22] Lloyd p. 215

[23] Egharevba, Jacob *A Short History of Benin* p. 47 Ibadan 1960

[24] See pp. 10–11

[25] Succession to the Itsekiri throne was not based on primogeniture. The brothers, half-brothers and sons of the dead Olu were all qualified to contest for the throne. See C. O. Omoneukarin *Itsekiri Law and Custom* Lagos 1942 p. 26

[26] Moore, William *History of Itsekiri* p. 91 Stockwell 1936. This slave revolt would seem to have been different in aim and scope from those which were soon to take place in the eastern delta, for neither did the slaves seek to take over power for themselves, nor did slaves belonging to other masters join them in their revolt and so transform it into a general slave rising. The revolt by the slaves seems to have been content with preventing the installation of an Olu. But that they succeeded in doing this is an indication of the power that the slaves possessed in those days.

[27] See pp. 15–16

political nature. While the Olu lived he provided a much needed central authority which could exercise control over the Itsekiri people and attempt to solve some of the problems connected with trade. In the absence of an Olu there began a struggle for power among the leading Itsekiri traders. Where before descent was a major factor in determining the role a man played in the political and social life of the Itsekiri community, in the new situation created by the interregnum, wealth derived from trade increasingly became the surest qualification for the acquisition of power and influence. This situation made it possible for men with the necessary drive and organising ability to rise to positions of great power and authority within the Itsekiri community. This was the situation which produced the class of *nouveaux riches* to which Nana belonged and which dominated Itsekiri history throughout the second half of the nineteenth century.

The Itsekiri were normally ruled at the centre by their king, whom they called Olu, and an advisory council of state. The council of state was made up of seventy titled men, or Ojoye; the Ojoye date back to the foundation of the kingdom when the Bini prince, Ginuwa, the founder of the Itsekiri dynasty, who was said to have been accompanied by seventy sons of Bini nobles, conferred on the latter titles similar to those in use in Benin. The titles of all seventy are not now remembered but the most important were without question those of the Ologbotsere, Uwangue, and Iyatsere. The Ologbotsere was the Olu's prime minister and chief adviser, the Uwangue was the custodian of the Olu's regalia, his chief spokesman in council and, most important of all, the person who crowned the Olu during his installation. The Iyatsere was the war captain.[28] Itsekiri usually seek to trace their genealogy to the royal family or to one or other of the other important families. Princes and princesses of the royal house were called Oton-Olu. Strictly speaking only children born to the reigning Olu were expected to use the name Oton-Olu.[29] In practice, however, all those used the name who could trace any connection between their ancestors and any of the Olu who have reigned since the foundation of the kingdom. Indeed the Itsekiri are extremely touchy about their *ebi*—their family group. Inability to

[28] Omoneukarin pp. 26-7   [29] Omoneukarin pp. 26-7

trace one's genealogy satisfactorily is often regarded in Itsekiri society as evidence of a slave origin.

Earlier it was stated that during the interregnum wealth rather than birth became the surest qualification for wielding power and influence. This statement now needs to be qualified and amplified. While it still carried some prestige to belong to one of the important *ebi*, one's fortune in the context of the entire kingdom was determined by ability in commerce. The men who wielded influence in Itsekiriland in the second half of the nineteenth century did so not mainly because they were Oton-Olu or belonged to the *ebi* of the Ologbotsere, Uwangue or Iyatsere but rather because they succeeded in building themselves up as wealthy traders. Yet, as will be shown,[30] there was a way in which birth into a particular *ebi* influenced and sometimes virtually decided the role people played in the trade and politics of the kingdom during the interregnum.

The two diagrams below show the genealogies of the leading characters mentioned in this study.[31] First the royal family group, which has been divided into two for convenience. The group which concerns us more is that which has been styled the 'House of Emaye'. Emaye was the daughter of an Ijo woman married to an Itsekiri man, Egharegbemi who was at the time the Iyatsere. The Olu Erejuwa I married Emaye who bore for him two daughters, Uwala and Iye. On the death of Erejuwa I Emaye was inherited by the former's son who became the Olu Akengbuwa I and for whom she bore one daughter and two sons, Omateye and Ejo. Emaye thus had five children from her two marriages. Of these five Iye was perhaps the best known for she seems to have possessed a forceful character and personality. European travellers and traders sometimes referred to her as 'Queen Dola', which was a corruption of her other name Idolorusan. Akengbuwa's reign was a long one and some of his more obvious heirs died before him. Consequently by the time he died, Omateye had become recognised as the heir. But there were

---

[30] See the account below.

[31] The genealogies are taken from Lloyd p. 213. I am heavily dependent on Lloyd for the account which follows. Lloyd for his part follows very closely on William Moore.

2. Itsekiri Ceremonial Canoe

5. Nana's state canoe

4(*a*) Nana's Palace Koko (Outside View)

4(*b*) Inside View of Nana's Palace

5. Johnson Nana in 1944
(By courtesy of Nana's family)

6. Newton Celleone Nanna
in 1965 (By courtesy of
Nana's family)

THE ROYAL LINE

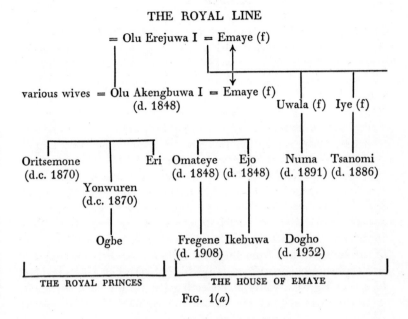

THE ROYAL PRINCES   THE HOUSE OF EMAYE

Fig. 1(*a*)

THE HOUSE OF OLOGBOTSERE

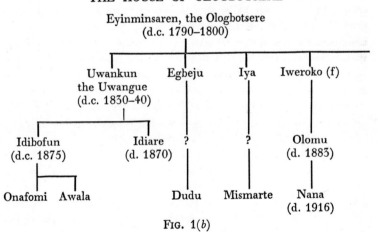

Fig. 1(*b*)

other children, born to Akengbuwa by other wives, and between these and the children of Emaye there was great rivalry often marked by considerable animosity. Of these other children the best known in Itsekiri tradition is Ugbaga. According to Moore the rivalry between Ugbaga and Omateye was extremely fierce. He states that Akengbuwa intended that Ugbaga should succeed him but that Omateye contested the succession with the latter. Both princes engaged in all sorts of intrigues against one another to the great unhappiness of their royal father. The kind of rivalry that took place is best illustrated by the comey episode. The Olu Akengbuwa appointed Ugbaga Governor of the River and gave him the traditional staff of office as well as a flag, both of which were to serve as emblems of his authority to collect the comey from European traders.When Omateye saw that Ugbaga had been appointed Governor of the River he sought a way of wresting the office from him. After consultation with Iye, he ordered replicas of the staff and flag from England. When these arrived Omateye waited for an opportunity to dupe his half-brother. News reached him that Ugbaga would be collecting the comey on a particular day. He therefore set out before the rightful governor to the Benin River, where most of the European traders were anchored. When the European traders saw his staff and flag, they paid the comey to him in the belief that he was the Olu's accredited representative. Some time afterwards, Ugbaga arrived to demand the comey and was told that Omateye had already collected it. Ugbaga was extremely angry and went back to complain to the Olu who was unable to do anything to Omateye. Moor implies that the death of Ugbaga soon after this incident was brought about partly by the disappointment which he felt on this and similar occasions. At any rate after Ugbaga's death Omateye became recognised as the undisputed heir to the throne.[32]

The death of Ugbaga did not remove the basic conflict between the children of Emaye and the other princes. If anything the recognition of Omateye as heir merely worsened the situation. Indeed there was the fear that on Akengbuwa's death an open conflict would break out between the two rival groups within the royal family. Batere on the Benin River was founded by Uwala

[32] Moore pp. 63-6

and Iye to provide a refuge for their brothers, Omateye and Ejo, should the latter be forced to flee from the capital as a result of armed conflict. Batere on the southern bank of the Benin River thus became associated with the house of Emaye. Tsanomi, Numa and Dogho[33] belonged to this house as can be seen from the diagram.

During the reign of Erejuwa I in the eighteenth century, the then Ologbotsere, Eyinmisaren, founded the settlement of Bobi, also on the southern bank of the Benin River. Some time in the nineteenth century, Uwankun, who was the Uwangwe and who is believed to have been one of the junior sons of Eyinmisaren, founded Jakpa on the northern banks of the Benin River in the general exodus from the Itsekiri capital of Ode-Itsekiri for which the reign of Akengbuwa I is remembered. Other children of Eyinmisaren hitherto resident in Bobi joined Uwankun at Jakpa. The 'house of Ologbotsere' thus became established on the northern bank of the Benin River.[34] Idiare, Olomu and Nana belonged to this house (see diagram).

There were thus three groups—the royal princes at Ode—Itsekiri, the 'house of Emaye' and the 'house of Ologbotsere'—sufficiently well organised to influence the running of the affairs of the Itsekiri kingdom during the second half of the nineteenth century. In fact the commercial and political rivalry between these groups, and more particularly between the 'houses' of Emaye and Ologbotsere, was to be the main feature of Itsekiri history during the period.

As already indicated two British firms, Horsfall and Harrison & Co, were established in the 1850's along the Benin River. Although about half of Harrison's trade was done with members of the Ologbotsere group, there is no evidence that this firm was in any way hindered from trading with members of the other two main groups. In 1863, for example, those indebted to the

---

[33] Tsanomi's full name was Oritsetsaninomi. The shortened form Tsanomi is given as Chanomi in the consular records. Dogho's full name was Omadoghogbone. This was shortened to Dogho and is rendered in British accounts as 'Dore'. Except when quoting, the proper shortened form, Dogho, is used throughout this work.

[34] This account is based on Lloyd and Moore.

firm included persons from all three groups.[35] What was true for
Harrisons was probably true for the other firms. It was thus a
matter of open competition for the rival groups to secure a fair
amount of trade from the various firms established on the Benin
and other rivers in Itsekiriland. As political power was in this
age dependent on commercial success, the rivalry expressed itself
in political terms as well. The career of Nana Olomu was pro-
foundly affected by this fact.

The beginning of the interregnum virtually coincided with
the appointment in June 1849 of the first British consul for the
Bights of Benin and Biafra in the person of John Beecroft, a
British merchant already familiar with the trade and politics of
the Niger Delta.[36] The appointment by the jingoistic Palmerston
was a recognition of the fact that there was enough British property and investment in the Bights of Benin and Biafra to justify
the cost. The consul's primary duty was to protect the lives and
property of British traders in the Niger Delta. And the lives and
property of these British traders did require protecting. The
turbulence of the age was caused mostly by the difficulties and
problems of the palm oil trade. Now the British traders were provided with an authorised agent of their home government to
whom they could cry for help in times of difficulty. The appointment was, in the context of this work, even more important
in another respect: the era of consular authority was the immediate prelude to the establishment of British rule in the Niger Delta.
Nothing was more decisive in the career of Nana than the establishment of British rule over Itsekiriland in 1884.

Two years after his appointment Beecroft paid his first official
visit to the Benin River at the request of the British traders there.
Some of their factories had been looted in the period of general
confusion immediately following the death of the Olu.[37] They
were convinced that the absence of an Olu was responsible for the
'depredations' committed against them. While the lack of a central authority must have been one factor responsible for the outrages about which the white traders complained, it was not the

[35] F.O. 84/1203 Freeman to F.O. 10 April and 29 Aug. 1863
[36] Dike, p. 95
[37] F.O. 84/858 Beecroft to F.O. 24 March 1851

whole story. One has only to study the situation in the eastern Delta at the time to realise that the presence of a king or other traditional ruler did not prevent clashes between white traders and coastal peoples. In Bonny, for instance, Anna Pepple once imprisoned British merchants with whom he had a quarrel arising from trade.[38] The real cause of the unrest of the period lay in the nature of the trade and the character and aspirations of the two groups of people actively involved in the drama of delta trade and politics. The men concerned—white and black—were men schooled in the rough and tough days of the slave trade. 'Chopping', high-handed and rough and ready justice (often injustice) characterised the period.

Beecroft's aim in visiting the Benin River was thus twofold— to obtain redress and to get the Itsekiri to elect a new Olu in the hope that he would keep a firm grip on his people and so prevent a recurrence of the kind of incidents that had brought him to the Benin River. Strangely enough the Consul left no details of the complaints of his countrymen. But while he was actually in the district, the people of the town of Bobi, led by their chief Tsanomi, attacked and looted Horsfall's factory.[39] The cause of the attack is not known but, judging from subsequent incidents,[40] it is unlikely that it was undertaken out of sheer desire for loot. Beecroft was filled with great indignation. In a note to the naval authorities, he requested that a gunboat be sent to the Benin River to mete out condign punishment: 'The sooner a man of war arrives the more pleasing it will be to me, for these scoundrels must be well chastised with powder and shot.'[41] This was characteristic. Beecroft was determined to leave no doubts as to the power and authority which the Consul could bring to bear on these perennial disputes between white traders and the delta peoples. The gunboat requested did arrive, and Beecroft proceeded to bombard and burn down Bobi,[42] thereby establishing the pattern of Afro-

[38] Dike, pp. 74–5
[39] F.O. 84/858 Beecroft to F.O. 20 March 1851
[40] See pp. 19–23
[41] F.O. 84/858 Beecroft to the 'first man-of-war' in the Bight of Benin 19 April 1851
[42] *Ibid*

British relations in this as in other parts of the delta: whenever a dispute arose between British traders and the delta middlemen, the latter had almost invariably to face punishment irrespective of the rights and wrongs of the case.

Beecroft's second objective was to get the Itsekiri to elect a new Olu. His failure can be partly explained by the fact that his endeavours were inseparable from the punitive measures against the Itsekiri. Naturally Beecroft first discussed the issue of a new Olu with the royal princes. The royal princes could not agree among themselves as to which of them was to be raised to the high office. Oritsemone and others suited by their wealth to fill the office were disqualified by the fact that they were children of slave women. The other princes were too poor to command respect in an age in which wealth and political authority went hand in hand. Beecroft's suggestion that Ebrimoni be made Olu was unanimously rejected because it was contrary to well-known Itsekiri law and custom: no slave could occupy the Itsekiri throne.[43] Beecroft made another unsuccessful attempt in 1853. Thereafter no other efforts are recorded as having been made to elect an Olu and the Itsekiri kingdom thus passed into an interregnum which lasted till 1936.

Having failed to get an Olu elected, Beecroft got the Itsekiri to appoint a 'Governor of the River'.[44] This was not a new office created to meet the needs of the interregnum. It had developed earlier as a result of Itsekiri commercial activity with the Europeans. The duty of the 'Gofine', as the Itsekiri called him, was to collect the 'comey' due from the vessels before the Europeans were allowed to trade in the Olu's territory. As trade was the main source of wealth and so of prestige for the royal household, so the office of Governor became of great importance, and by the beginning of the nineteenth century it had developed into a very important office of state. In addition to collecting the comey, the Governor had the duty of generally supervising the Olu's commercial activities, the Olu himself being the chief trader of the nation.

[43] Lloyd p. 216
[44] An account of the proceedings during which the Governor was appointed is given in Cal. Prov. 5/7 Vol. I.

In normal circumstances, the appointment of the Governor was the sole responsibility of the Olu. He did not, it would appear, have to consult his council, and the bearer of the office did not have to be an Oton-Olu or a descendant of one of the noble houses of Itsekiriland.[45] As long as there was an Olu, the appointment of a Governor was a relatively unimportant matter, as he was essentially the ruler's servant. In the changed circumstances of the 1850's, however, the status of the Governor became radically altered. First, there was the intervention of a British consular authority to bring about his election. From 1851 till the fall in 1894 of Nana Olomu, the last Governor of the River, the British authority in these parts was always involved in the choice and deposition of successive Governors of the River. Secondly, having been elected, the Governor became the only duly appointed executive authority in Itsekiriland a circumstance which, while enhancing the stature of the Governor, rendered his position extremely difficult. From the point of view of the Europeans, the Governor was a necessary officer of state who was expected to keep some hold on his people and to protect their lives and property. They looked on the Governor as head of the Itsekiri whose responsibility it was to ensure peace and order in commerce. The Itsekiri themselves had their own conception of the duties of the Governor. They saw in him their leader under whom they could combine against the white traders in the difficult matter of fixing acceptable prices. This was clearly incompatible with the European conception of the duties of the office, and was to produce future misunderstanding and strife.

When Beecroft summoned leading Itsekiri men to the meeting at which the Governor of the River was elected, neither the royal princes from Ode-Itsekiri nor members of the 'house of Emaye' attended,[46] because it was immediately after Bobi had been 'chastised with powder and shot'. Thus it was mainly the Ologbotsere house that was represented at the meeting at which Idiare was elected Governor. In view of the enhanced status of the Governor it is easy to see how the election of Idiare from the Ologbotsere group was bound to lead to resentment among the

[45] Omoneukarin, C.O. p. 28
[46] Cal. Prov. 5/7 Vol. I Beecroft to F.O. 20 March and 19 April 1851

royal group. It was probably in an attempt to lessen the tension arising from this situation that the Itsekiri sought to rotate the governorship of the river from one to the other major group. Idiare having been elected in 1851, in 1870 it was the turn of Tsanomi from the royal group. When in 1879 Nana's father, Olomu, from the Ologbotsere group was elected,[47] the pattern was maintained. But on Olomu's death in 1883 it was not another royal 'chief' who became governor but Nana. The pattern was thus disrupted and the Ologbotsere group appeared to be in the ascendant. It can be argued that by 1884 Nana was so powerful that it was politic to appoint him Governor rather than appoint someone else whose authority Nana could flout with impunity. Be that as it may, it is most likely that the royal group felt cheated and that therefore the opposition of Dogho from that group to Nana, as will be seen throughout this work, was explained by political as well as economic considerations.

The election of a Governor of the River was only one aspect of the general desire to protect the interests of the British traders in Itsekiri territory. One of the first things that Idiare did as Governor in 1851 was to sign an agreement with Beecroft aimed at regulating the commercial relations between the Itsekiri and the British traders. It is difficult to imagine a more one-sided document.[48] It is unnecessary to discuss here every clause of the agreement, but a few of the more important provisions may be examined. The first clause provided that the detention or molestation of any white trader on shore 'under any pretence whatever' would be regarded as an offence against Her Britannic Majesty and would involve the sending of a man-of-war to 'protect British subjects and property', a refined way of threatening that a gunboat would be sent to mete out fiery justice. Article 3 made it obligatory for the white traders to pay the traditional comey before commencing to trade. But, according to the provisions of Article 4, if for some reason the Governor refused to accept the comey when offered, the white traders could go on and trade. Article 5 imposed a fine of one puncheon of oil

[47] See p. 25
[48] Cal. Prov. 5/7 Vol. I. See Appendix I for a full text of this agreement

per day on every '100 tons of Register' on the Itsekiri in the
event of the trade of any vessel being stopped 'upon any pretence whatever' once the comey had been paid. Article 8 summed
up the purpose of the agreement:

> Whereas several boats have been plundered and lives sacrificed, it
> is deemed just and right, that all such aggressions, and depredations,
> committed upon British subjects and property crossing the Bar or
> otherwise within the limits of the chief of the River Benin domin-
> ions shall be satisfactorily adjusted by the said chief.

As the territories of the 'said chief' were not defined in the
agreement, the way was left open for the Governor to be held
responsible for adjusting 'acts of aggression' committed in areas
over which he had no *de facto* jurisdiction. While every provision was made to protect the whites against the blacks, no
provision was made to protect the blacks against the whites. The
Governor was expected to punish his people if they destroyed
property belonging to the white traders. What happened when
the reverse was the case? The Governor had no powers to act. It
was hardly conceivable that, given such a system, the Itsekiri
traders would wait for the Governor to act on their behalf when
their oil or other property was 'chopped' by members of a white
community that was as 'lawless' as the Itsekiri were often
portrayed in consular reports. In fact the turbulence of the age
was partly due to this kind of agreement. Despite the obvious
unfairness of the agreement, however, it remained the only
instrument duly signed and executed which guided Afro-British
relations in the Benin River during the period up to 1866 when
a new but equally one-sided agreement was signed.[49] Not even
the 'protection' treaty signed by Nana and other leading Itsekiri
citizens in 1884 corrected the element of injustice noticeable in
the 1851 agreement.

Throughout the era of consular authority, the relationship
between the Itsekiri and the white traders was uneasy. It was
not easy to tackle the two main factors responsible for this uneasiness—the fixing of prices acceptable to both sides, and the
question of debt inherent in the trust system. The fixing of

[49] See p. 23

c

prices for palm produce was complicated. The white traders had their eyes on the European market and tended to offer such prices as would assure them what they considered a reasonable profit. The coastal middlemen, unable to check on the European market prices and so uncertain about the fairness of the prices which the white traders offered, tended to resent any fall in prices. When there was a fall in prices, it was the practice of the middlemen to hold up their palm produce in the hope, thereby, of forcing up the price. The white traders invariably resented this economic sanction which the leading Itsekiri traders, and more especially the Governors, were able to bring to bear against them, and their usual reaction to such a situation was to send a protest to their consul and request his intervention with a view to the resumption of trade. One of Nana's offences in the opinion of the British authorities was that he adopted this sanction of stopping trade in 1886 at a time when the price for palm produce had fallen by about forty per cent.[50]

By far the greatest source of disagreement between Itsekiri and the white traders in the period up to 1884 was the question of the debts which were the inescapable concomitants of the trust system. There were many instances when a disturbed situation arose in the Benin River district, either as a consequence of parties failing to agree on the amount of debts outstanding, or white traders seizing oil belonging to Itsekiri traders in an endeavour to make good outstanding debts. To take an instance: on 24 May 1862 the factory of a Mr Henry was plundered by the 'boys' of an Itsekiri trader named Ikebuwa. The events which led to the incident are typical of the relations between the white traders and the Itsekiri middlemen. It is best to quote from the report of the Consul, Freeman, to the Foreign Office: 'In the spring of the year 1861 Mr. Henry, by one of those acts of prepotency to which coast Traders frequently resort to obtain a settlement of their claims, seized fourteen puncheons of oil belonging to a chief of the name Akebua having first pretended he would pay him a good price for it.'[51] As a matter of fact, Ikebuwa at the

---

[50] See F.O. 2/64, Evidence of Nana at his trial.

[51] F.O. 84/1201 Freeman to F.O. No. 9, 10 April 1863. The following account is from the same despatch.

time only owed Henry six puncheons of oil. Naturally, therefore, Ikebuwa went 'several times' to demand payment for the other eight puncheons. But 'Mr. Henry at last seized him and kept him in confinement and according to the general report in the river, which is however denied by Mr. Henry, kept him chained by the neck.' Ikebuwa was eventually released.

On 22 April 1862 a number of Ikebuwa's slaves, probably with their master's consent, attempted to steal a new anoe belonging to Mr Henry as a reprisal for the rough treatment handed to their master. Henry's krooboys gave chase, brought back the canoe, and took prisoner one of Ikebuwa's slaves. The prisoner was severely manhandled by the krooboys and was only handed over to a friend of Ikebuwa a few hours before he died. Ikebuwa immediately demanded not only his outstanding debt but compensation for the loss of his man. He was ordered out of Henry's premises. Ikebuwa left with a threat that when he did return he would obtain payment by force. By this time Henry himself had left the Benin River for England. His agent, fearing that the threat might be executed, applied to Governor Idiare for protection. The Governor dutifully sent an armed guard to Henry's premises. 'But Mr. Henry himself arriving a day or two after sent away this guard saying he could protect his own premises, thus taking the responsibility on himself.' Exactly a month after this demonstration of ingratitude to the Governor, and expression of confidence in his own powers, Ikebuwa's men attacked Henry's factory and carried away various articles including cases of gin. Henry immediately requested the consul to come to the Benin River and execute justice.

Freeman's settlement is interesting. He realised fully that Henry had, to a great extent, brought about the events which had taken place. He discovered that the white traders had stopped paying comey for some years and commented:

> This alone is sufficient to account for many of the irregularities and abuses of such frequent occurrence in the Benin [River], for it cannot be expected that chiefs who are such merely in name and have not the means of supporting their authority, should be held responsible for acts which they have not the power to prevent.[52]

---

[52] *Ibid*

In his letter to the various agents on the River requesting their assistance in fixing the value of the goods stolen from Henry's factory, Freeman wrote, 'You will understand that in requesting this information I am actuated by a desire that both the white man and the black in this river should obtain strict and impartial, and if necessary severe justice'.[53] The British Government, the consul warned, would not allow the coastal peoples to commit unprovoked outrages on the factories of the white traders. At the same time, the British Government would never allow the English traders 'to violate all principles of law and justice' and then hope to be protected by the might of the British navy when the coastal people reacted to the provocation. But despite this bold declaration of his determination to mete out impartial justice, the consul imposed a fine of thirty-five puncheons of oil on the Governor and other chiefs whose armed guard Henry had insolently sent off his premises, and twenty puncheons of oil on Ikebuwa himself. Henry received no punishment. Why this settlement? Freeman himself provides the answer:

> Notwithstanding the circumstances which led to the attack on Mr. Henry's factory in which I consider him so much to blame as to have deprived himself of any right to claim compensation still such an outrage would not be allowed to pass unnoticed or unpunished by Her Majesty's Government.[54]

This was a far cry from the lofty ideals of justice propounded by Freeman. It is significant that the Foreign Office did not censure the Consul or reverse his settlement.

In circumstances such as these, the Itsekiri could hardly be expected to put much confidence in either the white traders or their consul. It was therefore not surprising that they should have decided to take the law into their own hands on a number of occasions. In 1864, for instance, a Mr Hineson of Harrisons was seized by an Itsekiri trader because his firm had refused to pay an outstanding debt. Hineson was beaten up and detained until he paid a three puncheon ransom. Immediately the consul heard

[53] F.O. 84/1201, Enclosure 6
[54] *Ibid.* F.O. 84/201

of it he steamed to the Benin River and imposed a fine of twenty-five puncheons on the Itsekiri concerned.[55]

For the Governor, who was supposed to hold the Itsekiri in check, the position was extremely difficult. He could scarcely keep his men under control when, in fact, he had no guarantee that he would obtain redress for injuries done by the white traders against the Itsekiri. In 1866 the Governor Idiare had to stop all trade with the whites by 'placing armed canoes on the river and occupying the beach with an armed force' in an effort to secure the settlement of a dispute with Harrisons.[56] The whites were not paying the comey which Freeman had enjoined them to pay. There seemed to be no means of coercing the white traders to meet their obligation in this regard, for the consuls never seemed to have found it possible to insist on the payment of comey as a qualification for the right to protection.

In an effort to find some solution to the continued strife in the Benin River, Elmes drew up a new agreement with the Itsekiri traders in 1866.[57] Briefly, the new agreement provided that the Itsekiri (including the Governor) were never to stop trade, but that 'all disputes and questions involving prohibition of trade' were to be decided by the British consul. The chiefs were charged with the responsibility for punishing their men who attacked British property or persons. But where the British traders wronged the Itsekiri the issue was to be referred to the consul for trial and settlement.[58] This was hardly an improvement on the former situation. The Itsekiri were still left with no immediate means of securing redress. At any rate previous trials and settlements by the consul were not such as to inspire confidence.

Events which followed the agreement of 1866 made by Elmes, the Acting Consul, showed quite definitely that no real solution had been found. The *status quo* remained unaltered. The British traders continued to refuse payment of comey and the Itsekiri

[55] F.O. 84/1221 Freeman to F.O. No. 6, 9 June 1864. See also F.O. 84/1250 Commander Wilmot to Acting-Consul Glover 6 Jan. 1865—Enclosure 1 in Glover to F.O. No. 1, 3 Feb. 1865

[56] F.O. 84/1265 Elmes to F.O. No. 4, 9 June 1866

[57] F.O. 84/1265 Elmes to F.O. No. 5, 8 July 1866

[58] The text of the agreement is an enclosure in the despatch cited above.

continued, when they could, to seek redress in their own way. In 1868 a Foreign Office despatch to the Consul, Livingstone, requested that he inform British traders in the Benin River that they should not expect the British Government 'to enforce upon the African chiefs an observance of their treaty engagements unless British subjects on their part set an example by fulfilling their treaty obligations'.[59] But what was required was more than a theoretical recognition of the faults of the British traders. Such a theoretical recognition needed to be translated into practical policy: refusal by the consul to inflict punishment and fines on the coastal peoples unless their guilt was, in fact, proven and punishment of British traders who dealt unjustly with their African customers. The consuls did not ever seem able to achieve this degree of fairness in their dealings with the Itsekiri people. It is important to remember that this was the situation into which Nana was born and in which he grew up. His attitude to the British was, up to a point, conditioned by the prevailing Itsekiri ideas of British justice.

Although, despite such incidents, trade seems to have gone on satisfactorily most of the time, there can be no doubt that in the relations between the British and the Itsekiri the balance was still heavily tilted in favour of the former. The deciding factor was without question the might of the British navy. Britain was determined to protect the lives and property of her nationals even when this meant it was necessary to jettison ideals of justice and fair play. If in an age when British interests were mainly economic the people of the delta were subjected to injustice it was unlikely that, in the age of the scramble for Africa—an age which coincided with Nana's rise to power in Itsekiriland—when international competition and diplomacy exerted additional pressure on policy, Britain would allow considerations of strict justice to stand in the way of her imperial ambitions. The Nana episode showed that where ideals of justice clashed with British economic and political interests the former were relegated to the background.

Between 1857 and 1884, when Nana became Governor of the River, there were three Governors—Idiare (1851–70), Tsanomi

[59] F.O. 84/1290, F.O. to Livingstone (Draft) No. 10, 13 April 1868

(1870–9) and Olomu, Nana's father (1879–83). It is impossible to examine in any detail the career of these Governors. Although the records say nothing about regular meetings of Itsekiri elders summoned by the Governors, the likelihood is that the Governor consulted the elders when he found it possible and necessary to do so. It should be stressed that the Governor's position in this regard was difficult. The Itsekiri social structure was at the time undergoing a change. There was no Olu and consequently no traditional nobility. The old sanctions which regulated social and political behaviour could not be rigidly applied. The Governors, despite their links with either the royal or Ologbotsere house, were chosen more because they belonged to the class of new men with the wealth and power to enforce a measure of political control than because they belonged to the traditional nobility. While the Governor was a welcome agent for dealing with white traders, he could not always command the loyalty of all the Itsekiri. His immediate kith and kin and all those involved in his commercial ventures constituted his most loyal supporters. The other leading Itsekiri traders were either active or potential rivals and could not be expected to co-operate fully with the Governor in settling the affairs of Itsekiriland. In such a situation the authority of the Governor over his own people was necessarily circumscribed and a great deal depended on the personality of the holder of the office. Added to this internal difficulty was the problem of dealing with the white traders. Both Idiare and Tsanomi certainly found their task difficult. The Henry affair indicated some of Idiare's difficulties. As already stated, Idiare had to stop trade in 1866 over some dispute with the white traders. Tsanomi who succeeded Idiare also found himself in a position in which he had to place a ban on trade with the whites, for which act he was deposed by the British consul in 1879.[60] The Consul, Easton, reported that Tsanomi's stoppage of trade was for 'purely personal reasons'.[61] It is doubtful if this was the case, for Olomu, who was at this time one of the most wealthy and powerful Itsekiri traders, observed the ban. Olomu himself was appointed Governor in Tsanomi's place in 1879 and retained

[60] Lloyd p. 220
[61] F.O. 84/1541 Easton to F.O. No. 4 December 1879

the office till his death in 1883. By this time the general situation along the delta was changing. Nana, who succeeded his father as Governor, had not only to face the old question of acceptable prices; he had also to face the new problem posed by Britain's imperial interests in this part of West Africa.

CHAPTER II

Nana Olomu's Antecedents

THERE WERE two major factors which determined Nana Olumo's rise to eminence and fall from power; one was his inheritance, while the other was the age in which he lived. Nana was the son of Olomu. Olomu's father was Asorokun. His grandfather was Ofoluwa who, according to Lloyd, 'was perhaps a governor at Bobi at the turn of the century'.[1] Olomu's family traced their descent through Ofoluwa's father, Mufeme, to the Olu Abejioye whose son, Udefi was Ofoluwa's grandfather.[2] It would thus appear that by tracing his descent through five generations Olomu could establish some connection with the Itsekiri royal family. Olomu's mother was Iwereko, a daughter of the Ologbotsere Eyinmisaren. Nevertheless, despite these connections with the two most important family groups in Itsekiriland Olomu's career, like that of his son after him, was determined not by family connections but by his own application and drive.

Olomu, it has been suggested, was born about 1810.[3] He was thus born and gew up at a time when the trade of the Benin River was reported to be on the decline.[4] This was the period, as was pointed out in the last chapter, when the trade in palm oil replaced that in slaves and, in the process, called for new techniques and a great deal more organisation; a period when rivalry between the leading traders was a regular feature of the commercial life of the Itsekiri; a period remarkable for its turbulence. Yet it was in this age that Olomu established himself as one of the wealthiest Itsekiri traders of his, and of all, time.

[1] Lloyd p. 222
[2] Interview with Chief Newton Celleone Nana, oldest surviving son of Nana Olomu, at Koko 2 Oct. 1963. According to William Moore, Abejioye was the tenth Olu from Ginuwa's time. He was followed by two others—Omagboye and Atogbuwa before Akengbuwa. See Moore p. 23
[3] Lloyd p. 222   [4] Owen p. 357

The fact of Olomu's wealth and power is not in any doubt. In 1851 he signed the agreement between Beecroft and the Itsekiri traders directly after Idiare, the Governor, and Idibofun, Idiare's elder brother[5]—an indication that by that time he was already one of Itsekiriland's leading traders. Twenty years later he was clearly the foremost trader in the Benin River area, for on the death of Idiare in 1870 the Consul, McLeod, wrote to the British Foreign Office suggesting the appointment of Olomu as Governor of the River as he was 'the only chief having intellect and a force sufficiently organised to keep peace in the river' In fact it was not until 1879 that he was appointed Governor as, in 1870, Tsanomi was appointed to the office.[6] Another British consul wrote of Olomu, 'Aluma is a very clever native, he is the oldest and richest chief in the country and never gives any trouble.'[7] It was the opinion of James Pinnock, a British trader who spent over forty years in the area, that 'the most powerful chief ever known to Benin [River] was Alluma'.[8]

Commercial success in the nineteenth century was not easy to come by. Olomu's success must therefore be seen as evidence of his organising ability and resourcefulness. As already pointed out, the development of the palm oil trade led to the growth, between the Itsekiri middlemen traders and the Urhobo producers, of the same kind of relationship as existed between the Itsekiri and the white traders. In the interest of their trade the white traders found it profitable and, thus, expedient to give credit to those Itsekiri whose wealth enabled them to wield political power. Similarly, in order to ensure a regular supply of oil from the Urhobo, it was the custom of the Itsekiri traders to give goods in trust to leading Urhobo men, and to make outright presents to those who were in positions of authority and who could therefore influence their men to sell oil to the 'boys' of their Itsekiri friends.[9]

[5] See Appendix I   [6] F.O. 84/1326 McLeod to Vivian 11 May 1870
[7] F.O. 84/1508 Hopkins to F.O. 4 Dec. 1878
[8] Pinnock, James *Benin: The surrounding country, Inhabitants, Customs and Trade* p. 32 Liverpool 1897
[9] The account of the commercial relations between the Itsekiri and the Urhobo given in this work is based mostly on my own field investigations over a period totalling six months.

Olomu's main sphere of influence was along the Ethiope River and also up the Warri River, through Evhro (Effurun), to the various settlements of the Agbarho clan such as Ukan and Mogba. Along the Ethiope the main centres were Okpara, Ukhuokori (Kokori), Eku, Igun, Oriah and Abraka. In the Agbarho clan his commercial success was closely connected with his deep friendship with one Ovwha who was then the Osivie Agbarho (clan head). Olomu, it is said, used to give generous presents to Ovwha as well as advance goods with which to secure oil. Ovwha on his side did his best to encourage his people to sell their oil to Olomu's 'boys'. Relations were extremely friendly between the Olomu and Ovwha families.[10] Although Olomu enjoyed great trading privileges as a result of these relations with the Agbarho clan head, he did not prevent other Itsekiri from trading to the area. Indeed a similar alliance to his existed between Numa, father of Nana's implacable enemy, Dogho, and the Mowarin family of Mogba. In the other places where Olomu traded, the pattern was the same. In Evhro not only did he establish profitable friendships but he married Memese, Nana's mother, and so established a strong connection which not even the rockets of the British navy succeeded in shattering.[11] Both at Okpara Waterside and Igun (in Agbon Clan) Olomu is remembered as having attracted greater trade to the area by widening the creeks, so that his trade canoes could more easily use them, and by establishing depots to which the Urhobo took their oil.[12] Here, as in Agbarho clan, other Itsekiri traders like Tsanomi, Numa and Dudu were allowed to do business though they could not rival Olomu in sheer volume of trade.

Olomu also traded with the Abraka area. Here, however, there was not that same cordiality which existed in the Agbon, Uvbie (Evhro) and Agbarho clans. There arose a number of disputes over trade which led to armed conflict, although it is not clear what led to the unrest. It would appear that the Urhobo people

[10] Interviews with Okpalefe, Ovwha's son, 9 Sept. 1963 and with Newton Celleone Nana 2 Oct. 1963

[11] The account of the burning of Evhro is given in chapter IV.

[12] Interviews with Akoko Oghoghovwe (aged c. 90) and Oraka Ukavwe (aged c. 65) on 16/17 Sept. 1963

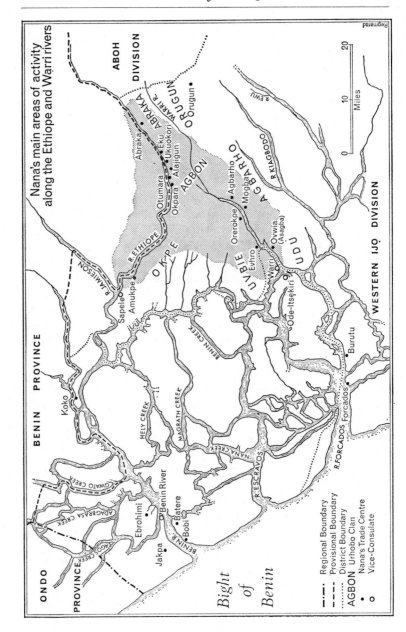

here were particularly difficult to deal with. Olomu complained that the Urhobo people demanded that he and other Itsekiri traders should pay a comey amounting to two-thirds of the oil they carried through the Ethiope River.[13] There was also a group of people who raided all canoes passing up and down the river. The result was tension which often led to stoppage of trade. Olomu, as a keen trader, was disturbed by these stoppages; on one occasion at least he had to take the field against the Abraka people in an endeavour, according to him, to force the people to reopen trade. On that occasion, Olomu was entirely successful and carried away eighty prisoners among whom were three 'chiefs'. It was the rumour that Olomu had murdered these prisoners in cold blood that took the British Consul, Hartley, to the Benin River in 1876. As Olomu was ill at the time, it was Nana who appeared before Hartley. Nana denied the charge of murder against his father. What had happened, he said, was that one of the 'chiefs' had died of self-imposed starvation, and the other two had committed suicide by hanging—an act which Nana explained in terms of the preference of the 'chiefs' to die rather than return to their country after the disgrace of being taken prisoners. To further convince the Consul that his father had not committed the atrocity which rumour attributed to him, Nana offered to take him to see the prisoners or else stand trial in a consular court where the charge could be proved or discredited.[14] The Consul seemed satisfied with Nana's explanation and so let the matter drop. It is significant that though the Consul warned against a recurrence of war, he did not express any horror or alarm at the fact that prisoners had in fact been taken. Events like the war against the Abraka over trade were inseparable from the commercial ventures of the time. Failure to meet one's commercial obligations was not infrequently met by some form of conflict during which it was customary to take prisoners who, if not redeemed, became slaves of the captors. By accepted

[13] F.O. 84/1455 Hartley to F.O. No. 54, 24 Nov. 1876. This particular episode is well remembered by the Abraka elders—Interview with Uwumiakpo Eyabere (well over 90 years old and of the Ovie family) and others at Abraka 27–29 Sept. 1963.
[14] *Ibid*

standards, therefore, Olomu had done nothing strange. It is necessary to stress the fact that, whatever the causes of tension in the Abraka area, Olomu's commercial activities there were not as peaceful as elsewhere. The tradition of hostility was to continue all through the period of Nana's ascendancy. The immediate prelude to the British offensive against Nana was commercial unrest in the Abraka country which the British blamed on the excesses of Nana and his 'boys'. The British were to find out for themselves later that the Abraka were an extremely truculent people.[15]

There were two other occasions, remembered by the Urhobo and Itsekiri alike, when Olomu's commercial activities led to war against certain Urhobo people. It has been pointed out that it was customary for the Urhobo to give to their Itsekiri customers slaves in lieu of oil owed. One of Olomu's wars in Urhoboland was caused by the complications which arose from this practice. Some Igun people had given slaves to Olomu in lieu of oil. A number of these slaves later ran back to Igun and Olomu demanded that they be handed back to him. The Igun people refused to comply with Olomu's request, and the outcome was a war from which Olomu emerged victorious, taking a large number of prisoners of war from the defeated.[16]

Olomu's second war was the Ogiegba war, as it is called. Ogiegba was an Urhobo trader from Amukpe in Okpe clan. The Okpe people, because of their geographical proximity to Itsekiriland, were semi-middlemen who did a profitable trade in slaves. Ogiegba, a leading Okpe trader, noticed that the Itsekiri, by going into the hinterland through the Ethiope, were undermining the trade of the Okpe people. He therefore decided to oppose the Itsekiri by raiding their trade canoes. As the Ethiope was one of Olomu's main spheres of activity, he found his trade canoes falling victims to Ogiegba's depredations. Accordingly, Olomu took the 'field' against Ogiegba and forced the latter to withdraw from the Ethiope and so desist from further attacks against Itsekiri trade canoes.[17]

[15] See Epilogue
[16] Interview with elders of Igun 16 Sept. 1963
[17] This episode is still well remembered by the Urhobo and is discussed by Moore p. 102

Olomu's victory in these wars was an indication of his strength in terms of war canoes and armaments. But it was not only against the Urhobo that Olomu fought. He also fought against the Ijo and his fellow Itsekiri. Olomu's war against the Ijo, according to Itsekiri traditions, was caused by their seizure of one of Akengbuwa's widows. Attempts by the royal family to ransom the widow failed. In the meantime, Olomu had been taken seriously ill and it looked as though his end had come. In traditional style Olomu consulted an oracle as to the cause of his illness. He was informed that the late Olu was angry with him because he had allowed his widow to remain in captivity even though he possessed the power to secure her release. Olomu thereupon promised to fight for the widow's release if he recovered from his illness. Soon afterwards Olomu got better and redeemed his pledge by going to war against the Ijo. He was completely victorious and not only secured the release of Akengbuwa's widow but also took many prisoners of war. This war is well remembered in Itsekiriland today not because of the supernatural aspects of Olomu's illness and recovery, but because of the great daring involved in confronting the Ijo whose power on the rivers was dreaded by all. As William Moore puts it 'nobody dared carry war into the Ijo country at this time, and expect to return to his home victorious'.[18] Yet Olomu dared. But he dared only because he was sufficiently equipped to take them on—another pointer to the tremendous power for which he is remembered.

Against his fellow Itsekiri men Olomu fought three wars. Two of these wars had to do with his trade to the Urhobo country. It was natural that there should have been rivalry among the leading Itsekiri traders at the Urhobo markets. Indeed the surprise is not that there was such rivalry or that there were skirmishes between 'boys' of rival masters, but that on the whole there were so remarkably few. It is all the more significant, therefore, that Olomu was involved in those few wars that there were among the Itsekiri of his day. The probable explanation for this was Olomu's outstanding success in trade—success which won for him the envy of the other Itsekiri traders.

Olomu's first war in Itsekiriland was against the royal princes

[18] Moore pp. 93–4

led by Oritsemone, and was occasioned by the success which attended Olomu's efforts at opening up trade at Ukan (in Agbarho clan). The royal princes resented Olomu's penetration into an area they probably desired to retain as an exclusive sphere of influence. In the war which resulted from Oritsemone's attempts to push Olomu out of the area, Olomu again emerged victorious.[19] The second war which took place in 1867 resulted from Olomu's insistence on reopening trade with an Urhobo market to which Idiare had closed all trade, because his canoes had been robbed there. Apparently, Olomu did not think that Idiare's stoppage of trade was in this instance justified and so on this occasion he defied the Governor.[20] He was again victorious in the war which followed. This war between Olomu and Idiare was an unusual event as it was rare for members of the same *ebi* to engage in war. This is why Itsekiri traditions tend to refer to it as a war between the slaves of Idiare and those of Olomu. Nevertheless this war, together with the others, indicate quite clearly that commercial success in those days had its peculiar hazards, and show that Olomu was on the whole a powerful trader. It is also important to note that on at least one occasion Olomu had to fight for his right to trade with an area from which others sought to exclude him. The desire to build up a monopoly was not peculiar to Olomu or Nana, though one of the ostensible reasons for the British offensive against Nana in 1894 was that he had established one.

Olomu's third war against his fellow Itsekiri was even more momentous for the later career of his son, Nana. This war, known as the Tsanomi-Olomu war, resulted from a debt owed to Olomu by Iye, sister to the Olu Akengbuwa. The matter of the debt had been adjudged in Olomu's favour by Akengbuwa before he died

[19] This and the other wars are discussed by George Neville in 'Nana Oloma of Benin'. The original manuscript can be found in Holt Papers Box 7/File 4; the published version in *Journal of the African Society* Vol. 14, 1914–5 pp. 162–7. (Later references are to the published version.) See also Lloyd, p. 223 and Moore pp. 95–9. The tension generated by the Olomu-Idiare war was not settled till Consul Livingstone visited the Benin River in 1868. See F.O. 84/1290 Livingstone to F.O. No. 7, 25 Feb. 1868

[20] See Lloyd p. 221

in 1848. But Olomu did not immediately ask for a settlement
of the debt until some years after the death of Akengbuwa.
Tsanomi, who was at the time managing the affairs of the
Iye household, refused to pay the debt on the grounds that
Olomu demanded more than was due to him. When it became
obvious that the dispute might lead to war, prominent Itsekiri
men like Idiare and Yonwuren sought to effect a reconciliation.
William Moore states that Olomu was disinclined to go to war
but that Tsanomi, goaded by his brothers, refused reconciliation
only to suffer a crushing defeat at the hands of Olomu. It has
been suggested that it was because of this humiliating defeat that
Tsanomi was offered the Governorship of the River in 1870,
instead of Olomu who, by virtue of his undoubted wealth and
power, was a strong candidate for the post; the hope was that he
could thereby make up some of the losses he had suffered as a
result of the war.[21]

Two of Olomu's wars against his fellow Itsekiri men were thus
waged against members of the royal house. Olomu's success in
these wars indicated not only his superiority in arms, ammunition and sheer numbers of fighting men but also his commercial
ascendancy; it was a source of humiliation to the 'house of
Emaye'. The feud between the Olomu and Tsanomi families
thus had its roots in the events of Olomu's lifetime. Numa, who
was Tsanomi's cousin, inherited this feud and was seen by the
British consular authorities as representing, among the Itsekiri,
the opposition to Nana's ascendancy. But it was Dogho, Numa's
son, who carried on the feud to its bitter end. The bitterness of
the feud was, as has already been suggested, worsened by Nana's
election as Governor of the River in succession to his father when,
in accordance with previous practice, the royal line would have
been expected to furnish the candidate for the governorship.
Moore suggests that the 'house of Emaye' deliberately brought
up Dogho to oppose Nana and so re-establish the primacy of the
royal group in Itsekiriland.[22] If this is true, then as this study will
bring out, Dogho lived up admirably to the expectations of his
family group.

[21] See Moore p. 98 and Lloyd p. 220
[22] Moore p. 108

D

Although it is impossible to express in exact terms Olomu's strength in arms, he could scarcely have become the richest trader in the Benin River, as described by the Consul, Hopkins, in 1878,[23] without amassing huge armaments to safeguard his canoes against Ijo attacks as well as against rival Itsekiri traders. Olomu lived at a time when the external slave trade had been abolished and when domestic slavery was the backbone of the Itsekiri economy. In these circumstances, it was possible to own a large number of slaves who carried on the actual trading. Each war canoe was said to be capable of carrying 40 paddlers and about 100 armed men.[24] Olomu's slaves have been variously numbered at 1,000, 3,000 and 4,000.[25] Nana was to inherit both his father's armaments and his slaves.

In the last chapter reference was made to the founding of Batere and Jakpa. The movement from the Itsekiri capital and its immediate environs to the Benin River reached its peak during the nineteenth century. The reasons given for this exodus are first, that it was a reaction by the leading Itsekiri families against the reputedly harsh and oppressive rule of Akengbuwa I. Secondly, the movement was inspired by the need to meet the European trade which was in the nineteenth century shifting from the Forcados to the Benin River.[26] The foundation of Jakpa by Uwankun is thus explicable by both these factors. However, once the movement away from the capital began, it became a regular feature of Itsekiri political and economic development. Every successful trader tended to want to found his own settlement to which he went with his immediate kith and kin. Thus Tsanomi left Batere to found his own village of Deghele, with which Dogho was later associated. Similarly Olomu left Jakpa for Ebrohimi which he founded in his determination to branch out on his own and expand his commercial activities.[27] The exact date of the founding of Ebrohimi is not known. Neville claims that Nana was born while Olomu was still at Jakpa,[28] which would indicate that Ebrohimi was founded after 1852, the year in which Neville claims Nana was born. Ebrohimi was situated inside a

[23] F.O. 84/1508 Hopkins to F.O. 4 Dec. 1878   [24] Lloyd p. 229
[25] Lloyd p. 218   [26] Lloyd p. 212
[27] Moore p. 93   [28] Neville p. 162

small creek off the Benin River. As became clear during the Ebrohimi expedition of 1894, the site could not have been better chosen for defence. The only approach to the town was through a creek which could be easily blocked and defended by a battery of guns. An advance through the mangrove swamps was a hazardous task which, as the British forces were to discover, entailed bridging or wading through innumerable creeks.[29] The land on which Ebrohimi itself stood was probably reclaimed, for the entire surrounding area was mangrove swamp. Most of the credit for the laying out of what has been described by various people as a model town[30] has tended to go to Nana, largely because it was made famous by his career. It seems more likely, however, that Nana merely improved on the work of his father, as the following description of Ebrohimi in 1894 tends to indicate:

> The different chiefs' houses were wooden, two-storey buildings on a European model, and roofed with galvanised iron.
>
> The principal street ran between Alluma's [Olomu's] house and Nana's battery; it was about 100 yards long and 40 yards wide, perfectly straight, and beautifully clean, with a surface of hard white sand. The houses each side were superior ones, and were roofed with galvanised iron. . . .
>
> The finest house was Alluma's, and it also contained the principal magazine. This was on the ground floor; the walls were 18 inches thick, of hard clay; outside these were iron wood piles, the whole faced with sheet iron. . . . The dwelling apartments were immediately above, and evidently well furnished, as the walls were almost covered with very large handsome mirrors. The bedrooms had beds with spring mattresses, etc . . .
>
> Nana's house was connected with an extensive range of warehouses containing his trade stores. . . . The store-houses were European built with iron roofs.[31]

One of the ironies of Itsekiri history is that, despite early missionary endeavour, the bulk of the Itsekiri did not embrace

[29] See chapter IV

[30] See for example Geary, William N. M. *Nigeria Under British Rule* p. 109 London 1927; Johnston, Sir Harry *The Story of My Life* p. 212 London 1923

[31] Hickley, Lieutenant J. D. 'An Account of the operations on the Benin River in August and September, 1894' *Royal United Services Institution Journal* Vol. 39 pp. 196–7

the Christian faith until the beginning of the present century.
Olomu played some part in bringing about this situation. After
the efforts of the Catholic missionaries had failed to produce any
permanent results,[32] no other attempts were made to convert
the Itsekiri till about 1875 when Bishop Ajayi Crowther once
more took up the task on behalf of the Niger Mission. The Bishop's
plan was to establish a mission centre among the Itsekiri. For this
purpose he sought an interview with Olomu, generally acknowledged by that time as Itsekiriland's most influential figure. The
interview between the Bishop and Olomu was interesting. The
bishop put his case strongly. Apart from the spiritual benefits
that would accrue to the Itsekiri on their conversion to Christianity, he pointed to the progress that had taken place in Lagos,
Calabar, Bonny and Brass where Christianity had secured a firm
footing. He particularly emphasised the benefits which the
education sponsored by the mission conferred on its recipients.
Olomu listened attentively to Crowther's arguments, but
refused to accept the Christian faith on behalf of his people. His
own counter-arguments were typical of the reaction of many an
African to the coming of Christianity. He feared the effects which
Christianity would have on the customs and culture of his
people. He argued that once the young generation acquired the
European habits which tended to go with Christianity, they
would ignore their own indigenous customs and traditions: they
would acquire, for instance, the habit of shaking hands with their
elders instead of going on their knees in true Itsekiri fashion.
As for education, Olomu feared that it would produce a class of
indolent youths, unwilling to do any form of manual work. In
vain did the Bishop point out that European manufactures were
produced by an educated and Christian people. Olomu refused to
be convinced about the necessity of a Christian mission centre in
Itsekiriland, and so Crowther had reluctantly to give up the
struggle.[33] No other attempt was made to convert the Itsekiri

[32] For an account of these efforts, see Ryder, A. F. C. 'Missionary
Activities in the Kingdom of Warri to the Early Nineteenth Century'
J.H.S.N. Vol. 2 No. 1 Dec. 1960

[33] C.M.S. Archives. CA/013, Crowther, D. C. 'A missionary Trip to
the Benin River' Oct.–Nov. 1875

people until after the establishment of Sir Claude Macdonald's administration in 1891.

Some of Olomu's objections to the introduction of Christianity and education were justified. Christianity and Western European forms of education did tend to create a social revolution which was hardly to the advantage of the elders of traditional society. Over a century has elapsed since the introduction of Christianity and western education into certain parts of Africa, and educationists are still concerned with evolving a system that will produce educated men who do not resent or despise manual labour. It might here be pointed out that in 1875 Olomu did in the religious sphere what his son was to do in the political and economic spheres in the 1890's, but with very different results. In 1875 Olomu held his ground against an African missionary and got away with it. In 1894 Nana held his ground and refused to give up the accustomed ways of doing things. But this time he was not dealing with an African bishop, but with an imperial power. In this regard 1894 was a far cry from 1875.

It was a fitting end to what was decidedly an illustrious life that Olomu should have filled in his last few years the highest office of state available at the time. For following the deposition of Tsanomi in 1879 for stopping trade, the Consul, Easton, appointed Olomu as Governor of the River.[34] He held that office until his death in 1883.[35] All the accounts are agreed about Olomu's greatness which he acquired through hard work and organisation and not just through position or influence conferred on him by birth. He must have left his son, Nana, a sizeable inheritance of trading and war canoes, a large number of slaves as well as a considerable quantity of armaments.[36] When, therefore, Nana followed his father as head of the Olomu family in 1883 and as Governor of the River in 1884, he stepped into a great inheritance.

Nana was not the oldest son of his father. In fact he was one of Olomu's younger sons born possibly in 1852 at Jakpa.[37] Nana was thus still a boy when his father engaged in some of the wars

---

[34] F.O. 84/1851 Easton to F.O. No. 41, 18 Dec. 1879
[35] F.O. 84/1660 Howett to F.O. 28 July 1884
[36] Neville   [37] Neville p. 162

described above. Neville claims that Nana served his apprenticeship in his father's war canoe, first as a paddler and then as one of his father's personal bodyguards.[38] If so, Nana's impressionable mind must have conceived of his father as fighting for his right to trade where he pleased. He probably realised early in life that in the age in which he lived success as a trader required not only business acumen but also ability and courage to fight one's way up to the top.

It is not clear how it came about that Nana succeeded to his father's entire heritage. The usual practice was to divide up the inheritance among the children. One source claims that Nana became sole successor because he was attentive to the needs of his father during the latter's old age.[39] A legend attributes it to some supernatural 'opening' of Olomu's eyes which enabled him to see that of all his sons Nana would make the most worthy successor.[40] Neville suggests that it was Nana's brilliance and courage as a warrior that determined his father to single him out as his successor.[41] Whatever the reasons for Nana's choice as sole successor, the fact that he succeeded to his father's entire inheritance was extremely important for his career. On the one hand he inherited his father's undoubted wealth and power and thus started his own career already Itsekiriland's wealthiest and most powerful man. Not only did he inherit the tangible asset of his father's wealth, but he also inherited the intangible but equally valuable friendships and goodwill which his father had established in the Urhobo oil producing area. On the other hand, however, he inherited his father's enmities both among the Urhobo and the Itsekiri. This was as significant a factor in Nana's life as the other aspects of his inheritance. Thus the hostility of the Abraka people and the hatred of the 'Emaye house' which developed during Olomu's lifetime continued to plague Nana, and contributed to the creation of the situation which ended with Nana's fall and eventual deportation.

The only description of Nana which has been discovered, is:

[38] Neville p. 162
[39] This is the view expressed by Nana's oldest surviving son, Chief Newton Celleone Nana
[40] Lloyd p. 224   [41] Neville

'The chief [Nana] . . . is a spare built man, standing about five
feet six inches with most intelligent features—a high forehead
projecting over a pair of keen piercing eyes, the face being
rounded off with a chin indicative of much determination.'[42]
There is no doubting his intelligence. All who met him were
agreed on that. After he had defended his father before the
Consul, Hartley, against allegations of the massacre of Abraka
prisoners in 1876, the British official described him as 'a very
intelligent young man . . . well acquainted with the English
language'.[43] Later Consuls and others were to uphold this
verdict.[44]

The picture of Nana the man has tended to be completely
obscured by that of Nana the Governor and trader. This is because
the official records were concerned almost exclusively with the
latter aspects of Nana's life. This is clearly an unsatisfactory position. It is worth quoting at length an account of Acting-Consul
Harry Johnston's visit to Nana in Ebrohimi:

Nana before 1888 was deemed to be a very truculent personage by
the traders. I went to the coast settlements at the mouth of the
Benin River to meet him in the winter of 1887–8, and found him
different to the trader's description: he was a fine looking Negro,
dressed in somewhat Muhammedan fashion in flowing garments. I
investigated his complaints and found them in most cases justified.
. . . Nana then gave me an invitation to come and see him at his
town in the interior. I decided to trust myself to him, and accordingly was taken up to his place in a magnificently arrayed canoe.
I was greatly astonished at its large buildings of white-washed clay,
neatly thatched, its broad and well-swept streets and the good order
of its population. I was lodged in a really comfortable house where
he fed me with well-cooked meals, and in the afternoons and even-
ings entertained me with interesting and sometimes spectacular
displays of athletic sports and dancing. It was almost like taking
part on the stage in a fantastic ballet. Hundreds of women dressed
in silks and velvets and armed with large long-handled fans of horse
hide or antelope hide executed elaborate and on the whole decorous
dances. Perfect order was maintained.

[42] *Lagos Weekly Record* 3 Nov. 1894
[43] F.O. 84/1455 Hartley to F.O. No. 54, 24 Nov. 1876
[44] See chapter III

I have seldom enjoyed more any African experience than my visit to Nana: the comfort of my lodging, the good, well-cooked food, the ordered quiet; his politeness and regard for the value of time. He himself talked fairly fluent 'Coast' English, so that intelligent conversation was possible with him. In addition he was a considerable African linguist in the tongues of the Niger Delta . . . I wish I had made his acquaintance a year earlier as he would have been a valuable adviser in Delta politics.[45]

Johnston was no over-enthusiastic negrophile. His account is therefore the more significant as testifying to the kind of person Nana was outside the uneasy spheres of trade and politics.

No doubt Nana had a good inheritance. He was not, however, the type who sat back and squandered it. In bettering his lot he followed in the footsteps of his father. Like him Nana concentrated on the Urhobo markets along the Ethiope and Warri Rivers. In the Agbarho clan he continued the friendship with the Ovwha family, cementing the relationship by marrying Ejemutohwo, a daughter of that family, as well as another Agbarho woman with the Itsekiri name of Emebiren.[46] These marriage alliances became a matter of general policy. In the Udu clan Nana took to wife Ikogho from the village of Ovwia, who was to be the mother of Chief Newton Celleone Nana, the present head of the Nana family.[47] In the Abraka area Nana sought to improve relations through marriage alliances and took two wives, one of whom, Agbemeta, was the daughter of Madubi, an influential trader.[48] Where Nana's father had not left behind friends who could ensure that trade was attracted to him he proceeded to make new friends. In Okpara (Agbon clan), for instance, he made friends with some of the leading traders such as Nwajeri, Ukavwe and Owere.[49] The fact that Nana was himself, through his mother, partly Urhobo was an added advantage.

---

[45] Johnston pp. 212–3

[46] Interview with Okpalefe Ovwha (son of Nana's great friend) 9 Sept. 1963

[47] Interview with Chief Aya Yovbake at Aladja (Udu clan) 22 July 1962, confirmed by Newton Celleone Nana

[48] Interview with elders of Abraka 27–9 Sept. 1963

[49] Interview with Oraka Ukavwe and others at Okpara Waterside 16 Sept. 1963

The organisation of trade remained very much along the lines laid down by Olomu. Nana sent his head slaves to establish depots along the watersides of Urhobo towns. There were many such depots dotted along the rivers, the most important areas of operation being the watersides of Okpara, Ukhuokori, Eku, Abraka and Otumara. The head slaves did not tour the Urhobo country buying palm oil and arranging to transport the oil down to their waterside depots. They depended on the Urhobo to bring the oil to them. This was why it was important that Nana should have friends and relations by marriage at the most important centres who could attract trade to him.

It was not only Nana's connections in Urhoboland which enabled him to achieve the monopolistic grip on the trade of the area about which the British administrators were to complain. After all other Itsekiri traders had similar connections, even though Nana's known wealth and power would obviously make him a much sought-after customer. He beat his rivals largely because of his great wealth, which enabled him to entrust more goods to his Urhobo customers than his rivals could. The Urhobo remarked on the promptitude with which he entrusted goods and on his generosity to his friends. He was never known to be indebted to any of his customers. It was more usual for the Urhobo to be behind in supplying oil for which goods had already been entrusted. This picture of Nana as a great and trusted trader is general in the Urhobo areas with which he traded, even including places such as Abraka and Eku which had suffered defeat in their wars against Nana.[50] He never seemed to have allowed past quarrels to influence his general trade relations.

In the age in which he lived, power and wealth went together. Nana's connections in Urhoboland, his trade organisation and his reputation as a trusted customer were backed up and made possible by his power in terms of war canoes and armaments. These factors taken together explain his virtual monopoly of the trade of the Ethiope and Warri Rivers. That Nana won such a monopoly must be conceded. There is, however, some room for debate about the particular methods he used for achieving it. The official records explain the monopoly solely in terms of Nana's

[50] See p. 44

raids which forced all other traders to keep out of his preserves.[51]
More imaginative writers have spoken of the suppression of
undue competition by fire and sword and of midnight raids on
desirable markets.[52] Enough has been said to make it clear that
Nana's success was due to other factors as well. This is not to say
that Nana's power in terms of armaments played no part in his
commercial success. He had the advantage of his father's reputation. Neville in his eulogy of Nana claims, with a touch of
exaggeration, that he had 20,000 war boys, a force of some 100
war canoes and over 200 trade canoes.[53] In these circumstances,
Nana's would-be rivals thought discretion the better part of
valour and withdrew from his known spheres of influence, thereby facilitating the building up of the monopoly. Nothing succeeds
like success.

In the Urhobo country also Nana's power stood him in good
stead. It seems that his career as head of the Olomu family began
with the war against the Urhobo of Eku. Igben committed
adultery with one of Olomu's wives and then fled to his mother's
town. Nana pursued Igben to Eku and demanded that Igben
be given up. The Eku elders refused to hand over Igben to Nana
and a war ensued. Eku appealed to Abraka, their close neighbour,
who readily came to their aid. Despite the Abraka aid, however,
Eku was severely defeated, after which Nana carried the war to
Abraka and harassed the people so much that they were forced
to flee to settlements in their hinterland so as to escape Nana's
severe punishment.[54] These wars, especially that against Abraka,
had the effect of continuing the hostility noticeable in the relations between the Olomu family and this part of Urhoboland.
Like the Itsekiri, the Urhobo were thus fully aware of Nana's
might. One consequence was the absence of keen competition,
which in turn meant that Nana could dictate his prices. Some of
the trade disputes between the Urhobo and Nana arose as a result
of low prices, though these would seem to have been peacefully

[51] See chapters III and IV
[52] Bindloss, Harold *In the Niger Country* p. 206 Edinburgh 1898
[53] Neville p. 164
[54] Interview with elders of Eku 22–4 Sept. 1963. See also footnote
48

resolved most of the time. Indeed despite Nana's strong position, the impression of him which has persisted among the Urhobo is that his methods were generally more pacific than aggressive.

Although most of the actual trading was left in the hands of the Oloruko[55] (as the head slaves were called), Nana was not content to leave his commercial affairs entirely in their hands. He himself toured the more important markets from time to time in order to strengthen personally his contacts with the Urhobo traders. If Nana was thus eager to maintain friendly relations with the Urhobo with whom he traded, he did not, it would appear, allow such relations to detract from a sense of his own importance. He seems to have been conscious of his wealth and power and to have wished others to see and recognise these and treat him with due deference. The story is told of a visit which Nana paid to Okpara. Ukavwe, one of his closest friends in that town, went out to meet him. Nana insisted that this man, who was much older than he, should kneel down before him as a token of respect. This was against traditional usage and Ukavwe refused to do Nana's bidding. As a result Nana ordered his 'boys' to seize Ukavwe and hold him captive, the close friendship notwithstanding. It cost Ukavwe's son nine slaves to redeem him.[56] This awareness of his power was one of Nana's traits which the British were to find irritating in the years after 1889. Ukavwe's reaction too was interesting. As Nana's friend he was no doubt fully aware of the physical force which the latter could command. But he stood on his dignity and preferred to be taken captive rather than abdicate his self-respect. This was typical of the relations between Nana and the Urhobo. The Urhobo were not always overawed by Nana's power as for instance the Eku war clearly demonstrated.

If Nana occasionally was guilty of such excesses and shows of

[55] The word Oloruko is generally translated 'head slave'. This is strictly speaking, wrong. Oloruko more accurately means 'captain of the canoe' and indicates that these so-called head slaves were not regarded as slaves in the western European sense. They were responsible members of their master's trading houses who were slaves only in the technical sense that they were not born into the master's household but had been acquired by sale, capture or pawning.

[56] The story was told by the son of Ukavwe himself by name Oraka at Okpara Waterside on 16 Sept. 1963.

power, his 'boys' were even more so. It is said that it was sometimes the practice of these 'boys' to invite children and women to
their canoes to buy fish and other local and imported goods.
They would carry their own wares into the canoes and, when the
bargaining had started, the head slaves would give the order to
shove off and all these people would be carried away as slaves.
Some of the women so seized would be married to other slaves
and their issue helped to swell the number of Nana's slaves. These
exploits were said to have been more common when trade
was bad, as the head slaves sought to have something to show
for their ventures, rather than merely report that trade was
bad.

It is unlikely that Nana himself was always aware of these
events, for the number of slaves and free men who traded for
him was so large that neither was it possible for him to have
known all of them, nor was it likely that they all reported directly
back to him. On some occasions, however, when Nana did get to
know of the escapades of his 'boys' he sought to make amends.
One of Nana's wives, Ikogho, was first carried off as a slave in
this manner. Tradition has it that the head slave who seized
Ikogho presented her as a wife to Nana. But before accepting the
offer, Nana made enquiries about how the girl was obtained. On
being told that the girl was lured into a canoe and so taken captive,
not only did he order that the head slave concerned be punished,
but he sent the woman back to her people with presents and
apologies for the affront done to them, as well as an offer to
marry her if her people were agreeable. The girl's people, over-
joyed at Nana's action, readily agreed and Nana proceeded to
marry the girl in the traditional manner.[57] On another occasion
one of Nana's 'boys' killed an Urhobo girl from Udu clan because
she had resisted capture. When Nana got to hear of the matter, he
is reported to have ordered that two canoes be filled with goods
and a seemly slave girl sent to the family of the murdered girl as
compensation.[58] Acts such as these restored the confidence of
the Urhobo in Nana himself, as distinct from his 'boys', as a

[57] See footnote 47. The story was confirmed by other elders of Udu at
various interviews during the month of Sept. 1963
[58] See footnote 47

man of peace and a lover of justice—the view which even today still remains.

One of the charges which has been most persistently levied against Nana is that of indiscriminate and large-scale slave raiding. Something may here be said about how Nana and others of his age obtained their slaves. As pointed out in the last chapter, the system of pawning constituted one source of slaves and as a great trader Nana must have thus obtained a considerable number of slaves. Then there were captives of war and victims of the kind of trick described above. In addition there were the occasional raids attendant on disputes over trade or in reply to other provocation. In 1885, for instance, Nana organised a raid against the Abraka because his canoes and produce had been seized by them and one of his 'boys' killed in the process. On this particular occasion only a few captives were taken and these, according to Nana, were subsequently ransomed.[59] It should be remembered that the Urhobo themselves continued to deal in slaves throughout the period of Nana's ascendancy. Therefore the Urhobo slaves found in Ebrohimi were not all the products of raids or of the escapades of Nana's 'boys'. Some were obtained through the normal trade in slaves in the area. As the children of slaves were slaves, and as the slaves were not so barbarously treated as to cause a higher rate of mortality among them than among the free born, the slave population was bound to increase from year to year irrespective of annual replenishments.

One question which arises from Nana's activities in the Urhobo country is whether in view of his power and wealth he established some kind of political hegemony over the Urhobo. Did, for example, the Urhobo pay tribute to Nana in order to win his goodwill and protection? Investigations among both the Urhobo and the Itsekiri have failed to bring to light any such relationship. Neither Olomu nor Nana, it would appear, strove to impose their rule over those Urhobo with whom they dealt. Their friendships and marriage alliances constituted the cornerstone of their policy. In Nana's case, in particular, the fact that his mother was an Urhobo woman and that he spoke the Urhobo language made him

[59] F.O. 2/64 Evidence of Nana at his trial: Enclosure in Macdonald to F.O. No. 49, 13 Dec. 1894

welcome in many an Urhobo town. Wars there were, but these were not wars of conquest but clashes arising from trade disputes. True, Nana's Oloruko stayed almost permanently in the depots in Urhoboland, merely going back occasionally to report to their master. These Oloruko were, as far as can be ascertained, essentially trading agents, not political 'residents'.

Nana is often compared with Jaja of Opobo. Like Nana, Jaja had his slaves living in the hinterland markets where they collected the palm produce and then conveyed it to Opobo for sale to European merchants. If the accounts of the Acting-Consul, Johnston, are true, there was at least one instance in which Jaja was influential and powerful enough to have secured the deposition of the head chief of a hinterland town, and to have replaced the deposed chief with one of his own head slaves. This was at Ohambele where Jaja removed Baba, who was the chief of the town, because the latter favoured direct trade with Europeans and replaced him with one Ekike Notsho, his own head slave, who proceeded to reverse Baba's policy.[60] No such active intervention in the political life of the Urhobo has ever been attributed to Nana. When, therefore, British official reports describe Nana as ruling the hinterland, they are to be understood to be referring to the monopoly of trade which Nana was able to establish over many of the Urhobo markets.

In 1883 Nana succeeded his father as head of the Olomu family. In 1884 he followed his father as Governor of the River after his election to that office by the Itsekiri elders. Trade and political relations between Nana and the British are discussed elsewhere. Here all that needs be said is that from the purely Itsekiri angle, the records are just as silent about the governorship of Nana as they are about those of earlier governors. It does appear, however, that he sometimes summoned meetings to discuss pressing matters, and that he took care to give a portion of the comey to the royal princes.[61] On the whole, Nana would seem to have exercised great control over the Itsekiri people, and it has been suggested that the absence of any so-called outrages against the white traders during his tenure of office was due to the effectiveness of

[60] Cal. Prov. 2/2 Vol. 5 Johnston to F.O. No. 12, 1 Aug. 1887
[61] Moore pp. 107–8. Lloyd p. 228

his control.[62] There is a tradition which recalls how Numa, Dogho's father, insulted Nana at a meeting summoned by the latter as Governor and was forced to pay a fine of many cases of gin.[63] If this tradition is true, the incident would scarcely have reduced the enmity between the Olomu and Numa families, and would indicate that Nana wielded sufficient influence in Itsekiriland to make it unwise to oppose him openly. Yet from the nature of Itsekiri society, as already described, it would be wrong to give the impression that Nana's political control over the Itsekiri was complete and unchallenged. It was in Ebrohimi and among the members of his own family group that he enjoyed the greatest support. The members of the royal house could hardly have been expected to give Nana their complete loyalty, and there were those who regarded him as an upstart. By and large, however, Nana's wealth and power enabled him to exercise a fairly effective authority over the greater part of the Itsekiri kingdom. Such active opposition as there might have been was apparently driven underground. Even the Numa and Dogho group seemed to have realised the danger of open opposition and so sought the downfall of their mighty rival through co-operation with the British who, for reasons of their own, were just as anxious to bring about Nana's fall.

[62] Lloyd p. 228   [63] Lloyd p. 228

CHAPTER III

Nana and the British, 1884-93

ON 12 JULY 1884 Nana was appointed Governor of the River at a meeting of the most prominent Itsekiri traders of the time.[1] As in the case of the election of previous Governors, the British Consul, Hewett, was present. In accepting the people's election of Nana as Governor, Hewett said that he looked to Nana 'to keep peace and good order in the country and to settle disputes at the markets'.[2] The appointment of Nana as Governor was a confirmation of the fact that he was by that time one of the leading traders in Itsekiriland, for an examination of the list of Governors since 1851 reveals the fact that only influential and powerful men were chosen for that office.[3] In other words the appointment of Nana was not, as claimed by Sir Alan Burns, the basis for his acquisition of power and wealth,[4] but a recognition of that wealth and power for which he was already known during the period. At the same time there is no doubt that, having been appointed, Nana stood a good chance of enhancing his already strong position, for the European traders tended to seek out the most influential men in society as their leading customers.

As already stated, the position of the Governor was difficult in the years after 1848.[5] If this was true for the years before 1884, it was even more true for the years after that date, for Nana succeeded to the office of Governor at the time of the scramble for Africa when, as a result of international diplomacy and competition among European powers, Britain was seeking to establish a claim, through treaties, to the Niger Delta as a British sphere of influence. This fact was to make Nana's position even more difficult and, as it turned out, more irksome than that of previous

[1] F.O. 84/1660 Hewett to F.O. 28 July 1884

[2] *Ibid*

[3] Idiare, Tsanomi, Olomu—the three Governors of the River before Nana—were all wealthy and powerful traders. It was necessary to appoint as Governor one whose wealth and power could command respect and obedience from his people.

[4] Burns, Sir Alan *History of Nigeria* p. 172 6th ed London 1963

[5] See chapter I pp. 12–13

Governors. Hewett had, for instance, charged Nana with responsibility for keeping the peace and settling disputes at the
markets. How was Nana to do this? Was he to adopt the time-
honoured methods of settling disputes as already described, or
was he expected to seek new methods acceptable to the British
Consul?

One of Nana's first acts as Governor was to sign, together with
other leading Itsekiri men, a treaty which brought Itsekiriland
under British 'protection'.[6] Article I contained the usual fiction
about British 'protection' being extended to the Itsekiri at their
own request. Articles II and III were straightforward enough:
the former bound the Itsekiri not to enter into an agreement or
treaty with any other foreign power without British sanction,
while the latter granted full and exclusive jurisdiction over British
subjects resident in Itsekiriland to the British Consular Officers.
Articles IV and V, though simply stated, were in fact complex and
Nana was later to be charged with breaking both of them.
Article IV provided that all disputes which could not be amicably
settled, whether among the Itsekiri themselves, with the white
traders, or between them and the neighbouring peoples, were
to be referred to the British Consul or similar officer. By Article
V the Itsekiri chiefs undertook to assist the British consular or
other officers in the performance of the duties alloted to them as
well as to act upon their advice 'in matters relating to the administration of justice, the development of the resources of the
country, the interests of commerce or in any other matter relating to peace, order, good government, and the general progress
of civilisation'. One question arises here: were the Itsekiri by this
article compelled to seek such advice or were they to decide when
they stood in need of British advice on the many issues listed?
Furthermore, could the Itsekiri be reasonably expected 'to act on
the advice' of British officers in the administration of justice
when traditional Itsekiri justice was, in certain important respects,
vastly different from British ideas of justice? Could the Itsekiri be
expected to act on the advice of British officers in matters connected
with the development of the resources of their country if and

[6] F.O. 93/6/10 Treaty with Chiefs of Jakri (Benin River). See
Appendix II

E

when their own interests differed from, or clashed with, British interests? Apparently the British regime established in the Itsekiri country in 1891 expected that the Itsekiri would. Nana refused to seek advice which was bound to be inimical to his own interests. Herein lay part of the crime for which he suffered bombardment and exile.

The Itsekiri refused to accept Articles VI and VII. In a despatch to the Foreign Office, Hewett confessed that he had failed to persuade Nana and Tsanomi, who was still an influential man at the time, to accept the whole of the treaty. He had therefore to content himself with getting them to sign the usual treaty form, with the proviso that Articles VI and VII were 'to be left for negotiation on a future occasion'.[7] Article VII provided for freedom of religious worship as well as freedom for all ministers of the Christian religion to practise in Itsekiriland. The Itsekiri were obviously concerned about the consequences of the spread of Christianity in their land, especially with regard to their polygamous way of life. Article VI laid it down that: 'The subjects and citizens of all countries may freely carry on trade in every part of the territories of the kings and chiefs parties hereto and may have houses and factories therein.' The Itsekiri were quick to grasp the implications of this article. As middlemen, the Itsekiri realised that to accept the article which provided for free trade would be prejudicial to their commercial interests. Nana was clearly not alone in holding this view, and it was not only the Itsekiri middlemen who refused to accept Article VI of the treaty. The Preliminary Treaty signed by Hewett with 'the king and chiefs' of Opobo on 1 July 1884 did not include this clause.[8] When the full treaty was eventually signed on 19 December 1884, Article VI as printed in the treaty form was expunged on the insistence of King Jaja and his chiefs.[9] During the conflict which later developed between the British Consul and Jaja, the latter

[7] F.O. 84/1660 Hewett to F.O. No. 15, 30 July 1884. The proviso is written at the end of Article IX of the printed treaty form, see F.O. 93/6/10

[8] Jaja 3, Preliminary Treaty with the King and Chiefs of Opobo 1 July 1884

[9] Jaja 3, Treaty with King and Chiefs, 19 Dec. 1884

argued that his refusal to accept Article VI of the 'protection' treaty justified his seeking to protect his hinterland markets from direct exploitation by British merchants.[10] But little attention was paid to Jaja's decidedly strong argument by the British administrative officers who, in Jaja's as in Nana's case later, found it convenient to ignore the fact that these middlemen traders had deliberately, and after full discussion, rejected free trade as part of the obligations they undertook to fulfil when they accepted British 'protection'. Free trade might have been necessary in the interests of British commerce and in the development of the hinterland of the Oil Rivers. Nevertheless, coastal middlemen like Jaja and Nana were, strictly speaking, within their treaty rights when they refused to allow free trade, and sought to protect their own interests in the face of increasing tendencies towards free trade. Nana's clash with the British administration of the Niger Coast Protectorate which ended with his deportation had, among other things, to do with the question of the trade of the hinterland from which by the treaty of 1884 Nana understood the white traders to be excluded, but in which, for obvious reasons these white traders were immensely interested.

The staff of office of the Governor was formally handed over to Nana by the Vice-Consul, David Blair, at an assembly of Itsekiri elders on 6 May 1885.[11] The Vice-Consul took the opportunity of reminding the assembled Itsekiri that they had passed under the 'protection' of the Queen of Great Britain by virtue of the 1884 treaty. Addressing himself to Nana, the Vice-Consul said that he looked to Nana as the executive power through which the decrees of the British Government and the Consul were to be implemented.[12] The British Government, continued Blair, was prepared to support Nana in the exercise of his authority so long as that authority was used in the interests of 'good government', amicable relations with neighbouring peoples and 'the furtherance of trade and civilisation'.[13] Having made these two extremely

[10] See Jaja 1/3, Cookey Gam and others to Salisbury 27 Aug. 1887 and Jaja to Queen Victoria 30 Aug. 1888

[11] F.O. 2/64 David Boyle Blair to Nana 6 May 1885. Paper submitted at Nana's trial marked E.

[12] *Ibid*   [13] *Ibid*

authoritative pronouncements, the Vice-Consul attempted to reassure the Itsekiri elders: it was not the intention of Her Majesty to interfere with the 'native laws and customs' of the Itsekiri people, so long as these laws and customs were in accord with those of civilisation and not cruel or conducive to degradation.[14]

On first reading, there was little wrong with the statements made by Blair. But a few questions arise from his address. Did he mean that henceforth Nana was to take his instructions from the British Consul? How was 'good government' to be interpreted? About which civilisation was Blair talking in his address? These questions indicate the difficulty which existed for those African leaders who, during the years of the scramble, had to deal with various European powers. For the Europeans came to Africa with their own ideas of what was conducive to good government or the furtherance of civilisation. They proceeded to set up these ideas as a model[15] to which Africans had to conform or face charges of barbarism and inhumanity. The sin of Nana and others like him was that they did not conform readily and quickly enough to the ideas of good government and civilisation which the British sought to impose. Clearly Nana could not in 1885 realise that even as the Vice-Consul was handing over to him the staff of office, he was by his pronouncements undermining the very position which he had built up for himself, as a consequence of which he had been elected Governor by his people. Nor could Nana have understood that the British Vice-Consul was implicitly enjoining him to give up long established customs and ways of doing things. Yet all this was implied by Blair's address, as future events were to show.

[14] *Ibid*. It is not known exactly when the British began to present the staff of office to the Governor of the River. Originally it was the Olu who gave a staff of office to the Governor as token of authority to collect the comey. By taking over the presentation of the staff, the British Consul was enabled to exercise a measure of control over the Governor. As Anene has pointed out, Vice-Consul Blair's whole speech was, from the point of view of the Itsekiri, superfluous since the office and functions of Governor were well established by practice. See Anene pp. 80 & 126

[15] See Oliver, R. and Fage, J. D. *A Short History of Africa* Penguin 1962

The conclusion of the Itsekiri treaty of 1884 was neither an isolated event, nor did Hewett undertake it on his own initiative or authority. After a long period of indecision as to what was to be the policy towards the Oil Rivers, the British Foreign Office realised by the end of 1883 that it was necessary to take more effective measures to protect existing British trade in the Oil Rivers and to make provisions for its further development, especially as it was held at the time that if the resources of the Oil Rivers were properly husbanded, they would prove more valuable to Britain than the other West African colonies.[16] Hewett was accordingly empowered to enter into treaties with the peoples of the Oil Rivers with a view to securing three main objectives: to ensure the protection of the lives and property of all the British subjects trading in that part of West Africa; to secure freedom of trade; and to secure freedom of worship.[17] This explains Hewett's treaty-making tour of the area between the Cameroons and the Forcados River in 1884, preparatory to the establishment in 1885 of the British Protectorate of the Oil Rivers.

This treaty-making assignment was, by Hewett's own testimony, made the more urgent by the fact that Germany had forestalled Britain in the Cameroons, a fact which filled him with the fear that the German Commissioner had the same ambitions as 'regards other rivers in this part of Africa'.[18] Hewett further reported that he had reason to believe that Germany's next target after the Cameroons was the River Forcados area. It was therefore to prevent the Germans gaining control of this area that Hewett hastened to conclude treaties with the Itsekiri and others who inhabited the Forcados River district in the months of July and August 1884.

Some days after the signing of the Itsekiri treaty, Hewett took Nana, Tsanomi and some of the white traders in the Benin River area on a tour of the Rivers Escravos, Forcados, Ramos and

[16] Tamuno, S. M. (now T. N.) *The Development of British Administrative Control of Southern Nigeria, 1900–1917* p. 24 Ph.D. Thesis London University 1962

[17] Tamuno p. 24

[18] F.O. 84/1660 Hewett to F.O. No. 18, 25 Aug. 1884. The discussion which follows is based on this same despatch

Dodo. The aim of the tour was to bring the peoples of the area under British 'protection'. At one of the towns on the Escravos, the Ijo who inhabited it claimed, according to Hewett, that they recognised Tsanomi as their ruler. They were therefore informed about the Treaty of 16 July of which Tsanomi, Nana and others were signatories and warned, under pain of severe punishment by Governor Nana, not to enter into a treaty with any other European power. At Burutu and 'Goolah' and other towns along the Forcados, Ramos and Dodo, Hewett reported that the people, though Ijo, acknowledged the fact that they were subject to Nana and were consequently made to understand that the Itsekiri 'protection' treaty was binding on them. A distribution of presents to the various peoples of the area marked the end of the tour.

It is easy to imagine how much was made of Nana on the trip. If the Ijo people did in fact acknowledge him as their overlord, then he had acquired that overlordship on his own merits before he was appointed Governor of the River, which was further proof of the wealth and power which excited the envy and hatred of less successful men. He was allowed by Hewett to warn the various peoples who were brought under British 'protection' that he would punish them if they broke the terms of the treaty or entered into other treaties with any other parties, even if these were British. Two years later Johnston, the Acting-Consul, confirmed Nana's powers over these Ijo people in a memorandum which he submitted to the Foreign Office.[19] At the beginning of British rule in Itsekiriland, therefore, not only was Nana used for the purpose of forwarding British imperial ambitions at a crucial moment, but his power and authority were confirmed by this fact. Only three years after Johnston's confirmation of Nana's jurisdiction over the Ijo people, that jurisdiction was called in question by a British special commissioner.[20] The questioning of Nana's power and authority was basic to his quarrel with the British in 1894.

For a while relations between Nana and the British remained

[19] F.O. 84/1882 Memo by Johnston—The Extent of Chief Nana's rule in the Bight of Benin
[20] See pp. 62-3

normal. This was largely because, despite the treaty of 1884, nothing was immediately done to set up an effective and formal machinery of government over the Oil Rivers Protectorate. An occasional visit by the Consul in a gunboat remained the sole reminder that this north-western extremity of the Niger Delta was a British sphere of influence. Hewett's and Johnston's advocacy of a more effective administration[21] did not produce any real response till 1891. In these circumstances Nana and others like him were left very much to themselves. Occasionally there arose situations which brought the British Consul to interfere in the affairs of the Itsekiri people. In 1886 Nana stopped trade with the whites in an endeavour to force up the price of palm oil.[22] A great deal was made of this act by the British authorities in 1894. Yet Nana's action was, in the circumstances, understandable and was definitely not the first of its kind. Idiare had stopped trade in 1886 and Tsanomi in 1879.[23] It is generally accepted that the 1880's were bad years for trade, during which period the price of oil in Liverpool fell by half.[24] The year 1886 in particular 'was a singularly bad year for business'.[25] For the Itsekiri this meant lower prices for palm oil. Nana as head of his people was directly involved in this situation. The Itsekiri looked up to him to take a lead in securing improved trading conditions. When therefore Nana stopped trade, he was acting in the interests of his people as well as of himself.

It might be argued that, if trade was generally bad, Nana

[21] F.O. 403/31. Suggestion by Consul Hewett as to the mode of maintaining (British) relations with the natives in the Oil Rivers; F.O. 84/1881. Johnston to F.O. No. 12, 16 March 1888

[22] F.O. 84/1749 Paton to Hewett 2 Dec. 1886; Enclosure in Hewett to F.O. No. 36, 23 Dec. 1886

[23] See p. 25   [24] Lloyd p. 225

[25] *The Liverpool Review* 1 Jan. 1887

The fact that 1886 was a bad year for trade is important, too, as part of the background of the quarrel between the British merchants and Jaja which ended in his deportation in 1887. In the face of low prices for produce both sides were undoubtedly eager to get the most possible out of their investments. For Jaja this meant control of the hinterland. For the British merchants and their Consul, it meant determination to penetrate the interior and trade direct with the producers. The resultant clash was in the circumstances understandable.

should have been aware of this and so desisted from the usual expedient of stopping trade to force up prices. The point, however, is that the middlemen were not always aware of what were the European prices for palm oil. What was more, a fall in the price of palm produce in Europe was not always matched by a corresponding fall in the prices of the manufactured goods which the Itsekiri bought from the white traders. The result from the Itsekiri point of view was an adverse balance of trade. In 1887, for instance, salt was said to be selling at ten to sixteen shillings per ton in Liverpool, but sold in West Africa at about thirty pounds a ton.[26] Since the white traders seemed always bent on forcing down prices, it was difficult for middlemen like Nana not to conclude that these traders were making an unfair profit at their expense.

The stoppage of trade lasted from June 1886 to the beginning of 1887. In January 1887 Nana was forced to write to Hewett to say that his people found it impossible to accept the prices being offered by the white traders, and could not therefore trade with them.[27] Hewett's reply to Nana is interesting. He attributed the stoppage of trade to two causes only: either Nana was incapable of dealing with the matter of low prices with the people at the producing markets, or he was unwilling to do so for selfish reasons. The Consul saw three possible solutions to the problem: Nana's removal from office as Governor; the establishment of factories at the hinterland markets by the European firms; or the total annexation of the protectorate of Itsekiriland. Nana was ordered to reopen trade immediately on receipt of the Consul's letter.[28]

Hewett was, of course, merely bluffing. He must have known that the British traders were not at the time eager to spend money on factories in the hinterland. His threat of annexation was even more of a bluff. Annexation could not solve the stoppage of trade. Yet the Consul's letter was a rude reminder that Itsekiriland was part of the British Protectorate of the Oil Rivers. And

[26] *The Liverpool Review*, 29 Oct. 1887

[27] F.O. 2/64 Hewett to Nana 24 Feb. 1888—submitted at Nana's trial, marked F

[28] F.O. 2/64

it was more than that. In Nana's letter and the reply to it can be seen first, the dilemma of the Governor whose actions in his official capacity and on behalf of the Itsekiri people as a whole could so easily be interpreted as being for selfish reasons. Secondly, there was a new authoritativeness in the tone of the Consul's letter in the new circumstances of Itsekiriland being part of a British protectorate. This authoritativeness was to become more noticeable in the years ahead and was to be a major cause of growing tension in the relations between Nana and the British.

In an earlier chapter it was shown how the British Consuls tended to ride rough-shod over the rights and feelings of the Itsekiri middlemen. In Hewett's reply can be seen a similar attitude. He was apparently satisfied that the British traders were offering sufficiently high prices for palm produce.[29] Yet there is no evidence that he made any effort to ascertain exactly what the situation was in the Benin River area, and he said nothing in his letter to demonstrate any concern for the adverse trade balance under which the Itsekiri were obviously suffering. He was convinced that Nana was just being difficult. The evidence does not, however, bear out any such conclusion. At the end of 1887 Johnston, the Acting-Consul, visited Nana who was at the time regarded by the white traders as 'a very truculent personage'. Johnston found him 'different to the trader's description'.[30] He investigated Nana's complaints against the traders and found them justified in most cases.[31] Such an opinion coming from Johnston must be taken seriously, especially when it is remembered that Johnston's visit was undertaken soon after he had secured the deportation of Jaja over matters that had to do with trade. Clearly Nana was not just an irresponsible and selfish past master in the art of closing markets.[31a]

Existing accounts of Nana tend to gloss over the period from 1886 to 1891.[32] In these accounts, events move from the trade

[29] F.O. 2/64
[30] Johnston, Sir Harry *The Story of My Life* p. 212 London 1923
[31] Johnston   [31a] Tamuno p. 58
[32] See for instance: Bindloss, Harold *In the Niger Country* p. 206 Edinburgh 1898; Crowder, Michael *The Story of Nigeria* p. 181 Lon-

stoppage in 1886 to the establishment of the Niger Coast Protectorate in 1891 and then to the expedition of 1894. This treatment leaves out an important facet of the developing relations between Nana and the British. In 1884, as described above, the Ijo people along the Rivers Escravos, Forcados and Ramos acknowledged themselves to be under Nana and, as such, bound by the Itsekiri 'protection' treaty.[33] Yet in 1888 these very people were reported to have signed treaties with the Royal Niger Company by which they ceded their territory to the Company. When Nana heard of these treaties, he immediately asked the Governing Council of the Benin River, at a meeting held on 18 September 1888 to protest to the British Consul on his behalf.[34]

This protest was responsible for the tour of the Forcados River area undertaken by Hewett in 1888. As in 1884, Hewett took Nana with him. He confirmed that Burutu and 'Goolah' had actually entered into treaty relations with the Royal Niger Company and caused these treaties to be handed over to Nana and, so eventually, to himself.[35]

Hewett reported the incident in full in a despatch to the Foreign Office. He noted that the Royal Niger Company had been trying to establish itself along the Forcados. He warned that to let the Royal Niger occupy the Forcados area and impose its high duties would cripple the trade of the Warri and Benin River districts, since the Forcados afforded the best entrance for steamers in the whole of this region.[36] He reminded the Foreign Office that private traders had sunk huge sums of money in developing the trade of the Benin River and Warri districts and that to allow the Royal Niger Company to come into the area at that stage could scarcely be regarded as just.[37] He recalled the dissatisfaction, which even then existed in the Akassa area over the Com-

---

don 1962; Mockler-Ferryman, A. F. *British Nigeria* pp. 98–9 London 1902; Geary, William N. M. *Nigeria Under British Rule* p. 109 London 1927

[33] See pp. 55–6
[34] F.O. 84/1881 Hewett to F.O. No. 34; 10 Nov. 1888
[35] F.O. 84/1881 Hewett to F.O. No. 33, 3 Nov. 1888
[36] *Ibid*
[37] F.O. 84/1881 Hewett to F.O. No. 34, 10 Nov. 1888

pany's duties and forecast that, in a similar way, the traders established along the Benin and Forcados Rivers would be subject to 'vexatious obstructions and troubles innumerable' if the Royal Niger Company treaties were ratified by the British Government.

The commercial and economic repercussions aside, Hewett advanced two further arguments against ratification of the Niger Company treaties. In the first place, he argued, the Itsekiri chiefs had already signed a 'protection' treaty which placed all Itsekiriland under direct British imperial control. If the Company were allowed to hold sway over the River Forcados area, part of Itsekiriland would pass away from the Oil Rivers Protectorate to the control of the Company. Such a situation, Hewett implied, was unacceptable and unfair to the Itsekiri people. Secondly, Hewett advanced the argument that the Royal Niger Company's treaties could not be valid because 'the native signatories thereto had no power to enter into them they being subjects of Nana and . . . included in the Jekri Protection Treaty of 1884'.[38] Hewett was clearly inclined, in this instance, to uphold the authority of Nana, though it is obvious that he was more concerned about the economic welfare of the British firms in the Benin River and Warri districts than about enhancing the authority of the Governor whom he had threatened to depose only the year before. But then this was one of those instances in which the economic welfare of the white traders coincided with that of the coastal middlemen.

The British Government did not, however, consider the matter one of great importance. As Lord Salisbury, the Foreign Secretary, noted in a minute, whichever British authority signed the treaties the area accrued to the Crown.[39] Nevertheless, it was probably as a result of Hewett's strong protest that Johnston was asked to write a memorandum on the extent of Nana's jurisdiction. Johnston confirmed in his memorandum that the chiefs and people of the Forcados River area had distinctly admitted to himself their political dependence on Nana.[40] He added further

[38] *Ibid*
[39] F.O. 84/1881 Minute by Salisbury on Telegram from Hewett to F.O. dated 5 Nov. 1888
[40] F.O. 84/1882, Johnston's memo already cited

that he had had occasion to use Nana's power over the people to support his own authority.[41]

In 1889 Major Claude Macdonald was appointed a Special Commissioner to examine and report on various complaints made against the Royal Niger Company and its administration. He was asked to take the opportunity to make a special study of the Forcados question. He was also to seek accurate information as to the extent to which the Protectorate and Niger Company treaties were consistent or inconsistent with each other, and to examine the validity of the titles on which the treaties rested. Finally he was to report on the expediency of leaving the existing treaties with or without modification in their operation.[42] Macdonald's report was a blow to Nana: 'After careful consideration, I cannot see that Nana and his advocates had made out a case with regard to Burutu and Goolah.'[43]

Macdonald based his report on what the people of Burutu and 'Goolah' told him at interviews which he held with them on 29 and 30 October 1889. According to Macdonald, the Ijo people told him that they had never been subjects of Nana, but that the latter was a good friend. This friendship they explained in terms of the fact that Nana's mother was a Goolah woman. As has been shown, Nana's mother was an Urhobo woman from Evhro (Effurun). One can only hope that this was not typical of the accuracy of the views of the Goolah people. Asked about a former treaty with the consular authorities, the Ijo elders claimed that they had never entered into any treaty before that into which they entered with the Royal Niger Company. This was of course strictly true, for in 1884 all that happened was that these Ijo people agreed to be bound by the treaty signed by Nana and the other Itsekiri elders. The Ijo further complained that Nana had come in a British warship and had compelled them to surrender their copies of the Royal Niger Company treaties. Macdonald

[41] *Ibid.* See also F.O. 84/1882 Minute by Governor Moloney in connection with his visit in April 1888 to the eastern limit of the colony of Lagos.

[42] F.O. 84/1940 F.O. to Macdonald Draft No. 1, 17 Jan. 1889

[43] F.O. 84/2109 Macdonald's Report chapter VII—The Forcados Question. What follows about Macdonald's mission is based on the same report

accepted the story of the Ijo elders whom, he said, struck him as being as intelligent as any he saw during his entire mission. It was on the basis of these interviews that Macdonald arrived at his conclusion.

In fairness to Macdonald it should be recorded that he also held interviews with Nana himself. Unfortunately he gave no details of the interviews in his report except in his conclusion where he stated that Nana failed entirely to show him that he ever had any right or power over the Ijo. Nana's failure to convince Macdonald of his authority over the Ijo need not surprise anyone. Macdonald was probably looking for some concrete evidence of suzerainty, some indisputable fact. It is easy to understand that there should have been no such evidence, no such fact, for the kind of power which Nana apparently exercised over these Ijo was *de facto* never *de jure* and had as its basis his wealth and power. At the same time Macdonald, in arriving at his conclusion, seems to have ignored Hewett's reports of 1884 and Johnston's memorandum. Although he noted that the Ijo people, like others who signed treaties with the Royal Niger Company, received an annual subsidy from the Company for signing the treaties, he did not see this as the possible explanation of the denunciation by the Ijo of the events of 1884. The Royal Niger Company was determined to become established in the Forcados River area, and in their drive towards this goal they did not scruple in the methods they adopted. John Flint has advanced the view that the Forcados treaties were forged, his argument being that the 'marks' of the signatory elders were too neat and unsmudged to have been made by illiterates.[44] While Flint's opinion might be true, it must be said that his argument is no conclusive evidence of forgery, for the elders might have declared their willingness to enter into, and their understanding of the terms of, the treaty and thereupon empowered the Company's officials to put down their names and marks. We have it on Hewett's authority that a great deal of secrecy surrounded the signing of these treaties by the Niger Company.[45]

[44] Flint, J. E. *Sir George Goldie and the Making of Nigeria* p. 188 footnote 1. London 1960
[45] F.O. 84/1881 Hewett to F.O. No. 34, 10 Nov. 1888

Whatever the rights and wrongs of Macdonald's understanding of the Forcados Question, the important thing from the point of view of this work is perhaps not whether Nana did exercise a *de facto* suzerainty over the Ijo people. What is important is to realise what Macdonald's report meant to Nana's pride and self-esteem. In 1884 Hewett had used Nana's power to bring these Ijo under British 'protection'. In 1888 Hewett had again confirmed and emphasised Nana's authority over the Ijo of Goolah and Burutu. Then in 1889 Macdonald's report questioned, and indeed denied, the very power which had been utilised by the British five years earlier. The crisis of 1894 was, partially at least, the outcome of dissatisfaction which arose out of situations like this. The longer Nana associated with the British, the more he realised, especially from this time onwards, that British interests and ambitions were at cross purposes with his. The result was mutual suspicion and antipathy which by 1894 ripened into open conflict.

At the time of the Macdonald mission, there was general uncertainty at the British Foreign Office as to how best to administer the Oil Rivers. The history of the struggle for the establishment of an effective administration over the Oil Rivers dates back to 1883 when Consul Hewett put forward a number of suggestions to the Foreign Office. One of these suggestions was that a number of Vice-Consuls be appointed to assist him in administering the Oil Rivers which, he proposed, should be divided into four districts. These Vice-Consuls were to be responsible for 'giving advice to the native kings and chiefs, and assisting them as best as they could in such matters as civilisation, the administration of justice, the development of the resources of their country and the interests of commerce'.[46] The upshot of Hewett's suggestion was no more than the appointment of a single Vice-Consul to assist him. But one Vice-Consul did not make for effective administration through the length and breadth of the Oil Rivers, especially as the Consul or his assistant was left alone during the absence on leave of one of the two consular officers. British authority therefore still consisted of the occasional visit of a gunboat. In 1888 Acting-Consul Johnston fulminated

[46] F.O. 403/31 Hewett's suggestions already cited

against a system in which one single individual had to govern an area the size of Burma, with an indigenous population of two million in addition to some six hundred white traders.[47] The Foreign Office had to do something to meet the criticisms of both the consular officers and the West African merchants who, after the Berlin West African Conference of 1885, had begun advocating greater British responsibilities in West Africa—both at the coast and in the hinterland.[48] In fact a year before Johnston expressed his views, the Foreign Office suggested the establishment of a colony over the Oil Rivers. But as the Colonial Office did not approve of the suggestion, the idea had to be dropped.[49]

The Macdonald mission was, therefore, another attempt at finding a solution to the problem of the Oil Rivers. Macdonald was to report, among other things, on the desirability of annexing the Oil Rivers to Lagos Colony as opposed to continuing the existing consular systems.[50] Macdonald's method during his mission was to hold discussions with the various peoples of the Oil Rivers in an endeavour to discover their own views on the mode of government they would prefer. The choice which Macdonald put before the people was between government by chartered company (the Royal Niger Company or the African Association) and direct imperial control in the form of a colony or Protectorate.

When Macdonald visited the Benin River for the purpose of finding out the wishes of the Itsekiri on this matter, Nana was the chief spokesman. The Itsekiri were categorical in their rejection of company rule. In rejecting company rule they were no doubt thinking of the Niger Company which, as seen from its efforts to establish along the Forcados River district, was a dreaded rival in trade. They however opted for a 'Queen's Government', but with two important specifications to do with slavery and polygamy. The Itsekiri reminded the British Commissioner that they were a polygamous people and on this matter were not prepared to be 'disturbed' in their 'domestic laws'. More important still they raised the question of slave holding, arguing that they depended entirely on slaves for their economy. As a plea for the

---

[47] F.O. 84/1881 Johnston to F.O. No. 12, 16 March 1888
[48] Tamuno p. 38   [49] Tamuno p. 32
[50] F.O. 84/1881 F.O. to Macdonald Draft 15 Dec. 1889

continuance in force of slavery, the Itsekiri argued: 'We treat them [the slaves] well, we feed them well, we do not kill them for any fetish purposes, they have certain rights in our country, and often become influential men.'[51] For the Itsekiri, as for other coastal middlemen of the time, the question of slavery was one of vital importance. Enough has been said about the role of slaves in the Itsekiri community to make it clear that to abolish slavery was to strike at the very root of their economy. Similarly the middlemen of Bonny, Opobo, New Calabar and Brass insisted on the retention of the institution of slavery.[52]

Macdonald sent in his report to the Foreign Office in June 1889. After the unanimous rejection of Company rule by the people of the Oil Rivers, he had little choice but to recommend the establishment of the Crown Colony system over the Oil Rivers.[53] Macdonald did not ignore the issue of slavery in thus recommending the inauguration of a colony system of administration. He thought, however, that the matter could be tactfully handled even within the framework of his suggestion. But Salisbury did not see the issue as being so simple and consequently restrained the Foreign Office from any immediate implementation of Macdonald's recommendation. In July 1890 Macdonald himself modified his original suggestion. He now recommended that the establishment of a Crown Colony be deferred till such time as 'the way had been prepared by an administration resembling that of a colony in that all officials would be directly servants of the Crown, but without the cumbersome machinery'. Macdonald's idea was to establish 'a vigorous administration' controlled by the Foreign Office which would undertake the task of pioneer development. Such an administration by imposing duties on the liquor trade of the Oil Rivers would raise a sizeable revenue which would enable it to undertake the effective government of the area under its jurisdiction; it should establish a capital in the hinterland and set about the task of social reform, preparatory to the establishment

---

[51] F.O. 84/1940 Enclosure 8 in Macdonald to F.O. No. 11, 12 June 1889   [52] Flint pp. 133–4

[53] Flint p. 135 *et seq*. Macdonald's report—its reception by the Foreign Office its eventual modification and acceptance—is discussed by Flint, pp. 135 & 153–4. See also Tamuno p. 32

of a crown colony. Macdonald did not accept the view that such an administration should interfere as little as was possible in the internal affairs of the African states. This is an important point especially in view of the fact that Macdonald himself was to inaugurate the system of administration which he advocated.

If the way were to be prepared for a crown colony, a necessary social reform was the abolition of slavery. Macdonald was apparently prepared to set about achieving this end. But such a policy was diametrically opposed to the known wishes of Nana and all other coastal middlemen who frowned on any type of social reform that not only struck a blow at their prestige and status in their respective communities, but undermined their economic position in one and the same process. Macdonald himself had heard and recorded the views of the coastal middlemen on the issue of slavery. Yet he was prepared to inaugurate a system which, by its declared aims, was bound to undermine that very institution. Little wonder if the administration soon to be set up clashed with some of those whose susceptibilities were to be thus set at nought.

The acceptance of Macdonald's modified proposals marked a significant change in British policy towards the Oil Rivers. Until this time, despite pressure from the men on the spot and British trading interests, the British Government had been unwilling to take greater responsibilities in the Oil Rivers than the maintenance of a consul there. Admittedly there had been various moves directed towards the desired end of greater control of the West African territories in general. Where in 1866 the four British 'settlements' of Sierra Leone, the Gold Coast, Gambia and Lagos had been brought under a single administration in the interest of economy, in 1874 these 'settlements' were constituted into two administrations—Gold Coast and Lagos, and Sierra Leone and Gambia. Then in 1886 Lagos was separated from the Gold Coast, while two years later the Sierra Leone and Gambia were split into separate administrations.[54] These developments represented a reaction against the policy ushered in by the 'Select Committee' of 1865, and indicated that in its usual slow-footed manner British colonial policy was undergoing a gradual change directed towards

[54] Tamuno pp. 19, 23 & 24

F

greater control in the affairs of the West African territories. In
the Oil Rivers in particular it has been shown how the Foreign
Office was led to send out the Macdonald Mission. The implementation of Macdonald's proposals was therefore the logical
end to a long process.

There was, however, more in the acceptance of Macdonald's
proposals than stated above. Britain's hands were, to some extent
at least, forced by the declarations of the Brussels Conference of
1889. For that conference urged on Britain and the other signatories of its General Act the progressive organisation of the
administrative, judicial, religious and military services in the
African territories placed under the sovereignty or protectorate
of 'civilised nations' as an effective means of suppressing the
slave trade. It recommended the setting up of 'strongly occupied
stations' in the hinterland of the territories controlled by the
signatory powers. It called for the mounting of expeditions to
suppress repressive actions and to secure the safety of the highways.[55] True these injunctions were not new or revolutionary.
British policy had, before this time, involved the carrying through
of some of these injunctions.[56] But this policy had not been general
and there were those who held that it was expensive and constituted an unjustifiable interference with the institutions of the
African peoples concerned. The Brussels conference presented
Britain with obligations towards the African territories over
which she had established colonies or protectorates—obligations
which now possessed international sanction. The Brussels stipu-
lations presented Britain with a ready-made programme which
she could proceed to implement. Henceforth Britain could, while
pursuing what were basically her own interests, claim that she
was doing no more than perform internationally-imposed duties.

In January 1891 Major (by now Sir) Claude Macdonald himself
was appointed Commissioner and Consul-General over what was
soon to be called the Niger Coast Protectorate, and sent out with

[55] Tamuno p. 33

[56] Hewett and Johnston had advocated more efficient administration,
Jaja had been deposed, allegedly for blocking highways of traffic, in
1887.

a team of Vice-Consuls and other necessary staff to inaugurate the
new era. The new regime was, like that of 1885, a protectorate
with the difference that Macdonald had all the staff he required
to make his administration really effective and so carry through
his own aims. In many ways Nana's troubles began with the
inauguration of this more regular and more formal machinery of
government.

Macdonald began his assignment with a tour of the entire area
committed to his charge, establishing vice-consulates at suitable
points along the rivers. In the area with which this book is
mainly concerned, two vice-consulates were set up, at Warri on
the Forcados River and on the Benin River. Macdonald's first visit
in his new official capacity indicated what the lines of future
policy were to be and, with regard to Nana's position, foreshadowed what lay ahead.

The Consul-General visited Warri on 19 August 1891. He
reported that the chiefs of Warri were Itsekiri who were 'under
Nana—the great middleman chief of Benin'. But, continued
Macdonald, the Warri chiefs were eager to be independent of
Nana. Then followed a statement which is totally neglected in
existing accounts of Nana's relations with the British, but which
in fact pointed to the crisis of 1894. It is best to quote from
Macdonald's despatch:

> As the trade here [Warri] promises to be one of the most flourishing
> in the Protectorate, and as Nana is already sufficiently powerful
> and threatens to become a second Jaja, I thought it politic to estab-
> lish a separate vice-consulate at this place, and to conclude with the
> chiefs of Warri a separate Protection Treaty.[57]

Thus at the very beginning of his administration and even before
he had had more time to study Nana himself, Macdonald had
come to the conclusion that Nana was a danger. In 1884 the
Warri people had accepted the protection treaty signed by
Tsanomi and Nana and others as binding on themselves.[58] The
aim behind their being made to sign an independent treaty in
1891 was to provide a legal document for the future which would

[57] F.O. 84/2111 Macdonald to F.O. No. 2, 1 Sept. 1891
[58] F.O. 84/1660 Hewett to F.O. No. 18, 25 Aug. 1884

alter the *status quo* of 1884. The establishment of a vice-consulate at Warri would therefore appear to have been a premeditated act directed towards reducing the power of Nana.

Macdonald's main aim in undertaking this tour was to explain to the people the implications of the import duties which he was about to impose in order to raise a revenue for the proper administration of the territory placed under his control. He reported that both at Warri and Benin River the chiefs consented to the imposition and thoroughly understood the implications.[59]

If the people understood the implications of Macdonald's import duties, did they also understand the full implications of the new regime? By his instructions Macdonald was directed to let the chiefs rule their people as previously. But he was to watch them 'so as to prevent injustice and check abuses'. The chiefs were to be made to understand that misgovernment would result in forfeiture of their powers. Macdonald was empowered 'in special cases', to insist on the delegation to himself of the powers of the chiefs if this would be 'for the benefit of the natives'. Finally Macdonald was to 'take under immediate control the inter-tribal and foreign relations of the native chiefs'.[60] These instructions virtually empowered Macdonald to take over the running of the internal as well as the external affairs of the Oil Rivers—a clear indication that the meaning of the word 'protectorate' was being decidedly extended. True, Nana and the Itsekiri did not, like Jaja of Opobo, request the definition of the word 'protectorate' as used in the treaty of 1884.[61] But Hewett's reply to Jaja on the issue can be taken as representing the British stand at the time. In that reply Hewett assured King Jaja that Britain did not intend to take Jaja's markets or country, but was anxious that no other country should. Britain was extending her 'protection' over Opobo but would leave the country still under Jaja's government. This explanation falls in line with the views

---

[59] See note 56

[60] F.O. 84/211 F.O. to Macdonald Draft No. 2, 18 April 1891

[61] Apparently Jaja wrote to Consul Hewett requesting that the word 'protectorate' be defined in order to make clear the full meaning of the Preliminary Treaty of 1884. I have not seen this letter, but Hewett's reply which clearly states that he was writing in reply to Jaja's request is to be found in Jaja 1/3, Hewett to Jaja 1 July 1884.

of the law officers of the crown up to 1889. In 1888 H. Jenkyns had in fact argued that the aim of declaring a protectorate was to avoid assuming jurisdiction over the internal affairs of the area concerned, and that all that a protectorate implied was the prevention of the indigenous government of the protectorate from entering into direct relations with other European powers. This view was upheld by C. P. Ilbert in 1889.[62] Macdonald's instructions went beyond this conception of a protectorate. He was left with a free hand to decide what the special cases were that justified his assuming the powers of the African chiefs for the benefit of the 'natives'. He was to take over control of inter-tribal relations. As inter-tribal relations consisted very much of commercial relations during this age, this meant that Macdonald could take over control of the commercial relations between the tribes. Clause IV of the 'Protectorate' Treaty of 1884 had laid a duty on the Itsekiri to hand over to the arbitration of the British Consul disputes which arose between them and the neighbouring tribes, but only when these could not be 'settled amicably'. But Macdonald's instructions bade him take over immediately the inter-tribal relations of these same people. There was a vast difference here between the situation in 1884 and that of 1891. Indeed Macdonald's instructions constituted, in certain important respects, a breach of the 1884 treaty.

It is unfortunate that Macdonald did not indicate in his report to the Foreign Office whether he explained to the people the full implications of his instructions. If the British interpretation of 'protectorate' had altered with and in their own interests by 1891, the African chiefs could not be expected to know or, if they knew, to acquiesce in, this fact. Macdonald's silence on the issue is therefore more regrettable since it meant that African chiefs like Nana were acting under a premise different in important details from that of the new British administration.

It is even more surprising that Macdonald did not mention in his despatch to the Foreign Office what settlement he came to with the Itsekiri chiefs on the thorny problem of slavery and

[62] Both Jenkyns, H. and Ilbert, C. P. were law officers of the crown. For a discussion of the changing conception and meaning of the word 'protectorate' at the British Foreign Office see Tamuno pp. 45–54

slave-holding. The Itsekiri chiefs had categorically asked for the preservation of the institution as a condition for their acceptance of a 'Queen's Government'. The slavery question was partly responsible for the modification of Macdonald's original proposal for the establishment of a colony over the Oil Rivers. Macdonald, by implication, had come out determined to prepare the way for the abolition of slavery, so that a colony could then be established. Yet in 1891 on his tour of the Benin River and Warri areas, he apparently glossed over this vital issue. The Itsekiri, in the circumstances, had the right to assume that their views on the subject were being respected, since they had made the point quite clear to Macdonald himself in 1889. And if their views were being respected, it was a short step from being allowed to keep slaves to augmenting the number of such slaves through time-honoured channels. The question of slavery was one of the issues that ostensibly led to Nana's fall in 1894. Yet in 1891, so far as can be seen from the records available, no final ruling was laid down.

The Benin River meeting gave Macdonald another opportunity of sizing up Nana; the first meeting having been during his mission in 1889. Some measure of Nana's wealth at the time can be seen from Macdonald's account of his entourage. Nana arrived for the meeting in a war canoe 'paddled by upwards of a hundred slaves, with four or five similar canoes in attendance'. He had a personal escort of twenty men armed with Winchester repeating rifles.[63] His business sense was demonstrated by the fact that he had a copy of the Proclamation containing Macdonald's import duties schedule which he assured Macdonald he had carefully studied in order to be ready for any white traders who might seize the opportunity to increase prices beyond the level justified by the duties. Macdonald came to the conclusion that Nana was 'a man possessed of great power and wealth, astute, energetic and intelligent'.[64]

After the meeting with the Itsekiri, Macdonald decided to hold a separate meeting with the European traders. As a result of this meeting he once again noted that he would have to 'combat another Jaja difficulty'. The Europeans gave conflicting views

[63] F.O. 84/2111 Macdonald to F.O. No. 2, 1 Sept. 1891   [64] *Ibid*

about Nana, lauding or vilifying him according to their trade
relations with him. Some of them complained that they could not
trade in the hinterland because they could not get fair play
'owing to Nana's great power and influence'.[65] Macdonald told
these white traders that it was for them to decide whether they
went to the markets to get the oil for themselves, or trusted the
middlemen to do so for them. His concern was that those who did
decide to go to the markets should obtain protection against all
forms of molestation.

The point raised by the European traders deserves further
consideration. What the white traders complained about was
Nana's power and influence and not any definite steps taken by
him to prevent their penetration of the hinterland. As a matter
of fact there is no record of attempts by Europeans to penetrate
the Urhobo or Kwale hinterland before 1891 which were frus-
trated by Nana or any other Itsekiri trader. In 1891 Gallwey,
the Vice-Consul in charge of the Benin River district, reported
that some Europeans had in the year before intended to move
into the hinterland but had not done so for fear of the hinterland
peoples. Hence these Europeans advised Gallwey to carry arms
when in 1891 he made his first trip into the Urhobo country.[66]
The account given by Lloyd of attempts to find a route to the
Niger proper, via Patani, can hardly be regarded as penetration
of the hinterland. For the attempt to develop the Forcados River
as a highway of trade was aimed at increasing the trade of the
Warri area as distinct from the Benin River district. Naturally
the Benin River traders—both Itsekiri and white—opposed a
move which would have reduced the volume of produce reaching
the Benin River. In other words this was a struggle between one
set of middlemen and another.[67]

It might be argued that the Europeans did not make any
attempt to penetrate the interior because they knew that the
Itsekiri middlemen would oppose such a move. But the point is
whether in the 1880's and early 1890's the European firms would

[65] *Ibid*

[66] F.O. 84/2111, Gallwey's Report on his visit to the oil markets of the
Sobo and Abraka Districts—Enclosure in Macdonald to F.O. No. 30, 12
Dec. 1891   [67] See Lloyd p. 226

necessarily have made more profits if they had decided to go to the hinterland themselves, buy the oil, and transport it in barges, where these could be used, to the river mouths rather than depend, as they did, on the middlemen. During his mission in 1889, Macdonald himself was surprised that although 'Ogbe Sobo' (Aladja) which was only '20 minutes launching above Warri' was a rich oil market, the European agents did not make any efforts to go there themselves.[68] One wonders if in the circumstances of 1891 the white traders brought up these complaints against Nana because they realised that their complaints were in line with the new policy which Macdonald was bound to pursue. As late as 1905 the firms were still content to remain at the centres where government stations were established, and were not setting up depots in the hinterland, even when it was clear that the Itsekiri could no longer stop them, which is evidence that these traders did not consider it necessary or profitable to take on the added responsibility of sending their agents direct to the producer areas.[69] The reluctance of the European firms to move into the hinterland was also noticeable in the eastern delta. C. J. Gertzel has shown that, although on the deposition of Jaja in 1887 the Acting-Consul, Johnston, helped the European supercargoes doing trade at Opobo to establish two hinterland 'factories' at Essene and Ohambele, 'they could do no business'. The cost of buying the produce and shipping it to the coast for export was so high that such produce as was eventually exported from these 'factories' was sold at a loss in Europe. Besides the producers, 'at the instigation of the Opobo chiefs', were unwilling to sell produce to these 'factories'. The upshot was that the supercargoes sold out their hinterland 'factories' to the Opobo middlemen chiefs and reverted to the old system.[70] As late as 1902, after the Aro expedition, Ralph Moor, the High Commissioner for Southern Nigeria, complained that the European merchants were still unwilling to invest money in transport development

[68] F.O. 84/2109 Macdonald's report already cited

[69] C.O. 592/3 Annual Report, Central Provinces 1906

[70] For C. J. Gertzel's views on this subject see her article, 'Commercial Organization on the Niger Coast 1852–1891', *Historians in Tropical Africa* pp. 301–2 Salisbury 1962

which would have enabled them to trade direct with the hinterland producers. They were apparently still satisfied with their trade at the coast. Moor complained that in this instance trade was waiting for the flag to take the initiative, a reversal of the more usual process.[71] There were thus two factors which governed the attitude of the European traders. On the one hand the middleman system was too well established for it to be toppled easily. On the other, especially in the years up to 1901, the road system of the protectorate was still so undeveloped[72] that it was much cheaper for the agents to depend on the middlemen using their canoes and slaves than for them to hire canoes and labour and penetrate the hinterland. Therefore, as in Jaja's so in Nana's case, the white traders were not complaining against middlemen in general, for they recognised the place of such middlemen in the economic set up of the age. Rather they were complaining against the power and influence of a particular African middleman—a chief whom they could not control.

So far as Nana was concerned, the real problem posed in 1891 was whether he was still to be regarded as Governor following the establishment of the Macdonald administration. Margery Perham states that Nana was recognised as Governor 'until he signed treaties accepting the British protectorate in 1884'.[73] This statement is obviously based on insufficient data. Lloyd holds the view that with the appointment in 1891 of Gallwey as Vice-Consul in charge of the Benin River Nana's office as Governor ceased to exist.[74] It is certain that Nana did not see things in this light. He attended the meeting of August 1891 in his official capacity and Macdonald recorded that the Itsekiri chiefs were headed by Nana.[75] Further, at that very meeting Nana spoke

[71] Tamuno p. 131
[72] See Tamuno p. 364 for a comment on the road development programmes of Moore and Egerton.
[73] Perham, M. & Bull, M (eds.), *The Diaries of Lord Lugard* Introduction, Vol. IV p. 50 London 1963
[74] This was the view expressed by Lloyd in 1957 in 'Nana Olomu—Governor of the River' June 1957, *West Africa* p. 109. In his article in the *Journal of African History* Vol. IV No. 2, 1963 p. 229 he maintains the view though he adds that Nana continued to use the title.
[75] F.O. 84/2111 Macdonald to F.O. No. 2, 1 Sept. 1891

strongly against the action of the Consul, Annesley, who had apparently declared him deposed in 1890 and broken his staff of office.[76] Nana had not accepted the Consul's action as final and had sent a letter of protest to the Foreign Office; the reply to this letter was still being awaited at the time of Macdonald's tour of 1891. Macdonald told Nana at the meeting that his letter was receiving the attention of the Foreign Office and that he would hear from the Foreign Office in due course. Macdonald himself still regarded Nana as Governor at this stage. It was not till 1894, at the beginning of the crisis which led to war, that he wrote to Nana to the effect that, as the British Government was already firmly established in the area, Nana was no longer to regard himself as head of the Itsekiri people as a whole, but as head of his own family alone.[77] No doubt the bulk of the Itsekiri continued to regard Nana as their head despite the establishment of the Niger Coast Protectorate in 1891. Yet his position was bound to get increasingly untenable. He stood for a system based on power, wealth and slavery; the new administration stood for a system which, while directed towards increasing the wealth available, not only set itself against slavery, but sought to make itself the ultimate power in the whole of the protectorate. It was in Nana's interest that the political, social and economic *status quo* should be maintained; the new order was for a reorganisation. In these circumstances a clash of interests was likely and, as will be shown, events moved quickly in that direction.

Nana's letter to the Foreign Office protesting against what he clearly regarded as wrongful deposition by Annesley is important as showing some of the traits that were to irritate the new regime. Nana was a man who was always aware of his position and power. Hence one of the things that infuriated him was that seven days after the Consul had arrived in the Benin River Annesley had not yet had the courtesy to send his compliments to him. Nana contrasted this attitude with his own, claiming that he always sent a messenger to the visiting consul to pay his compliments. From this it can be seen that Nana regarded him-

[76] F.O. 84/2111 Macdonald to F.O. No. 2, 1 Sept. 1891
[77] F.O. 2/64 Macdonald to Nana April 1894—submitted at Nana's trial marked M

self as an independent ruler dealing on a footing of equality with the representative of the British Government. This attitude, typical of the attitude of many an African chief in the age of partition, was bound to irritate British consular officials who could never put up with African rulers who looked on them as no more than equals.

Nana's other ground for protest was that Annesley listened only to the views of the white traders and did not so much as give him a hearing before declaring him deposed and breaking his staff of office. He resented the public calumny to which the Consul subjected him and marvelled at such a system of settling a 'palaver'. He ended with a plea that another Consul be sent out who could investigate the dispute and arrive at a more equitable settlement.[78] Unfortunately, nothing was done about Nana's protest until Macdonald's appointment and thereafter the Vice-Consuls found it convenient to regard Nana as already deposed while he for his part continued to regard himself as Governor of the River.

As we have seen one of Macdonald's plans for the protectorate was the establishment of stations in the hinterland. He did not waste much time before embarking on the implementation of this plan. For it was on his instructions that the Vice-Consul, Gallwey, undertook his first exploratory journey into the Urhobo hinterland in November 1891. The objects of the journey were, according to Gallwey, 'manifold'. One of these was the selection of sites suitable for the establishment of a vice-consulate, barracks and constabulary, the idea being that such inland government stations would embolden traders to move into the hinterland, as well as ensuring the maintenance of law and order[79]—a necessary condition for trade to flourish. As a result of Gallwey's journey one new vice-consulate was established, at Sapele.[80] For Nana and the other Benin River traders this was an important development. Sapele was much closer to the Urhobo and Kwale

---

[78] F.O. 2/64 Nana to F.O. 14 Dec. 1890—submitted at Nana's trial marked F

[79] F.O. 84/2111 Gallwey's Report—enclosure in Macdonald to F.O. No. 30, 12 Dec. 1891

[80] F.O. 84/2194 Macdonald to F.O. December 1892

oil producers than was the Benin River. Therefore the outcome of the establishment of the new government station was a movement of trade towards Sapele, which necessarily implied a falling off in the trade of the Benin River area.

It would be unfair to argue that the opening of a vice-consulate at Sapele was a step deliberately taken to reduce the commercial prosperity of Nana and the other Benin River traders. Nevertheless, there can be no doubt that the move into the hinterland, of which the establishment of a government station at Sapele was only a first stage, was inimical to the interests of the middlemen. Nana, as the leading middleman trader of this area, was clearly affected by the new situation. Yet although Gallwey noted that Nana and his satellites could not be expected to welcome the new order, there is no record at this stage of any large-scale opposition[81] to Gallwey's move into the hinterland. In fact Nana claimed during his trial that he helped the consular officials in their negotiations for land at Sapele.[82]

Thus, at the end of 1891 a new order had been established which represented a change in the attitude of the British to the Oil Rivers. The days of haphazard interference in the affairs of the peoples of the area were gone; the age of ordered administration dawned. The stage was set for a struggle between the British and the peoples of what was to become southern Nigeria; this struggle was occasioned by the determination of the British to impose their rule effectively on the Nigerian peoples, and the equally strong determination of the Nigerian peoples to resist the imposition of British rule. The Nana episode must be seen therefore as only one act in the drama that was to be enacted throughout southern Nigeria in the period from 1891 to 1914.

In the developing relations between Nana and the British, the years 1892 and 1893 constituted an uneasy interlude. One reason for the uneasiness of these years was the activities of the Royal Niger Company. In 1888, as has been already pointed out, the Royal Niger Company entered into treaties with a number of

[81] F.O. 2/51 Gallwey's Report on the Benin District July 1892—enclosure in Macdonald to F.O. 12 Jan. 1893

[82] F.O. 2/64 Nana's evidence at his trial—enclosure in Macdonald to F.O. No. 49, 13 Dec. 1894

Ijo towns in the Forcados River area. The signing of these treaties
was a pointer to the fact that the Company had plans to establish
itself in this area. Nana had protested against the Niger Company's activities in the Forcados region. He was not alone, however. Some of the firms interested in the trade of this part of the
Oil Rivers also protested to the Foreign Office. In July 1888
Blackstock & Co told Lord Salisbury that they were particularly
worried about the clause of the Royal Niger Company's treaty
which forbade the signatory chiefs having intercourse with
any strangers or foreigners except through the Company. They
argued that this clause would enable the Company to establish a
monopoly, contrary to the terms of its charter.[83] The Foreign
Office's attitude was that as long as the clause to which Blackstocks
drew attention was observed, there was nothing wrong with
the Niger Company establishing itself in the Forcados region.[84]

Two issues emerged from the new establishment. On the one
hand the entry of the Niger Company into the area constituted a
threat to the traders already established in the Warri and Benin
River districts. As an organised group the Company was in a
position to outrival the private firms which had been doing trade
in the area for some twenty-five years. Besides, the Company
imposed duties on exports passing through its area of jurisdiction,
thereby making it impossible for private enterprise to compete
successfully against it. On the other hand the entry of the Company into this area necessitated the fixing of a boundary between
the Company's territories and those of the newly reorganised
protectorate. In 1889 Macdonald had upheld the rights of the
Royal Niger Company. It now fell to him, on his appointment as
Commissioner and Consul-General of the Oil Rivers Protectorate,
to come to some agreement with the Royal Niger Company over
the question of a boundary between his administration and that
of the Company. Before he had left England to assume his duties,
that is before he had time to study for himself the movement of
trade in the area, he had proposed the following boundary line:

A line starting at a point at the mouth of the Forcados River
midway between the right and left bank, following that River to

---

[83] F.O. 403/76 Blackstock & Co. to Salisbury 30 July 1888
[84] F.O. 403/76 P. Anderson to J. Pauncefote 10 Sept. 1888

the mouth of the so-called 'Warri' creek up to a point two miles before reaching the mouth of the creek leading to Oagbie and Akiabodo.[85]

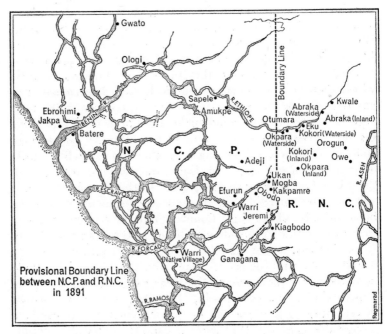

Provisional Boundary Line
between N.C.P. and R.N.C.
in 1891

He proposed that territory to the west of this line should be under the jurisdiction of the Oil Rivers Protectorate while territory to the east would be under the Company. The Foreign Office accepted his proposal with slight modifications and an important addendum, namely, that the proposed boundary was to be subject to modifications by further delimitation according to local requirements.[86]

The Foreign Office addendum was of vital importance as Macdonald was soon to discover. The boundary line as accepted by the Foreign Office virtually divided into two the Urhobo hinterland, from which most of the palm produce came down to the merchants established at Warri and Benin River. In other

[85] F.O. 84/2111 Macdonald to F.O. 13 June 1891
[86] F.O. 403/171 F.O. to Macdonald No. 45, 29 July 1891

words the Itsekiri middlemen traders would no longer be able to go to some of their old markets to buy oil, unless they were prepared to pay export duties to the Royal Niger Company. For some of the Itsekiri the new boundary spelt ruin as their best markets were now in the Company's territory and the Company was eager to attract as much trade as possible to itself.

The year 1892 opened with a flood of protests from interested trading houses in Liverpool and elsewhere. Echoes of Hewett's arguments of 1888 were heard once more as Ellis, Kinslingbury & Co, whose agents owned 'factories' both at Warri and Benin River, argued that it was unjust to hand over to the Royal Niger Company the trade of the area, and especially that of the Warri district, when in fact this trade had been developed by private enterprise.[87] Pinnock, who had traded in the area for over twenty years, was greatly surprised at the proposed recognition of the Company's rights in the Warri area and asked for a personal interview with the men at the Foreign Office.[88] The Liverpool Chamber of Commerce did not only cry out against the injustice to those who had laboured for years to develop the trade of the region but warned that the establishment of the Royal Niger Company in the Warri district would lead to conflict with the African traders.[89] The Foreign Office reaction to these protests was clearly not determined solely by the rights and wrongs of the matter or of the interests of the African peoples concerned, but rather by the international situation. For this was the period when European powers were busy deciding the frontiers of their respective spheres of influence. In these circumstances the Niger Company's claims to territory around the Niger and Benue were a useful diplomatic weapon in the international bargaining that was then going on.[90] This was a factor, if not the main one, in making the Foreign Office decide to uphold the rights of the Niger Company. In a letter to the various firms interested in

[87] F.O. 403/171, Messrs Ellis Kislingbury & Co. to Salisbury 12 Jan. 1892

[88] F.O. 403/178 Pinnock to F.O. 14 Jan. 1892

[89] F.O. 403/178 Liverpool Chamber of Commerce to Salisbury 25 May 1892

[90] For those negotiations see Flint chapter 8

the Forcados trade the Foreign Office argued that 'the Company had long been established on the Waree creek . . . and concluded Treaties on the Forcados River'. Therefore, argued the Foreign Office, the Company was perfectly within its rights in being granted jurisdiction over that district. In fact, concluded the Foreign Office, the boundary selected had confined rather than extended the Company's sphere of administration.[91]

It was one thing for Macdonald to propose the boundary line, and quite another for him to secure the interests of his area of jurisdiction. Soon after he arrived in the Oil Rivers, he began to face the problems created by the boundary line as accepted by the Foreign Office. In a despatch towards the end of 1892, he argued that after practical experience of the working of the boundary, it was his view that the existing line did not conform to any 'fiscal boundary' and that it was impossible to work under it. He proposed a modification of the old arrangement thus:

> The boundary should follow the Warri branch as at present laid down, as far as the mouth of the Oagbi creek, it should then follow the creek up to its source; the east or Niger side would be in the Royal Niger Territories, and the west or Warri side in the Oil Rivers Protectorate.[92]

Macdonald backed his proposed new line with practical arguments. The Itsekiri traders, he wrote, were accustomed to trade for some distance to the eastward of the Ogbe creek, that is in territory which by the old arrangement fell within the jurisdiction of the Niger Company. It would lead to friction and bloodshed if these Itsekiri were to be asked suddenly to give up their old markets, which they still regarded as justly theirs. Even if they were to lose these markets, Macdonald pleaded, the Itsekiri should be given time to collect outstanding debts and make arrangements for opening new markets. He requested that the Foreign Office give approval to his suggestion so he could put it into immediate effect.[93] It does not appear as if the Foreign

[91] F.O. 403/171 T. V. Lister to all firms interested in the Forcados River 18 Jan. 1892
[92] F.O. 403/171 Macdonald to F.O. No. 23, 12 Nov. 1892
[93] *Ibid*

Office gave any final ruling on the issue though, as Macdonald had consulted the Niger Company's Agent-General over the new line, it is likely that both sides respected it.

It probably will never be fully known how Nana reacted to the situation created by the inauguration of the Macdonald administration. But clearly matters were not made any easier by the commercial uncertainty which followed the establishment of the Royal Niger Company in the Forcados district. As the leading Itsekiri trader, his interests were greatly threatened by the Company's activities. Like other Itsekiri traders he was prevented from going to some of his Urhobo markets unless he was prepared to pay the export duties of the Company which, even by Macdonald's own account, were high and injurious to trade.[94] Towards the end of 1892 an incident occurred which showed clearly that unless something was done about the Niger Company's duties, the trade of the Warri district would be seriously endangered. In November 1892 two canoes carrying oil attempted to pass the revenue hulk of the Niger Company. The Company's launch gave chase. One of the canoes escaped. The other was forced to steer into the bush along the river bank and, when pressed, fired at the launch killing one person. The launch returned fire, and killed one man and wounded two. This caused general excitement in the district. Moor Harper, the Acting Vice-Consul for the Warri district, noted in a report to Macdonald who was on leave in England: 'The Itsekiri people are very excited and a small thing may put a light to the fire'. Various Itsekiri traders, he reported, still had plenty of oil, for which they had entrusted goods, to collect from the Company's side of the boundary, while all were irritated that they could not go to their old markets without the danger of being fired upon.[25] In forwarding Harper's report to the Foreign Office Macdonald condemned the action of the Niger Company and warned that the Company was introducing into this part of the Protectorate the same methods which were causing unrest in the Brass districts.[96]

[94] F.O. 84/2194 Macdonald to F.O. 8 March 1892

[95] F.O. 84/2194 Harper to Macdonald 8 Nov. 1892. Enclosure in Macdonald to F.O. 8 Dec. 1892

[96] F.O. 84/2194 Macdonald to F.O. 8 Dec. 1892

It was perhaps unfortunate for the British that the Royal Niger Company's decision to establish in the Warri district coincided with the inauguration of Macdonald's administration, for their activities clearly helped to render unpopular the new British regime not only with Nana but with all leading Itsekiri traders.

By 1892 Nana was unquestionably the greatest and most powerful person in Itsekiriland. In a report covering the years from 1891 to 1894, Macdonald stated that the trade of the Benin River was 'almost entirely in the hand of a powerful Jekri chief of the name of Nana'. He gave an account of Nana's strength— about 3,000 or 4,000 men and innumerable canoes, some capable of holding 40 to 50 paddlers and all of which could be mounted with guns. Nana's state canoe was a most beautiful one, made to order in England.[97] All this was a loud testimony to the wealth and power which, among other factors, were soon to lead to the fall of Nana.

The one shadow that for ever hung over Nana was the idea put abroad that he stopped trade whenever it suited his fancy to do so. Thus Macdonald recalled that some years before the writing of the report Nana, 'for some slight, real or fancied', stopped the entire trade of the Benin River district. Enough has been said about the incident to make it clear that the stoppage of trade in 1886 was not ordered to satisfy the whims and caprices of a tyrant-trader. Macdonald made another claim. Nana, he wrote, had been accustomed for many years to rule the Benin River by terrorism.[98] It was one thing to assert that Nana had won a near monopoly of the trade of his region, and quite another to presume to spell out the methods which had been employed for the winning of that monopoly. The existence of a monopoly was itself no evidence that this monopoly had been won through terrorist tactics, as many British accounts of Nana invariably suggest. Writing in July 1894 when the British offensive against Nana was nearly under way, Coxon, a British merchant trading in the area, claimed that Nana would not allow free trade; he said that in the Urhobo country Nana had established 'a scientific

[97] F.O. 2/63 Report on the Administration of the Niger Coast Protectorate, 1891–July 1894
[98] *Ibid*

frontier' made of broken bottles about three miles from the waterside of the towns where his trading depots were established, and had forced all the people within that frontier to trade with him alone.[99] Coxon's letter was one of the documents with which the Foreign Office was furnished during the crisis of 1894 as evidence of Nana's misdeeds. But most careful investigation has failed to produce any confirmatory evidence with regard to Coxon's claim. The general tone of the letter, which Macdonald himself described as 'somewhat highly coloured', leaves one in doubt as to the truth of Coxon's assertion.[100] Nor can much credit be given to the imaginative Harold Bindloss whose comments on Nana's methods have been cited elsewhere.[101] Itsekiri traditions have little to say about Nana fighting off his rivals in the Urhobo country. What these traditions emphasise is the power which made it dangerous to cross his path. Nana's trading organisation in the Urhobo country belies, to a large extent, a general accusation of terrorism. While Nana's acknowledged power in men and armaments played a part in the building up of his commercial position, that was only one aspect of the matter. He got the better of his rivals largely because of his superior wealth and organising ability.

Nana is sometimes accused of having used his great wealth and power only for his personal gain and not for the general development of his district.[102] This is scarcely a fair charge to bring against Nana in the age in which he lived, for which of the traders of the area—white or black—was not guilty of a similar charge? Not even the establishment of a British protectorate over the Oil Rivers can be said to have been altruistic.

The fullest account of the conditions in the Benin River district is to be found in Gallwey's report for the year August 1891 to July 1892. According to this report the trade of the district was far from satisfactory. Gallwey advanced a number of reasons such as 'the predominating influence of Chief Nana, and the monopoly of trade, held by him during the early part of the

[99] F.O. 2/63 Coxon to Pinnock 1 July 1894
[100] F.O. 2/63 Coxon to Pinnock 1 July 1894
[101] See chapter II p. 44
[102] F.O. 403/216 Annual Report Niger Coast Protectorate 1894/5

year'.[103] Gallwey briefly summed up Nana's position as it had developed since 1884. He recalled his appointment as Governor in 1884 and argued that this increased his self-importance. Inevitably he recalled that he had stopped trade in 1886. 'Prior to August 1891', the Vice-Consul reported, 'the trade of the district more especially in the Sobo markets, was more or less monopolised and entirely ruled by Nana.' Then came an important observation that during the year under consideration, Nana learnt that he must not interfere in other people's affairs. Although Nana naturally found it difficult to relinquish all his old powers, he was 'a fairly sensible man' and realised that it was foolish policy to thwart the aims of the British government of the Protectorate. Gallwey's summing up of the situation reveals that Nana was already beginning to adjust to the new policy of free trade advocated by government. He was consequently also beginning to lose his monopoly. Gallwey also recorded the fact that Nana's staff of office had been taken from him in 1890 and had not been returned at the time of the report. This most probably means that Gallwey and his staff were already treating Nana as a private individual and not as head of his people. Nana did not see things in the same light. The attitude of the Vice-Consul in this matter could not have been calculated to improve relations between Nana and the British political officers of the Benin River district.

The second reason given by Gallwey for the slackness of trade was the continual quarrels between the middlemen and the oil producers caused by the failure of the oil producers to pay oil for the goods with which they had been entrusted by the Itsekiri middlemen. The quarrels took the form of fights between the 'boys' of the Itsekiri middlemen and those owing oil, and ended in the Itsekiri carrying off slaves from the offending person or village. The disturbances caused often resulted in temporary stoppage of trade at the producing markets concerned. It would be unrealistic to argue that these quarrels and the adverse effect they had on trade were the work of Nana's 'boys' alone though,

[103] F.O. 2/51, Report on the Benin District, Oil Rivers Protectorate for the year ending 31 July 1892—enclosure in Macdonald to F.O. 12 Jan. 1893. The discussion that follows is based on the same report.

as he had an extremely large number of men working for him, attention was understandably focused on him. Gallwey claimed that just before his arrival in the district, there was one of these quarrels as a result of which Nana 'captured no less than 200 slaves from one man'. These slaves were, however, returned on the intervention of Gallwey. It is important to emphasise that, by Gallwey's own testimony, Nana agreed to return the captives even though this must have meant an over-all loss to himself. Nana was decidedly adjusting his ways along the lines of British policy.

The impression has been created through earlier works that the quarrels about which Gallwey complained were the result of Itsekiri, and more particularly Nana's, high-handedness. While it is true that Nana's 'boys' sometimes were high-handed, it will be stretching the point unduly to argue that these 'boys' relying on the acknowledged power of their master 'did pretty much as they pleased, as often as not seizing produce without paying for it'.[104] Gallwey's report corrects this impression as it makes it clear that the Urhobo and Kwale oil producers were sometimes responsible for the unrest in the hinterland. Admittedly Urhobo's refusal to supply oil was sometimes a reprisal against the actions of Nana's 'boys', for this was the only way of fighting back against any unwarranted attack. As has already been pointed out Nana did not always approve of these excesses. The truth about the situation in the hinterland was that the trading methods of the time tended to produce strife. The Urhobo themselves were not innocent of capturing slaves or even free men in lieu of outstanding debts. As Gallwey had undertaken a tour of parts of Urhoboland at the end of 1891, he had first-hand information of the situation as it actually existed. Thus at Eku he noted that the Urhobo were continually in a state of war with the Itsekiri traders there, or with neighbouring clans. At Okpara, Gallwey discovered that as a result of raids on one another, the Urhobo had seized '15 Jekri men' and the Itsekiri '13 Sobo men'. Gallwey ordered mutual restoration.[105] Concluding this aspect of

[104] Mockler-Ferryman, A. F. *British Nigeria* p. 99 London 1902
[105] F.O. 84/2111 Gallwey's Report on his visit to the Urhobo oil markets—enclosure in Macdonald to F.O. No. 30, 12 Dec. 1891

his report Gallwey claimed that the situation in the hinterland had improved since the establishment of the new administration. He realised, however, that these quarrels and stoppages of trade could not be finally eliminated until military posts had been established in the hinterland as distinct from the coastal districts. As events were to prove, the solution to the question of unrest in the hinterland could not be solved by the removal of influential men like Nana. The real solution lay in the inculcation of new habits, new modes of thought and new methods of settling disputes. It was not until a full decade after the fall of Nana that this solution was found.[106] By 1914 British penetration of the hinterland could be said to be complete. Until that time unrest continued.

Three other reasons were adduced for the unsatisfactory state of trade. One was the policy of the Oba of Benin who insisted on Itsekiri traders who operated in his domain paying a kind of trade tax. Failure to pay this tax often resulted in a stoppage of trade. Here once again was evidence that stoppage of trade was an accepted way of tackling disputes over trade. Another reason, discussed elsewhere, was what Gallwey described as the inability of the middlemen to understand fluctuating prices in the European markets. Finally the trade of the Benin River proper had declined as a result of the opening of Sapele as a government station and the movement there of some of the trade that was usually sent to the Benin River.[107] Everything considered, it is obvious that the causes of the slackness of trade were many and varied. Clearly the economic evils of the time could not be blamed on Nana as an individual, or even on his 'boys' alone.

Gallwey also commented on the political situation in Itsekiriland. According to him two factions existed in Itsekiriland. One of these occupied the right bank of the Benin River and was headed by Nana. The other occupied the left bank with Numa as its leader. Skirmishes between the two groups occurred frequently even after the establishment of the 1891 regime. Gallwey explained the differences between the two factions as 'simply the objection of the left bank people to be dictated to by Nana'.[108]

[106] See Ikime chapter IV.
[107] F.O. 2/51 Gallwey Report 1891–2   [108] *Ibid*

Little did Gallwey know that there existed a long-standing feud between the families of the leaders of the factions and that what appeared to him to be a struggle over trade was, in fact, a continuation of a feud which was to attain its worst dimensions under Numa's heir and successor, Dogho.

Numa died in February 1892, and was succeeded by his son, Dogho. Commenting on this fact Gallwey wrote:

> Numa was a particularly weak minded and incapable chief—but his son, who succeeded him, is a very superior man altogether, and in time is likely to improve very materially on his father's rule, and further he is not afraid of Nana. In addition to all this he is a very loyal supporter of Her Majesty's Government—His name is DORE.[109]

There is a tradition which states that Dogho's father carefully brought him up to oppose Nana.[110] Here, it would appear, was proof of the fact for Dogho, on loyalty (unquestioning loyalty in most cases) to the British administration and a dogged fight against Nana, built up a reputation which in after years made him one of the greatest British political agents in the whole of southern Nigeria.[111] In the same report Gallwey described an event which helps to show how Dogho proved his loyalty to the British. Gallwey had decided to make a trip to Lagos through the creeks. Nana furnished him with a large 'gig-canoe' for the journey but refused to supply the crew, arguing that, as Lagos was a British colony, his slaves might escape once they got there.[112] Dogho, who was probably happy at Nana's refusal, promptly made good the deficiency by supplying Gallwey with a crew of twenty-four slaves,[113] thereby winning the vice-Consul's gratitude. Dogho was already preparing the way for the part he was to play in securing the fall of his rival and enemy.

Another issue mentioned in the 1892 report was that of slavery. The lot of the slaves kept by the Itsekiri was considered 'a fairly happy one'. Gallwey did not seen any reason for the

[109] *Ibid*   [110] See Moore p. 108
[111] See Ikime, O. 'Chief Dogho: "The Lugardian System in Warri" 1917–1932' *J.H.S.N.* Vol. 3 No. 2 Dec. 1965 pp. 313–33
[112] F.O. 2/51 Gallwey's Report 1891–2
[113] *Ibid*

abolition of the system of domestic slavery as it operated at the
time.[114] After all, had he not journeyed to Lagos with a crew of
slaves? This commentary on the institution of slavery recalls
the argument put forward in the last chapter. Gallwey's judgment was a vindication of the points made by the Itsekiri to
Macdonald in 1889 as to why the institution of slavery should be
preserved. Again Gallwey's views raise a question posed earlier:
if slavery was not to be abolished, could the Itsekiri reasonably
be expected not to replenish their stock through the usual channels? One of the factors that ostensibly precipitated the crisis of
1894 was that Nana had raided the Abraka district and carried
away some slaves. In the circumstances in which the Itsekiri
found themselves, and bearing in mind the code of commercial
relations of the time, was Nana's seizure of Abraka men an
unusual event? It will be shown that there was much more in
the Nana episode than the evidence which was built up against
him in 1894.

The situation in 1892, as it emerges from Gallwey's report,
was one in which Nana and the other Itsekiri traders, as well as
the Urhobo, were to a large extent pursuing their accustomed
ways of life, and using the old sanctions with regard to securing
trade, and tackling the perennial question of debt, despite the new
fact of the establishment of British rule. At the same time, the
presence of British political officers was beginning to affect the
situation and to demand a modification of the old ways of doing
things. Both sides were beginning, however slowly, to react to
the new situation. Nana, by Gallwey's own testimony, was
definitely attempting to modify his position. Gallwey for his part
realised that time must be given to the Nigerian peoples to
adjust their way of life: 'I should be very sorry to see the necessity arise of using violent means to bring the natives to their
senses.'[115] It looked, therefore, as if there would follow a period
during which the Nigerian peoples and the British administration
would seek to find an acceptable *modus vivendi* through co-
operation. Yet in 1894 there arose a crisis which ended in war.
How does one explain this?

A few of Nana's papers captured after the Ebrohimi expedition

[114] F.O. 2/51 Gallwey's Report 1891-2   [115] *Ibid*

of 1894 provide some clue to the gradual worsening of relations
between him and the British. In June 1892 Gallwey, in a
peremptory note, ordered Nana to recall Ololu one of his head
slaves from the Urhobo country and restrict him to Ebrohimi.
If Ololu were seen on any of the beaches, Gallwey warned, he
would be detained and deported to Old Calabar.[116] Gallwey gave
no reason to justify this action. A week later, in another equally
brusque and mysterious letter Gallwey wrote: 'I wish to see
you on Thursday at 11. You are playing a very dangerous game
and I warn you that if I do bring gun boats into the River I shall
use them. You are fighting against the Government, and I warn
you to be very careful.'[117] That was all the letter contained.
There were no details of the dangerous game Nana was alleged
to be playing, nor was there any explanation of how Nana was
fighting against the government. In the absence of any letters
from Nana in reply to these two letters, it is impossible to make
further comment. Yet these letters are important as evidence
that, for one reason or the other, relations between Nana and the
British were deteriorating.

In August of the same year Nana received another letter from
a British administrative officer, this time from the Acting Vice-
Consul of the Benin River, Hally Hutton. He informed Nana that
the Vice-Consul at Warri had written to say that many of the
traders there were afraid to trade with the whites because Nana
and some of the other Benin River chiefs had not sent up 'a
proper message' to Warri allowing trade to go on. Apparently,
Nana had promised to send such a message and Hutton now held
him to his promise.[118] This letter confirms that Nana was a great
power in the area, and at the same time emphasises the difficulty
in which his power placed him. It would appear from a letter
written by Gallwey in 1893 that Nana did keep his promise,
asked the Itsekiri traders to resume trade, and himself sent up a
great quantity of goods to buy oil—for which latter act Gallwey
charged him with enlightened self-interest. In the same letter
Gallwey informed Nana that it was the policy of the British

[116] F.O. 2/64 Gallwey to Nana 15 June 1892
[117] F.O. 2/64 Gallwey to Nana 21 June 1892
[118] F.O. 2/64 Hally Hutton to Nana 9 August 1892

administration that everybody be free to trade where they pleased. He charged Nana with doing whatever he pleased, but seeing to it that nobody did anything against his own wishes. 'I am going to change all this,'[119] Gallwey declared.

In November 1893 matters reached a near crisis. Gallwey had gone up to Okpara and returned 'very dissatisfied with the state of affairs up there'.[120] In a letter to Nana at the beginning of December he wrote, 'You will have to give me a very clear explanation of your conduct or abide the consequences.' He charged Nana with pretending to be a friend of the government while in reality doing his best to undermine government policy. Nana's 'boys' were, according to Gallwey, 'spreading lies about the Government' and setting the Urhobo against the British administration. If he caught any of the 'boys', Gallwey fulminated, he would make a lasting example of him for the benefit of Nana, his 'boys' and his Urhobo friends. Once again no more details were given. From the tone of the letter it is obvious that he had not caught anyone actually setting the Urhobo against the British. Someone must have told him. Who did, and with what motives?

Gallwey in the same letter went on to describe two other incidents. While at Okpara he had sent for one Eddu, described by him as one of Nana's head slaves, to come aboard his launch to see him. Eddu refused to see the Vice-Consul on the grounds that, as Nana had not given him any such orders, he would be angry to hear that one of his head slaves had held discussions with the Vice-Consul on his own authority. Three times Gallwey sent for Eddu and three times did Eddu refuse to go to his launch. Gallwey in his letter to Nana claimed that all he had wanted to do was to discuss the current state of trade with Eddu as a sign that he took an interest in the markets. Eddu's attitude irritated Gallwey beyond measure and yet, granted that Eddu was in fact Nana's slave, the reply sent by him represented a perfectly understandable relationship between a head slave and his master.

Another of Nana's 'boys' called Ubari refused to sell chickens

[119] F.O. 2/64 Gallwey to Nana 7 Dec. 1893
[120] F.O. 2/64 Gallwey to Nana 1 Dec. 1893

to the Vice-Consul, arguing, according to Gallwey, that 'he and
the Consul did not agree; and that Nana was his master'. Again
Gallwey's pride was wounded to the core. Summing up these two
incidents Gallwey wrote to Nana:

> You ought to be very proud having such brave and big men on
> your side as Mude and Ubari. I look upon them as small boys and
> will treat them so when the time comes.
>   Had my soldiers been with me I would have made prisoners of
> Ubari and Eddu—and probably burnt Ubari's houses.[121]

Gallwey's reaction to the situation suggests that he regarded
Eddu's and Ubari's attitudes as a personal insult; for there was
scarcely any matter of government policy involved in these two
incidents, except in as far as they served to show Nana's great
influence and demonstrated that there were those who did not
yet regard the British government as the final authority in
the land. It might well have been the realisation of this fact
which increased Gallwey's fury. Gallwey ordered Nana to remove Eddu and Ubari from Okpara and punish them. When this
letter was tendered during Nana's trial as evidence of his
misdeeds, Nana remarked, 'I could not understand why Captain
Gallwey had spoken so strongly'.[122] According to Nana, Eddu was
not even one of his slaves but free born and head of the Itsekiri
community at Okpara. He had not sent Eddu to Okpara, yet on
receipt of Gallwey's letter he had recalled Eddu from Okpara
'and put him in chains'. He had inquired of Gallwey whether
Eddu should be sent to the Vice-Consulate but Gallwey had sent
to say that as Eddu had been recalled from Okpara he was
satisfied.[123]

As a consequence of what had happened at Okpara Gallwey
informed Nana that he was sending a strongly worded report to
the Consul-General. In the meantime he would stop Nana's
annual subsidy of £200 which, Gallwey claimed, was being paid
to him because he was regarded as loyal to the government.[124]
This was a misrepresentation of the facts. When the government

[121] *Ibid*

[122] F.O. 2/64, Nana's evidence at his trial—enclosure in Macdonald to
F.O. No. 49, 13 Dec. 1894

[123] *Ibid*   [124] F.O. 2/64 Gallwey to Nana 1 Dec. 1893

decided to introduce customs duties in 1891, it was realised that those Itsekiri elders who were accustomed to sharing the comey among themselves would suffer a financial loss as a result of the abolition of comey and the substitution for it of customs duties which were paid to the government and not to the elders. Consequently it was decided to pay those elders who could prove their entitlement to comey an annual subsidy calculated according to the amount that used to go to them in the pre-1891 era. Nana as Governor of the River no doubt received a fair share of the comey, hence his £200 annual subsidy. The British were not paying him £200 for being a loyal supporter. It would appear, therefore, that Gallwey was merely seeking to demonstrate that the British had been fair and generous to Nana, while the latter had proved ungrateful and recalcitrant.

Finally, Gallwey charged Nana with injuring trade without saying how. 'If I find you out', warned Gallwey, 'you must expect full punishment.' In a postscript Gallwey added that he had discussed the situation with a certain Harrison who was of the same opinion that Nana was definitely injuring trade both at Warri and in the Benin River.[125] This Harrison was the son of Dudu. Dudu had for some time stayed with Nana in Ebrohimi but had been obliged to leave because, in the face of Nana's influence and power, he had found no room for the expansion of his own trade. After he left Ebrohimi, he became one of the opponents of Nana's power.[126] His son, Harrison, was literate and often acted as an interpreter for the Vice-Consuls. It was hardly to be expected that Harrison would say anything in Nana's favour. It was the trio of Dogho, Dudu and Harrison who, together with all their henchmen, teamed up against Nana in 1894. It is, of course, possible that Gallwey did not realise that Harrison was one of Nana's personal antagonists. But as he had reported only two years previously the existence of two factions among the Itsekiri, he might have found out to which camp Harrison belonged. As it happened Harrison consistently worked against Nana's interests throughout the period of crisis.

The accusation that Nana injured trade does not seem to be borne out by the trade figures of the period. In the year August

[125] F.O. 2/64 Gallwey to Nana 1 Dec. 1893   [126] Lloyd p. 229

1892 to July 1893, the exports of the Benin River district totalled £78,272 5*s*. 8*d*. For the year August 1893 to July 1894 these exports had risen to £100,411 16*s*. 0*d*., an increase of over £22,000 During the same period there was an increase in the imports to the tune of £28,500. Yet if Gallwey is to be believed, trade was being injured in the second half of 1893. It was only in the Warri district that there was a fall in the export trade of some £10,500.[127] But then Macdonald had forecast that there would be a fall because of the export duties imposed by the Royal Niger Company on its own side of the boundary line which prevented many of the Itsekiri from going to their old markets.[128] Some indication that this must have been a major factor responsible for the fall in export trade in Warri is seen in the fact that, despite the fall in exports which meant the Itsekiri had less money to spend, there was still a £2,000 increase in imports. The combined trade of the two districts showed an overall increase of £132,000. In view of these figures one wonders exactly how much injury had been caused to trade by Nana.

About a week after the letter discussed above, Gallwey wrote another letter to Nana, the first paragraph of which reads: 'A short time ago I placed two red buoys about 1 mile this side of Aruea. They have been removed in the last week. As no other boys but yours would do this, I beg you will find out the offenders and hand them over to me.'[129] This was scarcely fair on Nana. Virtually every offence committed in the districts of Warri and Benin River was blamed on Nana or his 'boys', often without sufficient investigation. Nana's enemies would have been more than fools not to have cashed in on this situation to commit, or cause their 'boys' to commit, offences which they could then immediately report to the Vice-Consul as having been committed by Nana or his 'boys'. Nana was beginning to pay the price for his success, his wealth, his power and his obvious unwillingness to surrender his position before the onslaught of the imperial factor.

[127] For these trade figures see F.O. 2/64—enclosure in Macdonald to F.O. No. 44, 29 Nov. 1894
[128] F.O. 2/51 Macdonald to F.O. 12 Jan. 1893
[129] F.O. 2/64 Gallwey to Nana 7 Dec. 1893

Thus the year 1893 ended with the relations between Nana and the British in a far from satisfactory state. The reports and letters of the Vice-Consul suggest that while in some respects Nana was 'mending' his ways, in others he was unwilling to abdicate his power and position. When that has been said, it must be conceded that most of the charges brought against him by the British were either unproven, like those of setting the Urhobo against the government or injuring trade, or of a relatively minor nature, like Nana's men refusing to sell chickens to a British Vice-Consul. Yet these incidents were used to set the stage for the drama that was to be enacted in the following year.

CHAPTER IV

The Ebrohimi Expedition, 1894

THE YEAR 1893 had ended with a steady build-up of tension between the British administration and Nana. The trend of events did not change in the new year. If anything, events moved quickly to the crisis of August and September 1894. In March, Hugh Lecky, Acting Vice-Consul at the Benin River, wrote to Nana to the effect that it was being rumoured that Nana intended to 'chop' some Urhobo people at Oriah, in the Abraka district. Lecky warned Nana that he would be held responsible for any stoppage of trade or any other 'palaver' that arose out of the threatened 'chopping'.[1]

Whether as a result of the above letter, or as a result of the accumulated grievances of the British administration against Nana since 1891, Macdonald wrote to Nana in April. In the letter Macdonald informed Nana that as the British administration had been effectively established in the area, he was no longer to regard himself as 'chief' of the Itsekiri people. Every Itsekiriman, the letter warned, had the right to trade wherever he pleased and with whomsoever he chose. If Nana was caught intimidating any people—whether these were in his own town of Ebrohimi or elsewhere—the Consul-General would take 'very serious notice' of the fact.[2] It should be noticed that it was only at this point, April 1894, that Macdonald officially informed Nana that he was no longer to regard himself as Governor of the River. In 1891 Macdonald had promised Nana that he would let him know the decision of the Foreign Office about his alleged deposition by Annesley in 1890. Apparently the Foreign Office had not followed up the matter and Macdonald now took the decision on his

---

[1] F.O. 2/64 Hugh Lecky to Nana 27 March 1894. Exhibit L at Nana's trial. *All the correspondence between the British officials and Nana cited in this chapter are from this same volume.* Therefore the volume reference is omitted hereafter.

[2] Macdonald to Nana 5 April 1894 Exhibit M

own authority, invoking no doubt the instructions which gave him the right to take over power from the chiefs of the protectorate if and when this was in the interests of the people. In 1884 Nana had been elected Governor at a meeting of Itsekiri elders. In 1894 he was stripped of his office without consultation with those who had chosen him for that office. The reason for this was obvious: a Governor of the River in the situation of 1894 was an embarrassment to the British administration. Even more important was the fact that this particular person, who had held the office since 1884, was too self-willed, too influential, too aware of his own wealth and power to take directives from the protectorate government, especially when they clashed with his own interests. He was, therefore, no longer a fit instrument through which 'the decrees of Her Majesty's Government were to be enforced and executed'. In fact, from the point of view of the British administration, the office of Governor of the River had by 1894 become an anachronism. Nana did not reply to Macdonald's letter but it is easy to see that the letter could not have improved relations between him and the British administration.

In May A. F. Locke the Consular Agent, took over the Benin River vice-consulate, presumably in the absence of Gallwey who was at home on leave. According to Locke, it was brought to his notice early in May that the trade of the Benin River had been held up. He went on to investigate and was told by 'several of the Abraka and Uriah chiefs' that they had done no trade for a number of months. They blamed this on Chief Nana who, they said, made it impossible for them to trade at the waterside markets. That was not all. The chiefs declared further that 'in their interior villages their people were always being seized and taken away by Nana or by people acting under his orders'.[3] Locke obtained a list of those who had been seized and wrote to Nana asking that these people be returned.[4]

It was the news of this 'unsettled state of affairs' that brought the Acting Consul-General, Ralph Moor, to the Benin River on

[3] F.O. 2/64 Evidence of Locke at Nana's trial—enclosure in Macdonald to F.O. No. 49, 13 Dec. 1894
[4] Locke to Nana 10 July 1894 Exhibit 8

21 June 1894. He discovered on his arrival 'that matters were most unsatisfactory, trade being almost entirely stopped owing principally to the acts of the people of Chief Nana in seizing Sobo people and generally terrorising the locality of the Ethiope River'.[5] Therefore, he wrote requesting that Nana report at the Benin River Vice-Consulate to discuss, what were described by Moor as matters of vital importance to him and his people.[6] Nana informed the Acting Consul-General that there had been three recent deaths in his family and that his brother and second-in-command was seriously ill. He regretted his inability to leave Ebrohimi in the circumstances but sent Tonwe, a trusted relation and messenger, to the Vice-Consulate to represent him in the discussions that Moor wished to hold.[7] On receipt of this letter, Moor wrote back to Nana on 24 June. He commiserated with Nana for the misfortune that had befallen him and his people, but added: 'It is requisite that I should see you regarding matters of great importance and I must therefore direct that you attend here at 9 o'clock a.m. tomorrow without fail.'[8] It will be noticed that once again Moor did not disclose the nature of the issues to be discussed. Nana's answer on 25 June pleaded that it was against the customs of his people for him to leave the town so soon after the deaths reported in his previous letter; besides, he was too grief-stricken to undertake the trip requested by Moor. Once again he begged that Ralph Moor should transact whatever business there was through Tonwe.[9] Moor regarded Nana's letters as 'letters of excuse'. While there can be no question as to the correctness of Nana's claim that the customs of his people forbade his leaving home soon after the deaths reported, it is possible that Nana seized on the misfortunes in his family to avoid going to the Vice-Consulate. In this regard Moor's continued reference to unspecified 'matters of great importance' probably made Nana suspicious of the good intentions of the British administration. However that might have been, with the

---

[5] F.O. 2/63 Moor to F.O. No. 22, 6 Aug. 1894
[6] Moor to Nana 23 June 1894 Exhibit N
[7] Nana to Moor 24 June 1894 Exhibit O
[8] Moor to Nana 24 June 1894 Exhibit P
[9] Nana to Moor 25 June 1894 Exhibit Q

exchange of the above letters, the preliminaries were over and the real drama was about to begin.

As it had become quite clear after Nana's letter of 25 June that he had no intention of presenting himself at the Vice-Consulate, Moor wrote him a detailed letter. First, he told Nana that he did not consider the reasons advanced by him for not reporting to the Vice-Consulate sufficiently weighty. The government of the protectorate, Moor wrote, would not enter into communication with chiefs' messengers but only with the chiefs themselves. Moor then gave Nana a number of directives: Nana's people were, according to Moor, making it impossible for the Urhobo of the Abraka district to take their produce to the riverside markets. This was in direct contravention of government policy. Nana was therefore enjoined to take steps to remedy this situation and to send a message to the Urhobo concerned to the effect that he had ordered his people to desist from obstructing trade. He was to make it quite clear to the Urhobo that he was taking this step in obedience to the instructions of the British administration.

Next, Nana was ordered to recall Ologun, his head slave at Eku, and replace him with another. This step had become necessary, Moor wrote, because Ologun was terrorising and intimidating the entire district and had seized a number of Urhobo people. Ologun was further charged with having used abusive and threatening language to Harrison, guide to the Vice-Consul, Benin River district. Nana was also ordered to hand over to the British authorities the men seized by Ologun.

Moor gave Nana two weeks within which to carry out the above injunctions. The letter ended with a threat that if Nana failed to obey the orders given to him no canoes belonging to him or his people would be allowed to pass up or down the River Ethiope.[10]

Nana replied immediately. He once again apologised for his inability to report to the Vice-Consulate as Moor had earlier requested. He pointed out that the actions attributed to his boys in the Abraka area were without his authorisation and that as the matter had been brought to his notice, he would despatch instructions to those boys in compliance with the directives of the

[10] Moor to Nana 25 June 1894 Exhibit R

government. The Urhobo people alleged to have been seized by Ologun, he argued, were in fact men given in payment for outstanding debt. Various people in Eku, he explained, owed him oil valued at a total of 200 puncheons. He would recall Ologun—and did recall him—in obedience to the orders of the government, but added a plea that Ologun be allowed at a later date to return to Eku to collect debts still outstanding, as he was the only one among his head slaves really acquainted with the state of his business in Eku. He doubted the truth of the allegation that Ologun had abused Harrison without provocation and suggested that it was a matter of mutual abuse.[11]

After the above exchange of letters, the two weeks allowed Nana within which to carry out the instructions given to him were allowed to pass. On 9 July Moor returned to the Benin River with one officer and twenty men of the Niger Coast Protectorate Force to strengthen the contingent of one officer and fifty men stationed in the district.[12] According to Moor, he discovered on his return to the Benin River that his instructions had not been carried out. On 10 July, the day after his arrival, he wrote to Nana. He reminded Nana of Macdonald's letter of April and emphasised the fact that whereas Nana could settle disputes which arose among his own people according to 'native custom' he was obliged, in keeping with government policy, to take disputes between him and other people to the consular courts for settlement. By seizing slaves from those Urhobo owing him oil, Nana was taking the law into his own hands and thereby injuring trade. The head slave responsible for the seizure, Moor warned, was liable to severe punishment. While Moor was happy that Ologun had been recalled from Eku, he pointed out that the slaves seized by Ologun had not been released and instructed Nana to hand over the Eku people seized and take action in the consular court to secure payment of the outstanding debt. In other words Nana was called upon, as a consequence of the establishment of British rule, to abandon the use of the old sanctions for recovering debt. In the meantime, and until the Eku people were handed over to the consular authorities,

[11] Nana to Moor 25 June 1894 Exhibit S
[12] F.O. 2/63 Moor to F.O. No. 22, 6 Aug. 1894

reported Moor, 'I stopped the trading of Nana and his people in the Ethiope River, establishing a blockade against them at its mouth and seizing any of their canoes that attempted to pass.[13] The first physical sanctions had been applied.

Nana was kept informed of the blockade against his town. At the same time, in order to put an end to the general 'feeling of insecurity both to life and property caused by the parading of war canoes on the waterways', a proclamation was issued, dated 10 July, banning the use of all war canoes—they were described for the purpose of the proclamation as 'any armed canoe or canoe carrying armed men'.[14] Any war canoe found on the waterways would be liable to seizure and forfeiture and the chief to whom it belonged held 'guilty of hostility towards Her Britannic Majesty's Government of the Protectorate'.[15] Moor's letter ended, almost incongruously, with a message of condolence to Nana on the death of the latter's brother—the brother reported sick in Nana's letter of 24 June.

Nana did not send an immediate reply to Moor's letter of 10 July. Moor for his part returned to headquarters soon after he addressed the above letter to Nana. On 23 July Nana wrote to Moor. He reported that he had been informed by one Herbert Clarke, a messenger to the consular officers, that it was the government's intention to seize and remove him from the district. According to Nana, Herbert Clarke had felt compelled to warn him about the intentions of the government because of the blood relationship between them, Clarke being a member of the same *ebi* as himself. He expressed both surprise and fear that there should be such a plot against him when he felt that he had committed no offence against the protectorate government. In the circumstances, and remembering what had happened to Jaja of Opobo, he informed Moor that he would find it impossible to attend any meetings summoned by the Acting Consul-General. He renewed his plea that Tonwe be allowed to represent him at any meetings that it might be necessary to hold. The banning of war canoes, an act which was tantamount to disarming the

---

[13] Moor to Nana 10 July 1894 Exhibit T
[14] F.O. 2/63 Moor to F.O. No. 22, 6 Aug. 1894
[15] *Ibid* See also note 12

Itsekiri, was seen by Nana as further evidence of the government's hostile intentions towards him and his people.[16] In another letter addressed, 'My dear Clerk' and dated 24 July, Nana retold the Herbert Clarke story, and stated that some of his 'boys' had recently escaped from Ebrohimi and were probably telling tales about him in an endeavour to discredit him before the consular authorities. It was not, and had never been, his intention, Nana wrote, to enter into conflict with the government. He was apparently convinced that it was a foolhardy enterprise for 'blackman' to fight successfully against 'whiteman'.[17]

In the meantime, Moor who was at Old Calabar reported that he had received a cablegram, presumably from the Benin River Vice-Consulate, which stated that Nana was threatening to attack 'two friendly chiefs, Dore and Dudu'.[18] On the strength of this cablegram, Moor sent a further reinforcement of one officer and seventeen men to the Benin River, making a total of three officers and eighty-seven men already concentrated in the Benin River. In addition Moor requested that H.M.S. *Alecto* be in attendance at the Benin River. Moor then gave instructions that a meeting of all the important Itsekiri chiefs be summoned for 2 August.[19] It will be recalled that since 10 July a blockade had been established against Ebrohimi and that there was in force a proclamation against the use of war canoes. In these circumstances it was certainly not easy for Nana to carry out an attack on Dogho and Dudu without at the same time engaging in a war with the British forces charged with responsibility for maintaining the blockade and enforcing the proclamation. Besides, the fact that it was Dogho and Dudu that Nana was alleged to have been threatening to attack immediately raises doubts as to the truth of the accusation. For nothing could have been easier than for these enemies of Nana to make such a report to the Vice-Consul who, if past instances are anything to go by, would quickly see in the report further evidence of Nana's

[16] Nana to Moor 23 July 1894 Exhibit U

[17] Nana to 'My dear Clerk' 24 July 1894 part of Exhibit U. I have not been able to find out the identity of this Clerk.

[18] F.O. 2/63 Moor to F.O. No. 22, 6 Aug. 1894

[19] *Ibid*

'terrorist' activities. It is interesting to note that, so far as the evidence at present available goes, no inquiries were made locally before the Acting Consul-General was informed of Nana's alleged plan to attack these two 'friendly chiefs'. At his trial, Nana stated that he was unaware that any such accusation had been made against him.[20] Whatever the truth of the matter might have been, Moor seized the opportunity to build up a sizeable force in the Benin River. The request for the *Alecto* to be in attendance would tend to suggest that Moor was coming round to the view that force, or at least a show of force, was necessary for the settlement of the disturbed situation.

In accordance with instructions received from Moor, Locke wrote to Nana on 24 July inviting him to the meeting of 2 August and informing him that for the purpose of that meeting he could travel in his war canoes.[21] Moor himself arrived at the Benin River on 30 July, a day after the *Alecto*. It was only on his arrival that Moor received Nana's letter of 23 July in which he reported what Herbert Clarke had told him about the intentions of the government. Moor immediately wrote to Nana on the issue. First, he informed Nana that he had held discussions with Herbert Clarke who denied the story and that Tonwe, Nana's messenger who was said to have been present when Clarke made the alleged statement, confirmed Clarke's denial. He therefore urged Nana to attend the proposed meeting, at the same time making it clear that Tonwe would not be allowed to represent Nana at that or any other meeting. The object of the meeting, Moor wrote, was if possible to settle the existing unsatisfactory state of the district in a friendly manner. If not, he warned, other measures would have to be taken. He assured Nana that he would not be molested either on his way to or from the meeting. It was as a token of sincerity that Nana was to be allowed to go to the meeting in his war canoes. Moor seemed determined to convince Nana as to the falsehood of the alleged plot to deport him. He wrote: 'Any reports you may have heard regarding the Government seizing you are utterly unfounded. Such a course under the circumstances would be a gross breach of faith which I

[20] F.O. 2/64 evidence of Nana at his trial
[21] Locke to Nana 24 July 1894 Exhibit C

am surprised that you should have for a moment supposed the Government likely to adopt.'[22]

Nana wrote two letters in response to Moor's of 31 July. In one of these letters he requested that one chief Ogbe be allowed to represent him and that he was prepared to regard himself bound by any decisions taken at the meeting.[23] In the second letter he not only repeated the above plea but added that his suspicions about the hostile intentions of the government towards his people were confirmed by the fact that canoes carrying food to Ebrohimi were being seized by orders of the Vice-Consul. As a result, not only were his people facing the danger of starvation, but many of his men were being detained by the British forces. He made it quite clear that he could not, under existing conditions, attend the meeting on 2 August.[24]

The meeting was held as planned. Nana did not attend. Virtually all the other important traders in the Benin and Warri districts were present. Moor reported that all the chiefs who attended the meeting appeared to be anxious to carry out the orders of the government.[25] At the end a new treaty was entered into by the Itsekiri chiefs. This treaty was exactly like that of 1884 except for two factors: first, clauses VI and VII which had not been accepted in 1884 were now accepted—the Itsekiri chiefs had come round to accept free trade; and secondly, an additional clause was inserted which regarded the 1894 treaty as a ratification of the treaty of 1884. It was further stipulated that all offences committed against the provisions of the 1884 treaty were forgiven provided the new treaty was faithfully observed.[26] A copy of the new treaty was sent through a messenger to Nana who was informed that he was at liberty to enter into a similar form of treaty but only if he reported to the Vice-Consulate for the purpose.[27] In a letter to Nana after the meeting, Moor again requested that Nana carry out all the orders previously given

[22] Moor to Nana 31 July 1894 Exhibit V

[23] Nana to Moor 1 Aug. 1894 Exhibit W

[24] Nana to Moor 2 Aug. 1894 Exhibit X

[25] F.O. 2/63 Moor to F.O. No. 22, 6 Aug. 1894

[26] F.O. 2/63 Article X of the treaty—see Enclosure in Moor to F.O. No. 24, 15 Aug. 1894

[27] Moor to Nana 2 Aug. 1894 Exhibit Y

him, such as the release of the Eku people held in lieu of debt. Until this was done and until he reported to the Vice-Consulate for the purpose of settling matters,

> You and your people are hereby forbidden to appear on any of the waters of the Benin or Warri districts. Any canoe belonging to you or your people found on the waterways will be seized and forfeited and should the occupants of them not stop when called upon from Government launches or boats to do so they will be liable to be fired upon.[28]

It is difficult to say whether or not Nana's refusal to attend the meeting of 2 August was an error of judgment. On the one hand there was the presence of the British force and man-of-war; these were instruments of coercion sufficient to strike terror into Nana who must have known by now, taking into consideration all that had passed between him and the British authorities since 1891, that the British administration did not particularly desire to preserve him in his power and position. On the other hand there was the safe conduct offered him and the obvious fact that failure to attend the meeting would unquestionably single him out as opposing the wishes of the British administration. It was a difficult position to be in. The memory of Jaja's fate, despite a similar safe conduct, did not make things any easier for Nana. It would appear from all the evidence that Nana was, by 2 August, genuinely afraid for himself and that his refusal to be present at the meeting was due more to fear than to a desire to defy the authority of the protectorate government. As it turned out, however, the consequences of his failure to attend the meeting were as grave as any that would have followed on his going to the Vice-Consulate on 2 August.

At about the time of the meeting it was discovered that a strong barrier had been placed across the only creek through which access to Ebrohimi was possible. This, declared Moor, was in opposition to the directions of the government to the effect that all natural waterways were to be free for navigation. Nana was ordered to remove the barrier immediately on receipt of Moor's letter. Any delay in carrying out the order, he was in-

[28] Moor to Nana 2 Aug. 1894 Exhibit Y. See also F.O. 2/63 Moor to F.O. No. 22, 6 Aug. 1894

formed, would entail serious consequences.[29] It will probably never be known when the barrier was erected. Nana claimed that it was placed there by his father as a means of defence against rival Itsekiri traders as well as a safeguard against canoe robbers.[30] The British naturally assumed that Nana erected it as part of war preparations against the government.

The letter in which Moor ordered Nana to destroy the barrier was written on 2 August. On the next day, as the barrier had not been removed, Moor ordered Lieutenant-Commander Heugh of H.M.S. *Alecto* to remove it with mines. Some idea of the strength of the barrier can be seen from the fact that it took ten mines each with fifteen charges to blow it up. During the operation there was an exchange of fire between Nana's people and Heugh's party. Moor reported that four shots were fired at Heugh's party before he replied with half-a-dozen shots and two rockets.[31] Nana maintained at his trial that his men only fired in self defence.[32] The truth will never be known. At any rate, the first shots had been exchanged and Moor considered that a state of war now existed. From this time on he began to prepare for the final showdown. In a despatch to the Foreign Office he argued that the act of Nana's men in firing at the British forces materially altered the situation. The blockade of Ebrohimi was consequently to be more rigidly enforced to ensure that nothing entered or left the town. Moor's idea was that, as Nana depended for his food on supplies from the Urhobo country, this blockade would force him to surrender when the food supply in the town ran out. If Nana held out despite the blockade, it was Moor's view that more 'active measures' should be adopted. Should Nana indicate his readiness to surrender, Moor let the Foreign Office know what his terms would be—a £500 fine and the laying down of all arms and ammunitions save dane guns.[33] Moor was beginning to get irritated by Nana's continued resistance.

From this time on Moor concentrated on building up evidence

[29] *Ibid*   [30] F.O. 2/64 evidence by Nana at his trial
[31] F.O. 2/63 Moor to F.O. No. 22, 6 Aug. 1894
[32] F.O. 2/64 evidence by Nana at his trial
[33] F.O. 2/63 Moor to F.O. No. 22, 6 Aug. 1894

against Nana. He reported that there were strong grounds for
suspecting that 'atrocities' had been committed in Ebrohimi at
the funeral of Nana's brother which took place at the end of
June, and that this had probably been responsible for Nana's
fear of appearing at the Vice-Consulate. He was honest enough
to admit he had not been able to obtain reliable evidence about
the matter.[34] Surely one would have expected that Moor would
have waited until he had obtained information before making so
grave an allegation. James Pinnock wrote three years after the
Ebrohimi expedition that human sacrifices, the 'atrocities' Moor
implied, were within his experience, which spread over twenty-
five years, very rare among the Itsekiri.[35] It is difficult to resist
the conclusion that by sending what was in effect mere speculation as an official report to the Foreign Office, Moor was merely
attempting to prejudice that office against Nana and at the same
time preparing the ground for a justification of the steps which
he knew he was going to have to take against Nana.

It was further reported that 'a party of Idzos from a village
under the control of chief Nana' had attacked and burnt down
the Itsekiri settlement of Bobi at the mouth of the Benin River,
and carried off twelve persons as slaves. The Ijo chief was
ordered to report to the Vice-Consulate on 6 August to explain
his action but failed to turn up. According to Moor, it was reported that the Ijo chief 'had referred the matter to chief Nana
who directed him to keep the people seized and not to attend at
the vice-consulate'.[36] So Moor ordered Major Copland-Crawford
and Captain Scarfe of the Niger Coast Protectorate Force together with a party of marines under Heugh to arrest the Ijo
chief and, if that proved impossible, 'to take retaliatory measures'. The Ijo village, which was found deserted by the time the
British force arrived, was accordingly burnt to the ground.
Moor hoped that the punishment meted out to the Ijo would have
an excellent effect and prove to the neighbourhood that neglect
of government orders entailed serious consequences.[37] It is

[34] F.O. 2/63 Moor to F.O. No. 22, 6 Aug. 1894, see postscript
[35] Pinnock, James *Benin: The Surrounding Country, Inhabitants,
Customs and Trade* p. 32 Liverpool 1897
[36] F.O. 2/63 Moor to F.O. No. 23, 8 Aug. 1894   [37] *Ibid*

scarcely necessary to ask on whose evidence the conclusion was reached that Nana had instructed the Ijo chief not to report to the Vice-Consulate. The 'friendly chiefs' were obviously at work again.

Another incident which took place at Evhro (Effurun), home town of Nana's mother, was also attributed to Nana's influence. Apparently a dispute had arisen at the Evhro market on 26 July 1894. For some unstated reason Erigbe, described as the chief of the town, ordered his men to attack the disputants. During the confusion which ensued, goods were destroyed and a number of people injured. Like the Ijo chief, Erigbe was ordered to report to the Warri Vice-Consulate to explain his action. Until 8 August, when Moor wrote the relevant despatch, Erigbe had not turned up at the Vice-Consulate. On that day, Moor himself led to Evhro Major Copland-Crawford and five men of the Niger Coast Protectorate Force as well as four other European officers and a party of marines under Lieutenant-Commander Heugh. The aim was to get Erigbe to 'palaver'. He would not be persuaded, despite a threat that failure to negotiate would lead to the destruction of his town. In a last effort to persuade Erigbe to hold discussions with the British officers, he was given a half-hour ultimatum which, nevertheless, failed to produce the desired result. Moor thereupon decided that the only way open to him was the destruction of the town. Accordingly the greater part of Evhro was burnt down. Moor again hoped that 'this severe lesson' would have an excellent effect in settling the existing disturbed state of the district.[38]

The explanation for the heavy punishment inflicted on Evhro was that the Chief Erigbe was, as seen by Moor, 'a staunch adherent and friend of Nana' and as such his action, like that of the Ijo chief, was seen as a demonstration in favour of Chief Nana.[39] Hence it was necessary in the interest of the prestige of the British administration to deal seriously with the two cases. By August the general state of the Benin and Warri districts was reported to be greatly disturbed; government launches were patrolling the creeks and on land there was a concentration of the military. Yet Moor seemed to have expected the Ijo chief and

[38] *Ibid*   [39] *Ibid*

Erigbe to travel willingly to the Vice-Consulate. There was little evidence to show that either the Ijo chief or Erigbe had acted on the instructions or with the concurrence of Nana. Moor himself reported that Erigbe had 'caused much trouble for a long time past by his piratical acts in seizing boys, canoes and produce passing down his town'.[40] If this was based on fact, and not on a desire to paint Erigbe in such colours as would excuse Moor's action in burning down his town, it would further strengthen the argument that seizure of 'boys', canoes or produce was not confined to Nana or the Itsekiri. All whose power and geographical location enabled them to do so seemed to have engaged in it. Again, if the actions of the two chiefs were, in fact, a demonstration in favour of Nana, then he must have been well worth such a demonstration. It should be remembered that by this time Nana's town was already under blockade and he himself was unable to leave Ebrohimi. The trial of strength between him and the British had virtually begun, and the two chiefs in question must have been aware of this. If despite the evidence of British hostility towards Nana these men, who at the material time were not under the immediate control of Nana, chose to stand by him and risk their towns being burnt down, it is unlikely that Nana was the 'sable tyrant' and perpetrator of 'sickening atrocities' portrayed by Bindloss.[41] Such a tyrant would scarcely have kept the loyalty of the victims of his tyranny —for so are the Ijo and Urhobo generally portrayed—when once a new and, presumably superior, force arrived on the scene.

In the meantime Nana had placed a notice at the entrance of the Ebrohimi creek together with a flag of truce. In the notice he reiterated that the barrier across the Ebrohimi creek which had been blown up was not erected in preparation for war against the British and that he and his people desired peace.[42] On 13 August, while Moor was away from the district on a hurried visit to headquarters, Nana addressed a letter to the Acting Consul-General. For the first time since the crisis developed, Nana stated clearly that he considered himself to be 'the

[40] F.O. 26/3 Moor to F.O. No. 23, 8 Aug. 1894
[41] Bindloss pp. 206 & 209
[42] F.O. 2/64 Exhibit Z at Nana's trial

victim of a political intrigue caused by the conspiracy of surrounding chiefs and other wire pullers'.[43] He informed Moor that in view of the stern measures which the British administration had taken against him and his people, he had thought it expedient to seek the mediation of a third party. He had accordingly sent a deputation to Lagos to get the Governor of that colony to intervene in the dispute. The Deputy-Governor who had received his delegation had advised that Nana take up the question of peace negotiations direct with Ralph Moor.[44] Nana in this letter therefore declared his willingness to come to terms so that peace could once more be established on the rivers. It should here be mentioned that Lugard noted in his diary that he was informed by the Agent-General of the Royal Niger Company that Nana had also sought his intervention with a promise that he would abide by such arbitration whatever the result.[45] Apparently no notice was taken of this.

When Moor returned from headquarters and saw Nana's notice and flag of truce he immediately sent him a letter. Moor insisted as he had done from the very beginning that if Nana really desired a peaceful settlement of the dispute he should report to the Vice-Consulate. Moor noticed that Nana seemed afraid of being deported from the district. This, wrote Moor, was far from being the intention of the administration for, 'If you are prepared to carry out the directions and obey the orders of the Government and at the same time to rule your people in accordance with approved Native customs, it is to the advantage of the country that you remain as chief of your people'.[46] However, if Nana was not prepared to do these things, indicated Moor, the government had its duty to perform.

Nana's next letter, which according to both Nana and Claude Macdonald was written by a Lagos man on the run from his creditors, must have caused Moor a great deal of irritation. For while the letter contained essential truths it was written in a

[43] Nana to Moor 13 Aug. 1894 Exhibit 3
[44] *Ibid*
[45] Perham, M. & Bull, M. *The Diaries of Lord Lugard* Vol. IV, p. 85 London 1960 (entry for 1 Sept. 1894)
[46] Moor to Nana 15 Aug. 1984 Exhibit 1

pompous tone very different from previous letters written by
Nana's clerk. This letter regretted that Moor would not allow
Nana to be represented at meetings by anyone else, noting that
'former Consuls' had always allowed this. 'Chiefs in former
days', the letter ran, had 'full authority to govern', but since the
establishment of the 1891 regime, chieftaincy had lost its 'entire
prestige'. This being so Nana abjured all chieftaincy titles. It
was unfortunate, the letter pointed out, that the administration
allowed itself to be 'misled' by the influence of 'an interpreter
whose feelings were highly against [Nana] in consequence of a
private matter'.[47] Nana was ready for peace but he refused
Moor's essential condition that he must report to the Vice-
Consulate to discuss settlement.

Nana's letter seems to have convinced Moor that a greater
show of force was necessary. He reported that under cover of the
flag of truce Nana's people took to the rivers and plundered
passing canoes. On 16 August 'a small friendly village' was reported burnt down. Moor was of the view that the burning of the
village was 'probably' the work of Nana's people though he
admitted that he was unable to ascertain the facts before he left
the district for Old Calabar to secure two officers and one hundred
men as reinforcements.[48] At the same time he cabled the naval
authorities at Luanda for yet another gunboat and was informed
that the *Phoebe* would be at his service by 24-5 August. From the
Lagos Colony he requested the loan of seven-pounder field guns
with men to use them. In a despatch to the Foreign Office he
reiterated his previous stand that only 'absolute and uncondi-
tional surrender of Chief Nana and his advisers' as well as the
complete laying down of all arms save dane guns would meet the
situation. Failing such a settlement, it was imperative that active
measures be undertaken and that Nana and his advisers be removed from the district.[49]

While Moor was on his way to Old Calabar to secure reinforcements and arrange for another gunboat, the *Alecto* had
gone to the Forcados to refuel. The *Alecto* returned to the Benin
River on 13 August. On 17 August Lieut-Commander Heugh

[47] Nana to Moor 16 Aug. 1894 Exhibit 5
[48] F.O. 2/63 Moor to F.O. No. 25, 22 Aug. 1894   [49] *Ibid*

seized a number of 'hostile canoes' which he destroyed after transferring their cargo to his own boats. On 19 August Heugh led a force of nearly one hundred men in an offensive against Oteghele described as 'a large town of Nana's'. This town, Heugh reported, had threatened to fire on any canoe or boats passing up or down the creek leading to it. Like the Ijo village and Evhro, Oteghele was given to the flames after many of the inhabitants had been forced to desert the town and seek cover in the mangrove bush. Having destroyed Oteghele, Heugh devoted his energies to the effective blockading of Ebrohimi, and reported that as a result of the vigilance of the patrol boats a large number of canoes had been seized.[50]

It was at this stage that there occurred an incident which demonstrated the lengths to which Nana's men were prepared to go in the service of their master. The blockade was at its tightest. Every care was being taken to ensure that Nana did not leave Ebrohimi or receive anyone from outside. Suddenly a canoe with a single man in it appeared hugging the mangrove bush. The man was ordered to stop and come alongside the British patrol boats but he continued on his way. The British party then opened fire but although the man was hit several times he paid no heed, apart from quickening his pace, until he ran his canoe into a thicket, jumped into the bush and disappeared. When the canoe was eventually seized, it was discovered that the man had suffered a great loss of blood. Heugh was both amazed and impressed by this display of loyalty and courage and came to the conclusion that the man must have been carrying 'some important despatch' to Nana.[51]

If Heugh saw the above incident as demonstrating the determination of Nana and his people in their resistance to the British government in the Niger Coast Protectorate, he was soon to experience even greater determination. After destroying three villages at the mouth of the Ebrohimi creek, he decided to reconnoitre further up with a view to finding out what obstacles, if any, there were which could prevent an attack against Ebrohimi being made that way. Before setting out on the recon-

[50] F.O. 2/64 Heugh to Moor No. 6, 22 Aug. 1894 Exhibit 6
[51] *Ibid*

naissance, Heugh armour-plated his boat against rifle fire, apparently not expecting anything worse than a few shots from wandering riflemen. He miscalculated badly. For after going up the creek for some four hundred yards, Heugh and his party of eight ran into heavy fire from a masked battery somewhere in the mangrove swamp. Heugh's boat was pierced through in several places by shot which Heugh described in an exaggerated report as averaging 7–9 lbs. The casualty list included two dead, one man lost a foot, another an arm and four others were injured. In a self-flattering report Heugh spoke of how he steered the boat back to the ship in the face of heavy fire, with the wounded in the great traditions of the British navy, putting up a great struggle and keeping up a well-aimed fire which eventually silenced the guns of the enemy. The boat was all but sinking by the time the party got back to their ship.[52]

A day before the above incident, Frederick Lugard, then in the service of the Royal Niger Company, arrived at Warri on his way to Jebba. Lugard's impressions of the situation, recorded in his diary for the year, constitute a valuable commentary on the state of affairs at the time. There was considerable levity on the part of the British forces about the impending encounter with Nana. Lugard thought very little of the leadership, arguing that the militia was placed under an officer named Evanson 'with no experience at all'. The whole position, thought Lugard, was under-rated. Apparently no one realised at this stage how well armed Nana was or how strongly fortified the town of Ebrohimi. From what Lugard learnt about Nana he came to the conclusion that Nana would be 'a hard nut to crack' unless he gave in, although those actually engaged in the struggle did not share that opinion. 'Every one', noted Lugard, 'seemed to be looking forward to a great picnic.' Heugh's reconnoitring exercise of 25 August provided a foretaste of the 'picnic'. The result was 'a great scare'. Before the 25th the marines, in particular, hoped 'to goodness' that Nana would not give in after all the preparations that had been made. After the expedition, however, the men were horrified and their martial ardour cooled considerably.[53]

[52] F.O. 2/64 Heugh to Nana 25 Aug. 1894 Exhibit D
[53] Perham pp. 75–8

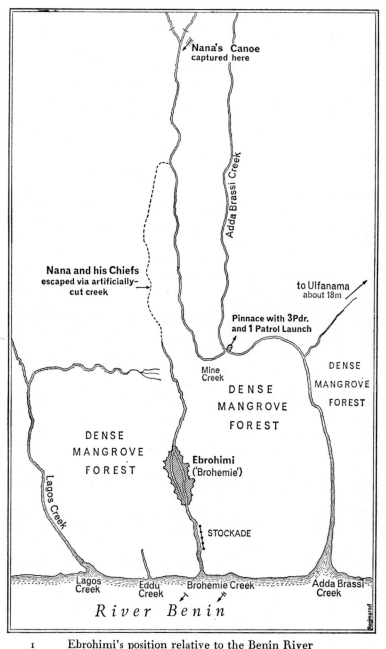

1   Ebrohimi's position relative to the Benin River

Heugh's reconnaissance had been undertaken on his own authority and against the express orders of Ralph Moor. Despite this fact, and despite the deaths and injuries, the venture did serve a useful purpose. It shook the British out of the dangerous complacency which Lugard had noted in his diary and, as Heugh himself pointed out, proved that Nana was a far more formidable enemy than had been supposed, and that it would be dangerous to attempt to take Ebrohimi by way of the creek. From this time on, therefore, preparations were made for a full-scale war.

Moor returned to the Benin River the day after Heugh's venture. He was greatly shaken by the 'disaster' that had taken place, and reported that the steadiness of the men had been affected by the outcome of the venture.[54] Nevertheless, the task in hand had to be accomplished. On the 28 and 29 August, therefore, Moor ordered a 'reconnoitring in force'. On the first day an attempt was made to construct a road through the swamps to Ebrohimi, using a 'party of friendly natives'. This attempt had to be suspended when it became known that the party was nearing the masked battery which had caused the disaster of three days earlier.[55] The next day the whole force available was landed with a view to proceeding towards Ebrohimi as far as was possible and ascertaining the possibility of taking the town by land. Once again 'native troops' led the advance. The party had gone as far as the point reached the previous day when spies reported that there was a powerful stockade some 200 to 300 yards off.[56]

The stockade which was eight feet high and had a 'face' of about 50 yards extended for 300 yards along the bank of the creek and was well masked by bush. It was made of hard wood logs firmly driven into the ground in rows of two or three. There were sleeping quarters for the garrison built near the stockade. Positioned at various points along the stockade were twenty-three heavy cannon.[57] Here was further evidence of the industry and skill of Nana and his men. It was Moor's opinion that the stockade which he described as 'a most powerful construction' had been built a year or two before. As it transpired at Nana's

[54] F.O. 2/63 Moor to F.O. No. 26, 31 Aug. 1894
[55] *Ibid*   [56] *Ibid*   [57] *Ibid*

trial this stockade was built during the period from July to August 1894, that is when it already appeared as if the crisis would end in war.

The first task of the reconnoitring party was to take this stockade. The seven-pounder field guns which had been sent up from Lagos were brought into operation and a heavy fire opened on the stockade. As the firing continued so a rapid advance was made. When within fifty yards of the stockade the British party encountered a deep creek. The party was forced to halt until trees had been felled across the creek. Whereupon the stockade was rushed. The garrison had retreated as a result of the heavy fire from the field guns. The British force was thus enabled to take the stockade without further fighting, though heavy but misdirected fire from Ebrohimi continued the while.[58]

By about 12 noon the British force had again advanced considerably nearer the town of Ebrohimi. But they again encountered a broad and deep creek which took a great deal of labour and time to bridge. The way to Ebrohimi seemed strewn with nothing but creeks. During this operation heavy fire continued from Ebrohimi as a result of which one African soldier was killed, a blue jacket shot through the back and one of the officers, Captain Scarfe of the Niger Coast Protectorate Force, shot in the head.[59] But for the misdirection of the fire, greater damage would have been done to the British force. At about 3 p.m. the outskirts of Ebrohimi were taken. Just when it looked as if Ebrohimi might fall to the British force, it was discovered that the intervening ground between the outskirts and the town proper was 'a regular morass with a network of small creeks throughout'. Consultations were at once held as to the wisdom of advancing on Ebrohimi and attempting to take it by storm. While consultations were in progress heavy firing both from cannon and rifle was kept up from Ebrohimi. This probably helped in deciding the British not to advance on Ebrohimi in its existing state of defence and with the forces then available for the attack. Orders were accordingly given to fall back on the ships. By 7 p.m. the entire force had returned to the ships, with the loss of the field guns which, because of high floods which had

[58] *Ibid*   [59] *Ibid*

washed off the bridges made during the advance, had to be spiked and thrown into a deep creek.[60]

Moor considered that the reconnoitring in force had been entirely successful in its aims. The exact distance and bearing of Ebrohimi were now known. It had been confirmed that advance through the creeks in boats was impossible, for it was discovered that many cannon were trained on the main creek from the town of Ebrohimi itself. To advance by that creek therefore would be to run into heavy fire. In addition the experience of the day had demonstrated that the defences of Ebrohimi were considerable and well manned. But for the misdirection and bad elevation of the guns the British force would, it was felt, have suffered heavy casualties during the day's operations. It was Moor's view that to attempt to take Ebrohimi with the forces then available would be disastrous. Hence it was decided 'to shell, blockade and invest the Town to either force a surrender or drive Nana and his people out of it'. In order to do this more effectively, two more gunboats were requisitioned from the naval authorities.[61]

The events of 25, 28 and 29 August 1894 administered a rude shock to the self-assurance of the beleaguering force. At the same time they forcefully demonstrated to Nana and his men to what length the British were prepared to go in their campaign against any persons whose power and influence threatened the effective establishment of British rule in the protectorate. Until this time Nana might have thought that the British would call off the blockade in the face of continued resistance. After 29 August any such illusions must have been dispelled, for the British now knew exactly what to do in the event of a final showdown which was by now all too likely. Moor's and Nana's letters immediately after 29 August show that both sides were sufficiently shocked to desire an end to the hostilities. On the 30 August, the day after the reconnoitring in force, Moor wrote to Nana:

> It is the desire of the government of this Protectorate to establish such peace and good order in the Benin District that trade may be carried on by all persons in safety and without fear. The present state of affairs is injurious to all, and I am therefore prepared on

---

[60] F.O. 2/63 Moor to F.O. No. 26, 31 Aug. 1894   [61] *Ibid*

behalf of the government to make such a settlement with you as
will allow of all persons carrying on their business without hesitation.

For this purpose hostilities will be suspended until I receive
your answer which should be sent by bearer.[62]

Nana might not have known it, but the tone and content of the
above letter were the highest tribute that could have been paid
to him by a British Consul-General. There is an unmistakable
earnestness in the tone of the letter and one can say that Moor
honestly desired a settlement at this point. Nana's reply ran:

I have to inform you that myself and people are still desirous of
making peace with the Government; I have asked for this before,
it was not granted.

I beg to apply through you again, to Her Majesty's Government
for the same and under what condition, the present hostility can
be terminated.[63]

There is none of that implied condemnation of British policy
noticeable in some of Nana earlier letters. The time and circumstance seemed most propitious for a settlement.

Yet a settlement was not reached. This would seem to have
been the result of Nana's refusal to accept Moor's conditions. On
4 September in response to Nana's letter quoted above, Moor
spelt out the conditions under which the hostilities would be
terminated. The only means by which Nana could obtain peace,
Moor wrote, was by 'an absolute surrender, and the laying down
of arms'.[64] There could be no other conditions except that the
lives of Nana and his men would be spared if they surrendered.[65]
Moor seemed to have recovered his self-assurance and to have
repented of his letter of 30 August. Nana's reply is rather difficult
to understand. He recalled that he had declined to attend various
meetings before the commencement of real hostilities on the
grounds that he feared what might happen to him. For the same
reason he could not be expected to give himself up. He argued
that it was possible for the government to make peace without

[62] Moor to Nana 8 Aug. 1894 Exhibit 7
[63] Nana to Officer commanding the Expedition 1 Sept. 1894 Exhibit 8
[64] Moor to Nana 4 Sept. 1894 Exhibit 9
[65] *Ibid*

the condition imposed by Moor. At the same time he protested his willingness to surrender.[66]

In Moor's next letter, he ignored the part of Nana's letter which stated that Nana thought peace could be arranged without Moor's essential condition of complete surrender. Instead, Moor seized on the last sentence of the letter which declared the willingness of Nana and his people to surrender. The first act of surrender necessary, Moor wrote, was that Nana and his principal chiefs and advisers should go on board H.M.S. *Phoebe*.[67] Nana was given until 6 p.m. of that day 4 September to take his men on board the British man-of-war. Until that time hostilities would be called off.[68] Nana in his reply did not shift his ground. He stated that the arms which he had acquired were not meant to be used against the government, but that all the coastal people of the Benin and Warri districts kept and carried arms for the protection of their lives and property and for use against the Ijo and Urhobo who were of a warlike disposition. He regretted that he had used his arms against the government but argued that he did so in self defence. Then he declared that he and his people were willing to lay down all arms and were prepared to carry out any laws the government might wish to enforce—laws which he hoped would be mutually beneficial to the British and his people.[69] He said nothing about going on board the *Phoebe*. Another exchange of letters did not materially alter the situation, except that Nana admitted that he had offended the government by not answering in person the various calls which had been made on him.[70] Then on 8 September Moor wrote yet another letter to Nana in which he explained in greater detail the terms the government was offering. If Nana and his people surrendered and laid down their arms, their lives would be guaranteed. If they continued to hold out and were eventually captured, their lives would be forfeited. If they escaped, they would be outlawed and if captured thereafter, their lives would be forfeited.[71] Nana replied: 'Your letter

[66] Nana to Moor 4 Sept. 1894 Exhibit 10
[67] Moor to Nana 4 Sept. 1894 Exhibit 11   [68] *Ibid*
[69] Nana to Moor 4 Sept. 1894 Exhibit 12
[70] See Nana to Moor 6 Sept. 1894 Exhibit 14
[71] Moor to Nana 8 Sept. 1894 Exhibit 15

to hand. I am very sorry to attend. I am afraid still. Please forgive me, I don't want to fight the Government, no blackman fitted the Government'.[72] The exchange of letters discussed above took place while Moor was awaiting the arrival of the two extra men-of-war he had requested from Luanda. While he waited for the gunboats to arrive, he also entered into correspondence with the Foreign Office. On 13 September he sent a telegram reporting that Nana was still holding out and that his removal from the district had become imperative.[73] It is noticeable that a despatch dated 15 September contained no new charges against Nana. According to Moor, Nana's letters showed that he thought it would be possible to come to some arrangement by which 'he could retain his position and power to a great extent'. The Acting Consul-General emphasised that no such settlement was acceptable and insisted on deportation as the only solution that would ensure the peace, good order and security to life and property necessary for the progress of commerce. The 'terrorism' exercised by Nana as well as the 'atrocities' perpetrated by his 'boys' were again recalled as evidence justifying deportation.[74]

In the same despatch Moor gave some details of what measures had been taken to restore order in the Warri and Benin districts. Both at Warri and Sapele the Niger Coast Protectorate troops had been reinforced by marines from H.M.S. *Phoebe*. Up the Ethiope and Warri Rivers 'the war canoes of friendly chiefs' were sent to protect any people who might be molested by Nana's sympathisers and friends. During this process two villages described as 'entirely hostile' were destroyed. As a result of these measures confidence in the government had been restored and many of those who had been disposed to assist Nana by obstructing the government had taken an oath of allegiance to the British administration. All that remained to be done was the destruction of Ebrohimi.[75]

On 18 September H.M.S. *Philomel* with the supreme commander of the African squadron, Rear-Admiral F. G. Bedford, C.B., on board, arrived off the Benin River. Three days later the

[72] Nana to Moor, Undated, Exhibit 16
[73] F.O. 2/64 Telegram from Moor to F.O. 13 Sept. 1894
[74] F.O. 2/64 Moor to F.O. No. 27 15 Sept. 1894   [75] *Ibid*

Widgeon, another gunboat, arrived. With their arrival virtually the entire naval strength of the West Coast together with nearly all the military might of the Niger Coast Protectorate was concentrated on Ebrohimi—undoubtedly the most impressive battle array assembled in the protectorate up to that time—and in a sense a tribute to Nana's power and organising ability. Moor was now in a position of strength and wrote to Nana on 19 September giving him one last opportunity to surrender.[76] Nana's reply was no different from his earlier ones. He was ready for peace but would not go on board a British man-of-war.[77] The die was now finally cast. The time for the final showdown had come.

On 21 September a reconnoitring party was landed under the overall command of the Rear-Admiral himself. It was discovered that it would be impossible to attack Ebrohimi by approaching it along the right flank of the town.[78] The next day another party was sent off to scout the country. All through the scouting operation Ebrohimi was kept under shell fire from the gunboats. It was noticed that, whenever the fire from the ships ceased, a return volley issued from Ebrohimi, indicating that the defences were manned and that the men took cover while the shelling was in progress and returned fire when they had breathing space. On 23 September it was decided to cut a track to the town as had been attempted on 29 August and in the same direction except that care was taken to avoid the zone of fire from Nana's town. The cutting of the track had proceeded for a distance of about 470 yards when a heavy but erratic fire opened on the British force. Ninety rounds were reported fired from cannons within an hour in addition to rifle, machine gun and blunderbuss fire. Apart from a bullet knocking the helmet off the head of one of the marines, no harm was reported to have been done to the attacking force. All the same the situation was threatening enough to force the British party to fall back on the ships. The next day the work continued and progressed satisfactorily as the party was by now safe from the zone of fire as calculated by

[76] Moor to Nana 19 Sept. 1894 Exhibit 17
[77] Nana to Moor 22 Sept. 1894 Exhibit 20
[78] F.O. 2/64 Moor to F.O. No. 28, 5 Oct. 1894. The following account of the final operations against Ebrohimi is taken from this despatch.

Nana's men the previous day. The track was cut to the outskirts of Ebrohimi, after which it was decided to fall back on the ships and make the final onslaught on 25 September.

The details for the final attack were minutely worked out. There was none of that levity of which Lugard had complained in August.[79] The Rear-Admiral himself drew up the plan of campaign. A General Memorandum was circulated to all sectional commanders. The stockade which had been captured from Nana's people on the 29 August was to be the base of operations and reserves of water and ammunition were stored there. The stockade was also to be used as a field hospital to which all wounded were to be taken.[80] The attacking force itself totalled over 300 men and 25 officers; there was also the force that was later to advance by the creek and eventually join the main force after Ebrohimi had been taken; and crew was left on the respective gunboats to man the boats and shell Ebrohimi. The exact strength of the defending forces is not known. Over 2,000 people were reported to have submitted to the British after Nana's defeat.[81] What proportion of the population was actually involved in the fighting it is quite impossible to say. The decisive factor in the encounter was, however, not numerical strength but the nature of the weapons of war and the training and discipline of the troops. In both these regards the British had the advantage over Nana.

The attack itself commenced at 5.30 a.m. on 25 September. It spoke well of the vigilance of the beleaguered that the attack was anticipated; for fifteen minutes after it had begun heavy fire was opened on the attackers from the town. Apparently the firing did no harm. By 6.30 a.m. the track had been completed right into Ebrohimi. The British force advanced—the marines were on the right flank, supported by blue jackets and guns from H.M.S. *Phoebe*; in the centre were the rocket party from H.M.S. *Alecto* and a maxim gun party of 'native' troops; another force of 'native' troops were placed on the left flank. Heavy fire

[79] See Nana to Moor 6 Sept. 1894 Exhibit 12
[80] The General Memorandum can be found as enclosure 2 in Moor to F.O. No. 28, 5 Oct. 1894 and as Appendix III.
[81] See p. 125

continued from Ebrohimi but caused no damage to the attacking force. Eventually the rockets and maxim guns did their work and not only set many of the thatched houses on fire but succeeded in silencing the fire from Ebrohimi. By 9 a.m. Ebrohimi had been taken.[82] The Ebrohimi expedition was virtually over.

Although the actual taking of Ebrohimi was something of an anti-climax, the whole operation was in fact a difficult one. Apart from earlier efforts in August, the entire British party had been kept busy since 21 September. Not only were parties engaged in cutting the track that eventually led the forces to Ebrohimi, but some were engaged in patrolling the creeks to prevent Nana escaping, for it had been reported that he was digging a creek through which to evacuate himself and his belongings. Further, the various advances were arduous because of the nature of the ground and the innumerable creeks that had to be crossed before Ebrohimi could be reached. For purposes of defence the site of the town could not have been better chosen. But this fact also made it difficult for Nana and his men to fight the British effectively. Most of the fire, the frequency and volume of which impressed the attacking force, was wasted because it was impossible for Nana's men to take proper aim at people concealed in the mangrove bush. Once the British force succeeded in getting into Ebrohimi, there was no doubt as to the outcome. Nana could never have hoped to win a pitched battle.

The town itself was largely deserted by the time it was taken. Despite the vigilance of the British, Nana himself was not in the town at the time of its capture.[83] Ebrohimi gave impressive evidence of the wealth and power of the fallen Governor of the River. In Nana's own house 'large stores containing munitions of war and trading material in very large quantities were found'. Cannon and swivel blunderbusses mounted on 'well constructed wooden carriages' were discovered placed in strategic positions. Leg and neck irons as well as handcuffs were found scattered about, sad reminders of the days of the slave trade. The large quantities of munitions of war were taken by Moor to be evidence

[82] F.O. 2/64 Moor to F.O. No. 28, 5 Oct. 1894
[83] See next chapter

of the fact that 'Nana had been preparing to try conclusions with her Majesty's Government for some years'.[84] While it is impossible to be categorical about Nana's intentions, it must be pointed out that arms and munitions were valuable articles of trade throughout the nineteenth century, and that being well armed was considered a sign of affluence. These facts together with Nana's claim that arms were necessary for self-defence furnish another and, indeed, the real explanation for the large quantities of arms and ammunition found in Ebrohimi.

After the taking of the town, a garrison was left there to guard it and receive refugees who came in from the surrounding bush. By 27 September about 1,000 such refugees were said to have come in, most of them in a bad state of starvation. Efforts were made to provide food and clothing for these people who were allowed to go back to their original homes, or settle with 'friendly chiefs' in the surrounding towns. By 5 October when Moor wrote his final despatch on the actual expedition, some 2,000 people—slaves as well as free men—had come in and had been dealt with as described above.[85] Nana's 'clan' had been broken, and the power of the last, and perhaps the greatest, of the Niger Delta middlemen chiefs had been broken for ever.

The events depicted above did not pass unnoticed by the press. Some of the press comments are interesting as showing the kind of information given out by the British; others are significant as representing the resentment of African opinion in the face of the increasing number of punitive expeditions then being mounted against various African rulers. Needless to say, some of the overseas papers put out disjointed explanations of the expedition. The *Journal of Commerce* reported how Nana's men had fired on the hulk housing the Vice-Consulate at Sapele and how Nana had actively opposed British traders going into the interior.[86] In an editorial on 8 September 1894, the *Lagos Weekly Record* deplored the expedition against Nana which it rightly saw as tending towards his deportation. It was the opinion of that paper that African 'potentates should continue to maintain their ancestral position and status under the light and influence of

---

[84] See note 82   [85] *Ibid*
[86] *Journal of Commerce* (Liverpool) 20 & 21 Aug. 1894

civilised government', and not be removed by force from their areas of authority.[87] But an article in the same issue of the paper declared that it appeared that 'Nana . . . had got himself into trouble with the Niger Coast Protectorate authorities by having offered human sacrifice or by practising some other of the abhorrent customs prevalent among the people of the region.'[88] In its first issue of October, by which time Ebrohimi had already been taken, the *Lagos Weekly Record* in yet another editorial condemned the expedition, noting that this kind of episode had become of too frequent occurrence in the history of Africa. It added: 'There is something desperately distressing in the spectacle of Native chiefs and tribes being hunted down and made fugitives all throughout Africa by civilized nations armed with the murderous weapons of modern warfare.'[89]

It was not only sections of the press that were ill-informed, or deliberately misinformed, about the real causes of the war. To most people the Ebrohimi war was fought because Nana indulged in slave trading, monopolised the trade of the district, stopped trade whenever it suited his fancy, and generally obstructed the forces of 'legitimate' commerce and 'civilisation'. This view of the episode which has been expressed in various publications since the event[90] merely adopts the opinion expressed by Ralph Moor in his despatches to the Foreign Office in the months from July to October 1894. Moor never tired of hammering on the 'terrorism' exercised by Nana over an area reputed to be a hundred miles long and fifty to sixty miles broad, or of how by force and threats he not only established a monopoly of trade but

[87] *Lagos Weekly Record* 8 Sept. 1894
[88] 'Warring with Chief Nana' *Lagos Weekly Record* 8 Sept. 1899
[89] *Lagos Weekly Record* 6 Oct. 1894
[90] Harold Bindloss is perhaps the worst offender in this regard. He wrote some four years after the event and virtually beat Ralph Moor to it when he talked about 'sickening atrocities', 'tangible proofs [of which] in the shape of decomposing corpses floated down the forest-shrouded creeks' (p. 206). J. C. Anene in his recent work, *Southern Nigeria in Transition 1885–1906* p. 156 apparently accepts the view of Bindloss which he quotes in a confirmatory manner. See also Allan Burns p. 172; Geary p. 109; Tamuno p. 58

sought to make impossible the establishment by the British of an effective government over the Benin and Warri districts.[91]

There was, however, more to the Ebrohimi expedition than stoppage of trade or even the question of Nana indulging in the slave trade. After all, the British administration did not abolish slavery till the first decade of the present century,[92] and some of the slaves released from Ebrohimi were sent to settle with 'friendly chiefs' whose slaves they in effect became. As pointed out in an earlier chapter the issue of slavery was not clearly settled in 1891 and if the Itsekiri continued to buy slaves the British were at least partly to blame. Dogho, one of the 'friendly chiefs', possessed slaves in 1892 and as late as 1911 opposed the abolition of the Native House Rule Ordinance.[93] The slavery question cannot satisfactorily explain the Ebrohimi expedition. Nor can the stoppage of trade be the reason. There had been stoppages of trade before. In 1879 Tsanomi, then Governor of the River, had stopped trade.[94] All that happened was that he had lost his office of Governor. There had been no war. In 1894 the British were not content to strip Nana of his office. They went all out to reduce him to nothing.

Admittedly Moor exercised some patience before the final debacle. But the events from 1892 to 1894 clearly foreshadowed the break-up of the power and influence of Nana. Nana's reaction to Moor's overtures were no doubt determined by a proper assessment of the situation. His refusal to report at the Vice-Consulate had not only the fate of Jaja to excuse it, but also the threatening letters written by Gallwey the year before. Nana is often compared with Jaja of Opobo. A full comparison cannot be attempted here, but it is significant to note the difference in the reaction of the British Foreign Office to the deportation of these two African personages. In the case of Jaja the British Foreign Secretary for a long time hesitated to give approval to Harry

[91] See for example F.O. 2/64 Moor to F.O. Nos. 27 & 28, 15 Sept. & 5 Oct. 1894

[92] The proclamation against slavery was not passed till 1901. C.O. 591/1 Proclamation No. 5 of 1901: The Slave Dealing Proclamation

[93] See Epilogue

[94] See p. 25

Johnston's action. In 1894 there was no hesitation, no note of disapproval. On the contrary the Foreign Office expressed 'cordial approval of Moor's proceedings' as well as 'appreciation of the able and energetic manner in which the position created by Nana's hostility to the Government [had] been dealt with'.[95] The difference in the reaction of the Foreign Office represented not so much a difference in the local circumstances which had led to the respective deportations, as a change in the tempo and aims of British colonial policy towards the Oil Rivers and West Africa in general.

It is in this change of colonial policy as well as in the purely internal rivalries among the leading Itsekiri traders that the real clue to Nana's fall is to be found. It will be recalled that in his 1892 report Gallwey had spoken of the two factions which dominated the Itsekiri political and economic scene. One of these factions was led by Nana and the other by Dogho. So far as Gallwey was concerned, Dogho's opposition to Nana derived from the latter's monopolistic tendencies. No doubt this was a factor in the situation. The fact that Nana enjoyed a near monopoly of the trade of the Ethiope River was a constant source of irritation to less successful men, and in this respect there must have been a large number of smaller traders who chafed under Nana's great power and influence and who would therefore welcome the break up of that power. Yet the real issue was not the *monopoly* but the *power* which had been used to build the monopoly for, as Nana argued, even his chief antagonist, Dogho, would not allow anyone to trade in areas the trade of which had been pioneered by Dogho himself or by his father, Numa.[96] There was, however, another factor operating throughout the period. This factor was the feud between the Olomu and Numa families; this was accentuated at this time by Nana's outstanding success in trade. Dogho representing the Numa family, therefore rallied round him all who

---

[95] C. 7638 Africa No. 3 F.O. to Macdonald 30 Nov. 1894. Compare with the attitude of the Foreign Office in the case of Jaja. F.O. 84/1828 Salisbury's minute on No. 12; 1 Aug. 1887 and also Salisbury's minute dated 29 Aug. 1887 and contained in Geary Appendix I.

[96] 'Interview with Chief Nana of Benin.' *Lagos Weekly Record* 3 Nov. 1894

stood to benefit by Nana's fall, and there were many. Under the pretext of fighting for economic freedom he used these men to wage a vendetta against his formidable rival. Prominent among those in Dogho's camp were Dudu and his son, Harrison.

For the anti-Nana group, the establishment of the British administration was a welcome event. The administration of the protectorate became, in a sense, an instrument of revenge in the hands of this group. By supporting the government over issues on which it was opposed by Nana, they helped to pave the way for his fall. Thus this group were seen by the British as standing for free trade whereas in 1884 Dogho's father, Numa, and Dudu were among the Itsekiri signatories of the 'protection' treaty which definitely excluded free trade. In 1892 Dogho found a slave crew for Gallwey when Nana on valid grounds refused to supply such a crew.[97] Throughout the years from 1891 to 1894, Harrison featured prominently in the developing conflict between Nana and the British. It was from him Gallwey sought confirmation of the fact that Nana was injuring trade. One of the offences committed by Nana's headman Ologun, was that he used abusive language to Harrison, guide and interpreter to the Vice-Consul of the Benin district.[98] When reports reached the Benin Vice-Consulate that the Abraka district was being disturbed by Nana's people, Nana requested that the Vice-Consul take one of his aides along with him to that district when carrying out his investigations. But it was not Nana's man but Harrison who accompanied Locke to Abraka. Nana had cause to argue that Harrison got the Abraka people to trump up charges against him.[99] At any rate, as Harrison did the interpreting, he had every opportunity to build up a strong case against Nana. Most of the letters written to Nana by the consular authorities in the years from 1891 to 1893 were based on reports from undisclosed sources. It does not require a great deal of imagination to guess from where these reports emanated. Nana himself was aware of these intrigues and warned the Acting Consul-General in 1894 not to

[97] See p. 89
[98] See p. 100
[99] F.O. 2/64 Evidence by Nana at his trial; see also *Lagos Weekly Record* 3 Nov. 1894

accept all the reports against him put abroad by his enemies.[100] Unfortunately for Nana, his power and influence, inimical as they were to the imperial power, militated against his protests being taken seriously by the British administration.

Not satisfied with undermining Nana's position with the British administration this rival group, referred to by the British as 'friendly chiefs', played a prominent part in the active operations against Nana in 1894. In fact at a point in 1894 Moor brought reinforcements to the Benin River because he had been informed that Nana threatened to attack 'two friendly chiefs', Dogho and Dudu.[101] The fact that Nana could scarcely have carried out such a threat—if he issued it at all—while his town was blockaded and war canoes banned from the rivers did not trouble the Consul-General. It was enough to have evidence of Nana's misdeeds, actual or intended. Once again the source of the information was not given. Nana denied ever having such intentions. In the circumstances suspicion for originating the alleged plot falls on those who stood to gain by putting such a story abroad. It was these same 'friendly chiefs' who in 1894 supplied war canoes and men used for patrolling the Warri and Ethiope Rivers and keeping in check any people who showed any desire to assist Nana against the British.[102] They provided the scouts who sent valuable information about Ebrohimi to the British party. In the attack on Okotobo, where Nana had reputedly escaped after the fall of Ebrohimi, it was Dogho who furnished the war canoes and it was his head man, Omota, who led this assault.[103] If further evidence of the important role Dogho played in bringing about the fall of Nana is required, it is furnished by the fact that he was awarded a commemorative medal for his part in the Ebrohimi expedition,[104] and appointed British Political Agent a few years after Nana's fall,—the first of a number of offices that Dogho was to hold in a career of loyal if extremely profitable service to the British colonial regime in this part of southern Nigeria.[105]

---

[100] See for instance Nana to Moore 16 Aug. 1894   [101] See p. 103
[102] See p. 121   [103] F.O. 2/64 Evidence of Omota at Nana's trial
[104] C.O. 444/3 Moor to C.O. No. 236, 30 Dec. 1899. Also Macgregor (War Office) to Under Secretary of State for the Colonies 29 May 1899
[105] Ikime chapter V

Dogho and his henchmen would not, however, have found things so easy had their desire to encompass the fall of their over-mighty rival not coincided with the aims and ambitions of the British administration. Although in the development of British imperial control of West Africa the period of 1891–5 has been described as that of 'the long standstill',[106] there is evidence that the period was not so much one of a 'standstill' as that of the beginning of the race for empire in this part of Africa. Chamberlain's rise to power at the British Colonial Office in 1895 might have increased the tempo of colonial development;[107] it certainly did not initiate it. In the Niger Coast Protectorate, for instance, the establishment of the Macdonald administration in 1891 was an important step towards greater colonial commitments in West Africa, a pointer to the fact that the British Government had abandoned their policy of indifference in the affairs of various peoples of Nigeria, and adopted a new one of active intervention. The 1890's therefore saw the beginning of a period during which various expeditions were mounted by the British for the purpose of 'pacifying' the hinterland of the coastal districts. But the 'pacification' of the hinterland would be useless unless all recalcitrant coastal chiefs were brought to their knees at the same time. It is against this general background that the Nana episode must be seen; for it was no more than one in a series designed to achieve Britain's imperial ambitions in this part of Africa, in the face of French and German rivalry in other spheres. Parallels to the Nana drama could be found elsewhere along the West Coast of Africa.

The Ijebu expedition of 1892, as A. B. Aderibigbe has argued, was organised not just because it was necessary to break up 'the intransigent Yorubas of the "coast" and force them to surrender their control of the trade routes' in order that 'Christianity, commerce and civilisation' might flourish in the hinterland. It was also and largely because the forward party at the British Colonial Office, ably represented by Gilbert Carter in Lagos, desired to extend British rule to Ijebu and beyond.[108] But it

[106] Robinson, R., Gallagher, J. & Denny, A. *Africa and the Victorians* p. 379 London 1961
[107] Robinson &c p. 395
[108] Aderibigbe, A. B. 'The Ijebu Expedition, 1892: An Episode in the

K

would have been naive to put this forward as the reason for the expedition. Instead, the Ijebu were accused of trade monopoly, of refusing to allow free passage of commodities through their territory, and of dishonouring the terms of a spurious treaty signed on behalf of the Ijebu by Carter's own pretentious nominees.[109]

In the Gambia in 1892 'strong measures', involving a punitive expedition in which the *Alecto* also featured, were taken against a local chief, Fodi Suleman Santu of Toniataba because, as J. M. Gray states quite bluntly, that chief refused to accept British authority.[110] Early in 1894 the *Alecto* again saw service in a punitive expedition against another Gambia chief, Foddi Silla, who refused to 'give up his old habits' and was charged with stopping trade and generally resisting British authority.[111] In Sierra Leone the Government was also busy extending its rule. Governor Fleming was reported to have said at a banquet in England in June 1893: 'Let us do all in our power to preserve the possessions we now have . . . Let us do all in our power to extend their boundaries into the interior of the continent.'[112] The preservation and extension of these possessions entailed loss of independence on the part of the West African peoples concerned, as was demonstrated by the case of Bai Bureh in Sierra Leone.[113] In the then Gold Coast, British policy towards Ashanti vacillated until about 1890. From that date, however, the British realised that the only way to consolidate their hold on the coastal area was to secure control of Ashanti as well. At the end of 1890 a treaty of 'protection' was offered to the Asantehene. When the Asantehene refused to accept British 'protection', it became clear that 'strong measures' would have to be taken against him. The assault on the Asantehene began in 1895, the year after Nana's

British Penetration of Nigeria Reconsidered' *Historians in Tropical Africa*, Salisbury, 1962 p. 267

[109] Aderibigbe p. 270

[110] Gray, J. M. *History of the Gambia* p. 467 Cambridge 1940

[111] Gray, p. 467

[112] Quoted by Crooks, J. J. *A History of the Colony of Sierra Leone, West Africa* p. 313 Dublin 1903

[113] Fyfe, C., *A History of Sierra Leone* p. 586 London 1962

fall. The ultimatum which was sent to him charged him with failure to keep open the roads, with hindering trade, and with engaging in human sacrifice.[114] There is a striking similarity between these charges and those levied against Nana only the year before, as well as those which were to be levied against the Oba of Benin a year after the Ashanti expedition of 1896. The similarity in the charges was not just an accident. It derived from the fact that these various expeditions had one thing in common —they were organised to further British imperial ambitions in West Africa.

The fall of Nana was, therefore, not encompassed just to save the Urhobo from his ravages, or to break the monopoly of trade which he held. As Moor wrote: 'It has too long been the custom of the people of Benin and Warri districts to say that they know no government but Chief Nana and it has now become necessary to convince them to the contrary.'[115] This declaration, rather than the case which Moor so laboriously built up against Nana in his despatches, lay at the root of the crisis of 1894. The British had discovered that only if they were in effective control of the protectorate could they successfully exploit its wealth and keep out rivals. Powerful chiefs like Nana, with a clear conception of their rights, were an obstacle to the attainment of this objective and therefore had to be removed. The circumstances and events of 1894 were more the occasion than the cause of Nana's fall.

This is not to say, however, that the personalities involved in the drama of 1894 did not affect the course of events. It has been argued that had Macdonald and Gallwey been in the protectorate in the months from June to September 1894, there might have been no armed conflict.[116] The advocates of this view hold that Nana trusted these two men more than he did Moor, who was more inclined to pursue a 'forward' policy. The evidence scarcely justifies the speculation. Macdonald had in 1891 predicted that in Nana he would have to deal with a 'second Jaja'. Gallwey had

---

[114] Claridge, W. W. *A History of the Gold Coast and Ashanti* pp. 352 *et seq.* London 1915

[115] F.O. 2/63 Moore to F.O. No. 23, 8 Aug. 1894

[116] Lloyd, P. C. 'Nana, the Itsekiri' in *Eminent Nigerians* p. 85 Cambridge 1960

demonstrated by his correspondence in 1892 and 1893 that given
the opportunity he would not hesitate to use gunboats against
Nana. There is therefore no reason to think that Macdonald or
Gallwey would have acted differently in 1894. Yet Moor did
stand for a 'forward' policy, pledged to establishing British authority through the length and breadth of the protectorate. Most of his
letters were written in terms which left no doubts as to whom
he considered was the 'master'. Throughout the events of 1894
he was always aware that the balance of power in the event of a
final showdown was in his favour. There was no question of
treating with Nana on terms of equality. Only once did he soft
pedal—after Heugh's disastrous reconnaissance—but he quickly
regained his confidence and self-assurance. It was not just Moor
who desired a 'forward' policy. He took his cue from the general
tone of British colonial policy. His actions were thus conditioned
by the knowledge that both official and non-official opinion in
Britain was disposed to accept a 'forward' policy.

As for Nana, he was genuinely concerned with the maintenance of the power, wealth, influence and prestige which had been
his since he succeeded his father in 1883. His resistance to the
British was therefore very much motivated by a desire to preserve
his position in Itsekiriland—a position which was being gradually
undermined by the British especially after 1891. The question is
sometimes raised as to whether Nana fully appreciated the meaning of the 1884 treaty or the significance of the inauguration of
the Macdonald administration of 1891. From what transpired in
1884, it is clear that Nana and the other Itsekiri elders realised
the seriousness of the signing of the 'protection' treaty. But their
attention was focused on the social and economic implications of
the treaty, as witness their refusal to accept Articles VI and VII.
It is doubtful whether Nana and the others fully appreciated its
political significance. Did they, for instance, understand that
signing the treaty compromised their sovereignty? Nana's attitude
during the years from 1884 to 1894 indicated that he still regarded
himself as an independent authority acting and negotiating on
terms of perfect equality with the British Consuls. But this was
the very point about which the British officers were extremely
sensitive, for they clearly saw the treaty as conferring on them

ultimate sovereign power over the areas to which they were appointed. As pointed out earlier the provisions of Articles II–V of the treaty—and these were the articles which dealt with the political relationship between the Itsekiri and the British— seriously undermined Itsekiri sovereignty. This was the point which Nana seemed to have missed. The fact that in 1887 Nana, like other middlemen chiefs of the delta states, agreed to accept a 'Queen's Government' also throws doubt on his understanding of the political implications of British 'protection'. In the circum- stances Nana's actions were guided by an understanding of the treaty completely different from that of the British officials who were inclined to be legalistic in their interpretations. This was undoubtedly one of the factors which produced the crisis that ended in the conflict just described.

If Nana missed the full political significance of the treaty of 1884, he did not fail to recognise that the establishment of a formal administration in 1891 was a veritable threat to his vested interests. Between 1884 and 1890 there were only a few incidents which reminded Nana and the Itsekiri that they were part of a British protectorate. As from 1891 there were many more such reminders. For the first time there was permanently stationed in the Benin River district a British Vice-Consul who soon began to insist on new ways of doing things. Above all the Vice-Consul began to take a great deal of interest not only in the trade of the area, coastal and hinterland, but also in the internal affairs of the Itsekiri people. In other words the British began to invade those spheres of life which the Itsekiri had endeavoured to protect in 1884, as they sought to establish a new social and economic order. Nana resented and resisted this change because it undermined his position. The incidents so far discussed would seem to indicate that Nana realised that the new order was threatening to reduce him from the status of an independent power to that of a mere subject no longer entitled to employ methods of self-help against rivals, enemies and debtors. This realisation together with the fact that the British were seeking to break his monopoly turned him against the British and so led to the events of 1894.

There seems to be some debate as to whether Nana and others like him should be described as African nationalists in the context in which they acted. Indeed T. N. Tamuno has warned that 'Nana's claims to be a significant place as a Nigerian nationalist should . . . be seriously modified'.[117] It is easy to point to the sectarian and almost selfish nature of Nana's resistance and to the fact that he did not command the following or sympathy of the entire Itsekiri. The services rendered to the British by the 'friendly chiefs' furnish incontrovertible evidence of the latter fact. It might even be argued that had Nana been the underdog in the internal political and commercial rivalry in Itsekiriland, he would have played a similar role to that of Dogho, Dudu and the other 'friendly chiefs'. But not even the accusation of self-interest can derogate from the essential truth that in taking his stand against the British Nana was actuated by the desire to maintain intact his economic and political heritage. No nationalism is ever completely divorced from this kind of self-interest. Tamuno, who apparently bases his judgment only on the events of 25 September 1894 rather than on a detailed analysis of the overall struggle from the month of July, further goes on to speak of the 'feeble' resistance,[118] put up by Nana's immediate following, the implication being that the 'feebleness' of the resistance was an indication of the unpopularity of Nana's cause. As a matter of fact, Nana's resistance, as has been shown in this chapter, cannot be fairly described as 'feeble'. In the final analysis the fact remains that what Nana and others like him stood for on a limited plane in the late nineteenth century was in essence what nationalists of the period after 1914 were to fight for on a larger plane, the freedom from alien control. The difference in methods and scope was little more than a difference in the age in which the respective groups of nationalists lived, the experience which guided their actions and the resources available to them in the fight against the imperial factor. Besides, it should be remembered that until April 1894 Nana was the recognised head of the Itsekiri people and that therefore his resistance to imperial control was, in some measure at least, 'national' in the Itsekiri context. Throughout the crisis of June-September, Nana was guided by

[117] Tamuno, T. N. 'Some Aspects of Nigerian Reaction to the Imposition of British Rule' *J.H.S.N.* Vol. 3 No. 2 Dec. 1965 p. 276
[118] Tamuno p. 277

the advice of the elders of Ebrohimi. His persistent refusal to hold discussions with the British political officers was not just a token of his own stubbornness, but a reflection of the opinions of his closest advisers.[119] In fighting to preserve his position and inheritance, Nana typified contemporary nationalist resistance to imperial control elsewhere in Africa. The fact that the interests of certain Itsekiri groups made them decide to join forces with the British to secure the fall of Nana cannot and should not blind us to this central fact.

[119] See pp. 154–5

CHAPTER V

Escape, Surrender, Trial

WHILE THE British force prepared for the final attack on Ebrohimi, Nana was busy working out a plan of escape. Apparently he realised that once the British succeeded in cutting their way to Ebrohimi his men would be no match for the trained troops of the British. Therefore he conceived the idea of digging a canal at the back of his town through which he could evacuate his family and belongings. But the digging of the canal was an arduous task and was not completed before Ebrohimi was taken on the morning of 25 September. In fact, Nana was still busy at the canal when it was reported to him that his town had fallen to the British. Thereupon he collected his immediate kith and kin and as much property as he could and left Ebrohimi through one of the creeks.[1]

The details about the cutting of the canal are not clear. Moor reported that many slaves were set to work to cut this canal. The fact that 'carters' whips' were found scattered near the unfinished canal was seen as evidence of the brutality with which the slaves were driven during those hectic days.[2] Nana for his part argued that the whips had not been used for a long time and had been dropped in the general confusion that followed the taking of Ebrohimi. As for the slaves he was reported to have driven with brutality while engaged in the task of cutting the canal, Nana stated that during the last few days before the taking of Ebrohimi so many of his slaves had fled into the bush that he had to fall back on the services of his immediate relations.[3] Whatever the truth of the matter, there can be no doubt that Nana's idea of cutting the canal was a brilliant strategem which gave yet more evidence of that intelligence which friend and foe alike admired.

In the meantime the British, having heard that Nana was

---

[1] F.O. 2/64, Moor to F.O., No. 28, 5 Oct. 1894   [2] *Ibid*
[3] F.O. 2/64 Evidence of Nana at his trial

planning to escape through the canal, sent patrol boats to keep watch over the creek from which Nana was expected to emerge. As soon as the British discovered that Nana was not in Ebrohimi and had not escaped through the unfinished canal, Moor issued a proclamation outlawing Nana and a number of his principal men. The proclamation enjoined 'all good subjects' to assist in the task of capturing Nana and his aides, and threatened severe punishment for any person who sheltered or otherwise assisted Nana and his men in their escape. A reward of £500 was offered to any person who captured and handed over Nana to the British administration; a reward of £100 each was offered for five of Nana's aides—Bizani, Ololu, Oko, 'Little Towray' and Ologun. The proclamation also declared 'all the goods and chattels, real and personal property, of the said chief Nana Alluma and his people' forfeited to the government.[4] Having issued the proclamation the British set about the task of capturing the fleeing Nana.

The task proved in the end to be impossible. This was largely because the attacking force was not familiar with the intricacies of the creeks, and also because information about Nana's movements could not be very accurate. On 26 September it was decided to attack a town called Eddu, some distance behind Ebrohimi, in the hope that Nana might be found there. The town was taken and burnt to the ground but Nana was not there. On 27 September a party of marines was sent out in search of Nana, but all that was achieved was the capture of Ologun, Nana's head slave whose activities in Eku had caused Moor to order his recall from that place. On the next day a canoe containing 'all Nana's valuables' as well as his papers was captured. Apparently a patrolling party had run into the canoe in which Nana and his people were travelling during the early hours of the morning. Despite heavy firing from the patrol boat, the occupants of the canoe, some of whom were wounded, succeeded in making their escape by jumping overboard and making for the mangrove bush.[5]

Nana's own account of his escape shows that he suffered considerable privations during this period. When the news came to him that Ebrohimi had been taken by the British he had to think

[4] F.O. 2/64 Enclosure in Moor to F.O. No. 28, 5 Oct. 1894
[5] F.O. 2/64 Moor to F.O. No. 28, 5 Oct. 1894

and act quickly. The canal through which he planned to escape was not yet complete. He therefore decided to clear a way through one of the small creeks that led out of Ebrohimi. Through this creek he escaped in eight canoes and with about 500 of his people. According to Nana, he and his party went a long distance into the mangrove swamp where they remained for three days. The searching protectorate forces caught up with Nana's party and Nana claimed that many of the soldiers passed close to him, but as these soldiers did not recognise his person, they probably thought the party was just another group of slaves or free men who had fled into the bush on the fall of Ebrohimi. Having by sheer luck escaped capture at this juncture, Nana left the main party and, taking his family in one canoe, continued his flight. It was this canoe that was fired on and eventually captured by the patrol boat on 28 September. Nana was obliged, in view of the heavy fire from the patrol boat, to run his canoe into the mangrove swamp and to flee with his family into the thick bush. Nana reported that he lost a child and a sister as a result of this adventure, as they had wandered off on their own into the mangrove swamps and died either of exhaustion or other misadventure. It was while he and his people were wandering about in the bush that Nana saw an Ijo man whom he persuaded to take him and his followers to Okotobo, a town where he had friends.[6]

Nana made his last stand against the British at Okotobo. When information reached the British that Nana had escaped to Okotobo, arrangements were at once begun for an attack on that town. A reconnoitring party was despatched by the British to Okotobo to ascertain the correctness of the information about Nana being there. Moor testified that this party ran into heavy fire and was forced to fall back on the ship.[7] By this time it had become quite clear that it would be difficult to employ regular protectorate troops for the capture of Nana, as most of these troops could not identify the object of their chase. So once again the British had to fall back on the services of 'friendly chiefs' who were only too willing to finish the work they had begun. A force of 400 men in

[6] 'Interview with Chief Nana of Benin' *Lagos Weekly Record* 3 Nov. 1894

[7] F.O. 2/64 Evidence of Moor at Nana's trial

fifteen war canoes was sent against Okotobo. This force was commanded by one Omota, Dogho's head slave. The plan was to make a joint attack by land and water. Accordingly about half the force was landed some distance from Okotobo, with orders to march on the town. Omota himself led the rest of the force that was to invest Okotobo from the war canoes. The water party arrived first and immediately engaged in hostilities. Omota claimed that his party only opened fire when the cannon mounted along the Okotobo beach was trained on them. The hostilities lasted only one day, during which the attacking force lost one man killed and five injured. The casualty list among the beleaguered is not known. By the end of the day Okotobo had fallen and all Nana's chief aides were captured. Some measure of the resistance put up at Okotobo can be seen from the list of ammunition captured on the fall of the town—thirteen cannon, five Winchester rifles and thirty-nine blunderbusses.[8]

Although all Nana's lieutenants were captured, Nana himself again succeeded in escaping capture. The attack on Okotobo must have taken place some time between 21 and 30 October. When Omota's men found that Nana had again escaped they organised a pursuit through the creeks, but failed to find the ex-Governor of the River who eventually found his way to Lagos on 30 October 1894.[9]

Nana's arrival in Lagos created a stir. The Lagos press, which had taken an interest in the Ebrohimi expedition, seized on the opportunity offered by Nana's presence in Lagos to interview the ex-Governor and so give him the only opportunity he ever had of stating his case before the public. The *Lagos Weekly Record* came out with a leading article and a report of an interview on 3 November. In its leader the paper expressed surprise at the fact that, though war had been declared and waged against Nana and though he and his people had been made fugitives, the public had no idea what the particular offence was which Nana was alleged to have committed. The paper condemned accounts of the episode published in British newspapers which it described as 'more in the form of an excuse or apology for the war, than a

[8] F.O. 2/64 Omota's evidence at Nana's trial
[9] *Lagos Weekly Record*. 3 Nov. 1894

honest and candid relation of the circumstances which led to it'. The *Weekly Record* drew attention to an article in 'a Liverpool journal' which explained the war in terms of Nana's obstructing trade and refusing to report to the Vice-Consulate. The same 'journal' while reporting that British gunboats had fired on and sunk canoes belonging to Nana's people, added that it was not ascertained that there were any people in the canoes at the time they were sunk.

In the interview with the press, Nana again pointed to the differences between him and the Dogho faction as the real cause of his troubles. He recalled that on his succession to the headship of his house he had taken up the task of conciliating the neighbouring Ijo who preyed on the trade of the Itsekiri. In this task he had sought and obtained the co-operation of the other 'chiefs' but not that of Dogho or Dudu 'who declined to take part in the matter'. He eventually succeeded in getting the Ijo 'to eat juju' with the Itsekiri and so bring to an end Ijo depredations on Itsekiri trade. By his own account, Nana next devoted his energies to the opening up of trade with various Urhobo people. The outcome of his efforts was that he increased his substance immensely, a circumstance which only succeeded in accentuating the hostility of the Dogho group towards him. But, according to the newspaper report, the particular event which led to open disagreement between Nana and Dogho was the seizure by Dogho of some Urhobo people at a market established by Nana in the Urhobo country. Dogho's reasons for the seizure was that the people at the market owed him twenty puncheons of oil. One should pause here to reflect that if Nana's story were true, this would be a confirmation of an argument advanced earlier that seizure of people for debt was an accepted practice of the time; Dogho would thus have been guilty of one of the offences for which he and the British harassed Nana. In the interview Nana claimed that Dogho was not ordinarily entitled to trade in the market concerned since he, Dogho, did not allow other Itsekiri traders to use markets established by himself or his father, Numa. But Nana had allowed him to trade there as an act of grace. As Nana feared that the seizure of the men would adversely affect the flow of his trade, he appealed to Dogho to hand over the men seized. Dogho,

however, refused to do this unless the debt was paid in full.
Nana was obliged to pay the debt, but thereafter he prevented
Dogho from trading in that particular market. This, claimed Nana,
was the immediate prelude to Dogho's plot against him. The
rest of the interview related the nature of the British attack and
the final taking of Ebrohimi. As Nana was for obvious reasons
seeking to win the sympathy of the press, one must be sceptical
about the story he told. Yet his explanation of the purely Itsekiri
aspect of the crisis fits well into the general pattern as described in
the last chapter. As for his dealing with the Ijo, Lloyd has pointed
out that there exist no reports of Ijo 'piracy' after 1870 and has
suggested that this might have been due to Olomu's or Nana's
influence and power over them.[10]

In Lagos Nana put up with a friend named Seidu Olowu. It is
not clear whether it was Nana's intention to surrender himself
to the Lagos Governor at the time he arrived in Lagos or whether
he took that decision on the advice of Seidu Olowo. However that
might have been, Nana did surrender himself to Governor Carter
who, though he provided a police escort to keep an eye on Nana's
movement, did not keep him in confinement. Macdonald was
later to complain about Carter's failure to keep Nana in prison.[11]
The *Lagos Weekly Record* reported that Nana had no hesitation
in surrendering to the British authorities in Lagos. This, continued the paper, was because Nana believed in the essential
justness of his case and the impartiality of the British Government—propaganda meant for the British administration. The
Lagos Weekly Record was obviously impressed by Nana's surrender and wrote:

> The confidence manifested by Nana in coming as he had, and
> throwing himself into the power and custody of the British Govern-
> ment, shows that he only desired to get beyond the adverse
> influence which he believed to be operating against him when
> he would be ready and willing to submit his conduct to any
> investigation desired. There can be no doubt that the act speaks
> volumes in his favour both as to his consciousness of innocence and
> his confidence in the integrity and honour of Her Majesty's

[10] P. C. Lloyd, pp. 225–6
[11] C.S.O. 1/13/4 Macdonald to F.O. No. 36, 12 Nov. 1894

Government; and it now remains to be demonstrated whether such confidence has been misplaced.[12]

The *Lagos Weekly Record* was clearly inclined to sympathise with Nana. If both Nana and the *Lagos Weekly Record* honestly believed in the honour, integrity and sense of justice of the British authorities, they were soon to receive a rude shock and to learn that the much vaunted British justice was not universal in its application.[13]

While the active operations against Nana were being undertaken, the Commissioner and Consul-General of the Niger Coast Protectorate, Sir Claude Macdonald, was away on leave. He returned to handle the trial, the last phase of the Nana episode. But a little difficulty arose before the trial could be arranged. Macdonald left England on 13 October and arrived at Accra on 2 November. At Accra he received a letter from Sir Gilbert Carter, Governor of the Colony of Lagos, to the effect that Nana had surrendered to him and that Macdonald should call at Lagos on his way to the protectorate. However, when on 3 November the mail steamer anchored off Lagos, Sir Gilbert sent Macdonald a letter. It informed him that some difficulty had arisen about handing over Nana to the Niger Coast Protectorate authorities and that the best way out was for Macdonald to produce a warrant for the arrest of Nana. On the strength of this letter Macdonald travelled to Forcados where he obtained the necessary warrant of arrest. On 6 November Macdonald returned to Lagos and presented the warrant of arrest.

Macdonald had expected that Nana would be immediately handed over to him on his presenting the warrant. He received a severe shock. He was informed by Sir Gilbert Carter that the law officers of the Lagos Colony were of the opinion that Nana could not be handed over to the Niger Coast Protectorate officers because he was 'a Lagos British subject', his town of Ebrohimi being situated on the right bank of the Benin River which, by a boundary proclamation made by a former governor of Lagos, was within the territory of the Lagos colony. In addition, Carter

[12] 'Chief Nana of Benin' *Lagos Weekly Record*, 3 Nov. 1894

[13] See account of Nana's trial below. See also Macdonald's comments on Nana's surrender in note 21.

reported that the Queen's Advocate in Lagos was of the legal opinion that Nana would be justified if he took action in court against the protectorate government for the operations which that government had taken against him and was further of the opinion that were such an action taken Nana would win his case.[14]

Macdonald was greatly taken aback by this unexpected development. He was amazed that a government which had lent to the Niger Coast Protectorate for the Ebrohimi expedition seven-pounder field pieces and the men to fire them could morally take up the stand of the Lagos authorities. But this was no time for pondering on morality. Macdonald had to find a way out of the *impasse*. He recalled the events of 1891. Macdonald informed Carter that, on his appointment as Commissioner and Consul-General in 1891, he had taken up the question of the boundary between the Niger Coast Protectorate and the colony of Lagos. According to Macdonald he had received a despatch from the Foreign Office dated 27 July 1891 in which the boundary had been laid down—a boundary which definitely placed the Benin River within the territories of the Niger Coast Protectorate. But Carter argued that he was not aware of such a boundary arrangement and could take no official or legal notice of it.[15] While Carter's attitude might have been dictated by purely official considerations it would appear that there were other influences at work. In a letter to John Holt dated 21 November 1894 Carter wrote: 'I did all I could for Nana and declined to make him a prisoner. He went voluntarily to Old Calabar with Sir Claude Macdonald and I felt that he might be safely left to be dealt with in that quarter.'[16] It would thus appear that certain commercial interests were, even at this stage, exerting their influence on the side of Nana. Macdonald probably did not realise this. In one last bid to find a way out of the difficulty Macdonald suggested to Carter that the archives of the Lagos administration be searched for a similar correspondence to that which he had received from the Foreign Office. When this was done, it was

[14] The account is taken from Macdonald's report to the Foreign Office. C.S.O. 1/13/4 Macdonald to F.O. No. 36, 12 Nov. 1894
[15] *Ibid*
[16] Holt Papers Box 12/7 Carter to Holt 21 Nov. 1894

discovered that a letter from the Colonial Office dated 25 July 1891 had laid down the boundary to which Macdonald had referred. This discovery undermined the position taken by the Lagos administration and Macdonald reported that Sir Gilbert Carter was thereupon prepared to accept the boundary as binding though it had never been officially proclaimed within the Lagos colony.[17]

While the search was going on for the correspondence from the Colonial Office, it was suggested that Nana might be asked to surrender himself to Macdonald and so put an end to the legal arguments. Accordingly Nana was sent for and, on being asked by Carter whether he would willingly surrender himself to Sir Claude, immediately agreed to do so.[18] As a result of this act the warrant of arrest was never executed. It is easy enough to see why Nana gave himself up to Macdonald. Having initially surrendered to the Lagos authorities, there was only the legal point raised by the Lagos law officers to stop his being handed over to the Niger Coast Protectorate government. As things turned out the legal argument was nullified by the correspondence from the Colonial Office. Therefore, even if Nana had not surrendered himself to Macdonald at the point at which he did, he would still have found himself given over to Macdonald through the execution of the warrant of arrest. When that has been said, however, one can still hazard the guess that Nana felt that a surrender would influence Macdonald in his favour. The events were to show that Macdonald was not so impressed.

Before the legal tussle between the Lagos and Niger Coast Protectorate authorities, Nana had sent a cablegram to the Foreign Office requesting that his trial be held in Lagos.[19] Apparently he had been advised to do so by some Lagos lawyers who had taken an interest—economic and otherwise—in the Nana episode. Macdonald reported that Nana had actually paid one such lawyer a retainer of £100. The main reason for these lawyers seeking to have Nana tried in Lagos was that they could then plead his case, whereas if the trial took place in the Niger Coast Protectorate there would be no opportunity for lawyers to represent Nana, since lawyers were not permitted to plead in the con-

[17] C.S.O. 1/13/4 Macdonald to F.O. No. 36, 12 Nov. 1894
[18] *Ibid*   [19] *Ibid*

sular courts. Macdonald considered that it would be detrimental to 'the cause of justice' for Nana's trial to take place in Lagos. He recalled a previous occasion on which he had taken a European who had deliberately murdered an African to Lagos for trial. Despite what Macdonald considered clear evidence of the European's guilt, he was acquitted by the mixed jury of Europeans and Africans.[20] In other words, it was Macdonald's view that Nana's trial in the Niger Coast Protectorate would guarantee greater justice being done than trial in Lagos. There was little in Nana's trial at Old Calabar to justify this stand.

As soon as Macdonald arrived at Old Calabar he began to make arrangements for Nana's trial. In a despatch to the Foreign Office in which he reported these preparations he discussed the issue of Nana's surrender to the Lagos authorities. He pointed out that emphasis was bound to be laid on this fact during the trial. He implied that such emphasis would be misplaced because, as he argued, Nana was virtually pursued into Lagos territory by the forces of 'friendly natives' and his surrender there was therefore really forced on him.[21] Both Nana and the *Lagos Weekly Record* had placed some hope on the fact of Nana's surrender to the Lagos authorities. It was hoped that this would influence the British authorities in Nana's favour. But even before the trial took place, Macdonald had made it clear in this despatch that he did not intend to be influenced by this.

The trial of Nana began on 30 November 1894 at the consular court in Old Calabar. The court was presided over by Sir Claude Macdonald himself. The charges levied against Nana were:

i. That he on or about the months of August and September 1894 with his people armed and arrayed in a warlike manner did levy and make war against the Government of Her Majesty the Queen in the Niger Coast Protectorate, and endeavour by force of arms to avoid carrying out the terms of a treaty entered into on 16th July 1894.

ii. That he has failed to carry out the provisions of the Treaty entered into on the 16th July 1884, in that he has acted in opposition to the British consular officers in the execution of the duties assigned to them and not taken their advice in

[20] *Ibid*   [21] *Ibid*

L

matters relating to the administration of justice, the development of the resources of the country, the interests of commerce, or in any other matter in relation to peace, order and good Government, and the general progress of civilisation.

iii. That he, on or about the months of August and September 1894, has committed a breach of the peace in the Benin district of the Niger Coast Protectorate.

iv. That by his conduct he, on or about the months of August and September 1894, has excited others to commit a breach of the peace in the Benin District of the Niger Coast Protectorate.[22]

Nana pleaded 'not guilty' and the prosecution thereupon opened its case.

The first witness for the prosecution was A. F. Locke, Consular Agent, Niger Coast Protectorate. His evidence was a straightforward narrative of the events which took place between May and 25 August 1894. He recalled how he had heard about the trade of the Abraka area being stopped and how he had gone to investigate the report. On the strength of what he was told by the Abraka people he came to the conclusion that Nana was responsible for the stoppage of trade. Another aspect of the situation which Locke stressed in his evidence was Nana's refusal to report to the Vice-Consulate despite, what Locke considered, sufficiently genuine written and oral guarantees of safety. Finally, Locke recalled how he had seen evidence on 25 August of Nana's armed aggression on the boat Heugh took out on his reconnoitring trip up the Ebrohimi creek. Nana promptly opposed the suggestion implied by Locke that his people had been the first to open fire on the reconnoitring party, arguing that his people were forced to fire only in self-defence. It is difficult to say exactly what happened. Heugh in his report which was tendered at the trial stated that Nana's men were the first to open fire.[23] But was Heugh a reliable witness? Is there any reason why his view should be accepted? According to Heugh, his party had travelled some 380 yards up the creek when he heard voices from the sur-

[22] The account of Nana's trial is to be found in F.O. 2/64, Enclosure in Macdonald to F.O. No. 49, 13 Dec. 1894. No further references are given in the discussion which follows.
[23] Exhibit D at Nana's trial.

rounding mangrove bush. Because of this fact he decided to 'turn about' and it was in this process that Nana's men began firing at the British party. There is reason to doubt the truth of Heugh's report. Before this day, Heugh had led the offensive against a number of villages without any great provocation.[24] Besides, if Lugard's observations are anything to go by, the prevailing mood of the British marines before the disaster of 25 August was one which looked forward to action—to a 'great picnic'.[25] It was unlikely in the prevailing mood of the British that Heugh decided to fall back on the ship merely because he heard voices in the bush. The more likely response to voices in the bush was the firing of a few rounds from his own guns 'to clear the bush'. It is quite possible that this was what in fact took place and that it was the unexpected promptness with which Nana's party returned fire that made Heugh decide to fall back. At any rate, Lugard's scepticism about the reliability of Heugh's report is unmistakable. On 27 August 1894 Lugard made the following entry in his diary about Heugh's reconnoitring venture:

> Heugh says he stood upright at the rudder, and the cannon balls whistled round him—he could see them pass his face in the air, and was struck on the foot by one, which riccochetted off, and did damage. It all but knocked him out of the boat, but he recovered himself—yet it did not even leave a bruise or mark of any sort!
> Heugh claims that there was none left to steer, so he did it himself. As a matter of fact, however, there must have been 3 other sound men in the boat.[26]

A man so obviously bent on self-justification would scarcely have reported that he had started off the hostilities. When later the awards were made for the Ebrohimi expedition, Lugard evidently was surprised that Heugh got a promotion. He noted: 'Heugh of the *Alecto* gets a D.S.O. and promotion for his business. There were some who expected a C.M. [Court Martial] instead!'[27] It would therefore appear that Heugh was an unreliable witness and that his report was a dubious document on which to base judgment as to who should take responsibility for the opening of hostilities.

[24] See chapter IV
[25] See Chapter IV
[26] Perham and Bull p. 77
[27] Perham and Bull p. 305

The court's cross-examination of Locke was at best half-hearted. The court asked whether Locke had ascertained the fact that the trade of the Abraka area had been stopped by Nana's men and was satisfied by Locke's 'Yes.' The obvious and logical follow-up to that question was never raised; Locke was not asked what methods he used to ascertain this fact. The court was not inclined to belabour the witness who was, after all, a consular officer. One can understand why Macdonald was concerned that Nana should be tried in Old Calabar. At the consular court, Old Calabar, there was no lawyer to ask embarrassing but relevant questions.

The second and chief prosecution witness was Ralph Moor, the man who had led the offensive against Nana. His evidence was virtually a recapitulation of the events of June to October 1894 described in his despatches with the exception that at various points he deliberately overstated and almost falsified the accounts of events with the obvious aim of securing conviction. Moor began his evidence by handing to the court various documents as exhibits; these were the same exhibits to which reference has constantly been made in this work. He not only handed in these exhibits but attempted to summarise their contents. It spoke little for Moor's integrity and sense of fair play that a number of these summaries were very different from the actual contents of the letters handed to the court. To quote from Moor's evidence at the trial:

> I hand in another document (marked I). This is a letter from Acting Vice-Consul Haly Hutton pointing out that Nana was not keeping his promise, and respecting the terms of his treaty whereby he is to encourage trade, and that he was oppressing the smaller traders. I hand in another document (marked J). This is a letter from vice-consul Gallwey speaking in strong terms of Nana's conduct in stopping trade, and intimidating the smaller trader, and pointing out to him that in thus failing to carry out the terms of his treaty the consequences for him would be very serious.[28]

Moor seemed to be making a desperate effort to relate his evidence to the charges levied against Nana. But he was doing this by sacrificing essential truth. Neither the letter marked I nor that marked J said anything about Nana's treaty obligations. Moor's

[28] The two documents I and J can be found in the Appendix V

interpretation of these letters was a projection of his own ideas. These letters have been discussed and need not further detain us here. It is, however, striking that despite the important difference between Moor's comments on these letters and their contents, the court did not see fit to ask any questions. It is possible to argue here that, as the despatches were not handed in as exhibits, it was impossible to spot the discrepancy. It is unlikely that Macdonald, the trial 'judge', did not read the despatches. At any rate, at another point in the trial, Macdonald did introduce extraneous matter and use this for cross-examination purposes.[29]

As most of Moor's evidence was a restatement, attention will here only be drawn to points of particular interest or to discrepancies between Moor's evidence at the trial and the accounts in his despatches. As evidence of how Nana contributed to the disturbed state of the Benin District, Moor recalled the attack on Bobi by the Ijo chief, whose name was now given as Dear, described by Moor as 'an adherent of Nana' whose action he regarded as 'tantamount to an act of Nana'. In the despatch in which he discussed the incident, Moor had reported that the British party sent to arrest chief Dear found the chief's town deserted though the party could hear the people shouting in the bush and firing guns. At the trial, Moor stated that the British party was fired on and that 'they therefore burnt the village'. As a matter of fact Moor had given Major Copland-Crawford definite orders 'to take retaliatory measures' if it was found impossible to arrest the Ijo chief.[30] The village was burnt not because, as Moor's evidence implied, the Ijo had first fired on the British force but rather because the village being deserted, the chief could not be arrested. Moor's account at the trial of the burning of Evhro also differed in an important respect from that contained in the despatch. At the trial Moor stated that when Chief Erigbe was summoned to the Vice-Consulate, 'he replied that Nana was his chief, and that he did not recognise the authority of the Government'. This was a new twist to the episode which was not mentioned in the despatch. It is possible to argue that Moor forgot this aspect of the matter while writing his despatch. But such an argument is difficult to accept when it is remembered that Moor went into great

[29] See p. 154   [30] F.O. 2/63 Moor to F.O. No. 23, 8 Aug. 1894

details to justify the burning of Evhro. It is difficult to imagine a
man who was content to report mere speculations to the Foreign
Office failing to report the kind of statement credited to Erigbe—
a statement which represented the kind of defiance for which
Moor sought to bring Nana to book. As in his despatches, so now
at the trial, Moor seemed preoccupied with painting Nana in
the blackest possible colours.

It will be recalled that in one of his despatches Moor had reported that Nana's people had, under a flag of truce, attacked
and plundered passing canoes. It transpired at the trial that these
canoes belonged to the same 'friendly chiefs' Dudu and Dogho
whom Nana was alleged to have planned to attack. When Moor
testified to this fact at the trial, he was no doubt mainly interested
in depicting the 'terrorist' activities in which Nana was supposed
to have indulged. But did it occur to Moor to ponder why Dogho
and Dudu featured so prominently in the events of June to
October 1894? Was Moor using these 'two friendly chiefs' or were
they using him?

Commenting on the state of Ebrohimi at the time it was taken,
Moor in his evidence stated that 'several decapitated bodies' were
found in the creek leading to the town. He was convinced that
the people had not been killed as a result of the constant firing
kept up from the British warships. The implication was that
Nana or his aides had deliberately murdered the people in question. Nana did not deny that such bodies were found. He merely
stated that he was not aware of any murder having been committed. Nana might well have known more than he owned up
to at the trial, but it should be pointed out that a state of war
already existed and that a fairly large number of people lost their
lives as a result of that war. The responsibility for this loss of life
must be shared by both sides engaged in the war. No one had at
any time before the trial accused Nana of wanton murder. The
situation described by Moor was essentially a war time situation.

On the issue of slaves, Moor claimed that Nana possessed over
5,000 slaves. Some of these slaves, he stated, had had their ears
cut off, this being the treatment allegedly meted out by Nana to
all slaves who attempted to escape. Although Nana denied this
charge and stated that he had passed a law against cutting off

the ears of slaves in Ebrohimi, mutilation of refractory or criminal slaves was an accepted practice among the Itsekiri,[31] a practice in which Nana's father had engaged.[32] Moor stated further that Nana acquired over 200 slaves every year, a statement which if true meant that between 1884 and 1894 Nana must have acquired 2,000 slaves. Undoubtedly Nana did possess a large number of slaves. It should, however, be remembered that Nana inherited some of these slaves from his father and that the number of slaves was bound to increase through ordinary natural processes, the children of slaves being slaves. Besides, there was the tendency to look on all who worked for Nana as slaves, whereas there were free men among Nana's 'clan'. Nana, in his defence, repudiated Moor's assertion that he obtained his slaves through 'regular raids', arguing that apart from slaves obtained during raids arising from trade disputes, most of the slaves were either bought or given to him as security for debt.[33]

Moor closed his evidence with a recapitulation of how he had toured the Ethiope after the fall of Ebrohimi, and how the 'sobos seemed delighted that Nana's power had been broken'. While there were undoubtedly some of the Urhobo who were happy that the mighty Nana had fallen before a greater power, there was also another explanation for the joy expressed by the Urhobo people. Since May the entire districts of Benin and Warri had been greatly disturbed. Normal life had been impossible in the prevailing conditions. Moor's tour of the Ethiope area marked the end of this disturbed situation. The Urhobo were happy that they could return to their normal lives and not just because Nana's power had been broken. At any rate, if Moor thought the Urhobo would willingly accept British authority in the new situation created by the fall of Nana, he was sadly mistaken as the events of the next decade conclusively proved. In their own way the Urhobo were to resist the imposition of British rule to an extent that called for the sending of British 'patrols' into their territory.[34]

Not a single question was asked by the court despite the various

---

[31] Omoneukarin p. 83   [32] Pinnock p. 33
[33] See Nana's statement of defence
[34] For details of British penetration of Urhoboland see Ikime, O. *Itsekiri-Urhobo Relations* &c Chapter IV Ph.D. Ibadan 1965

discrepancies between Moor's evidence and his despatches; and incidentally, these despatches were not submitted as exhibits as they should have been. One wonders how the truth was to be arrived at without questions being asked. Nana for his part declined to cross-examine Moor, merely stating that he would make a statement of defence.

The next prosecution witness was Dogho's headman, Omota, who merely described the attack on Okotobo. Omota was followed by two witnesses, Akpato and Macholo, who described themselves as 'the messengers who took up the messages to Brohemie' from the Acting Consul-General. The evidence of these messengers gave some idea of what went on inside Ebrohimi during the crisis. Moor's letters, the messengers stated, were usually handed over to Nana who gave them to his clerk who proceeded to read them before an assembly of the elders. Nana always asked from these elders what kind of reply was to be sent to the Consul-General. The messengers claimed that most of the time it was a certain Bazani, one of the 'head chiefs' who did the talking and led the others in deciding what kind of letter was to be sent to Moor. Cross-examined by Nana, the messengers revealed that Nana had often asked them to 'beg the consul to make peace'. The court which had sat silently through the two and a half days during which Moor gave evidence, was stirred and asked two questions. One of them was designed to find out whether Nana allowed Bazani's views to be discussed by the other chiefs or whether he was entirely guided by this head chief's opinion. The messengers answered that Nana always asked the views of the other chiefs before taking the final decision. The court then asked a question which certainly did not arise from the evidence of these messengers: 'Did you take any message from Mr Moor to Nana about the Lagos man Thompson?' The messengers replied that one of the letters sent to Nana was opened and read by Thompson and Jackson, Nana's clerk, and that Nana was not present when the reply to Moor's letter was written; and it was this reply which greatly incensed Moor and caused him to order intensified shelling. After reading this particular letter, Moor sent the messenger to warn Nana against Thompson whom he described as 'a rogue and a vagabond'.

The interesting fact is that not one of the prosecution witnesses had mentioned 'the Lagos man Thompson'. In other words, Macdonald was deliberately introducing into the trial information received from other sources which were undoubtedly from Moor's despatches. Yet when Moor's evidence differed from his despatches, no questions were asked. Macdonald seems to have been a little anxious to find some reason for pleading extenuating circumstances on Nana's behalf. The questions about Bizani and Thompson were clearly designed to demonstrate that Nana acted under a certain amount of pressure.

After the messengers came the most interesting witness of all— Tonwe, Nana's trusted messenger, who virtually turned Queen's evidence and proceeded to give what he no doubt thought was damning evidence. One wonders how it was he became a witness for the prosecution. Did he volunteer to give evidence or was he cajoled and bribed? The word 'bribed' is used advisedly. According to Alan Boisragon, one of the survivors of the so-called 'Benin massacre', 'Towey who had been with Nana when Brohoemi was taken . . . was then taken to Old Calabar and educated by the Protectorate Government for interpreter's work.'[35] Was this why he testified against Nana? Tonwe was to meet a luckless end. He was killed by the Bini when he accompanied Phillips's party to Benin as government interpreter.

Tonwe began by describing how Nana had ordered a certain Jack to be nailed to a tree for committing adultery with one of Nana's wives and for mortally wounding a certain Patapa, one of Nana's headmen. According to Tonwe, 'there was no evidence . . . brought to prove either charges'. True to its self-imposed taciturnity during most of the trial, the court engaged in no cross-examination even in face of a charge of 'unlawful murder'. Tonwe agreed under cross-examination by Nana that after Jack had been hanged, he was sent by Nana to the Vice-Consulate to report that Jack had been hanged for the murder of Patapa. The Vice-Consul did not, it would appear, raise any objection to what had been done. Nana would scarcely have volunteered the information about the hanging to the British authorities were he not sure that he had imposed the capital punishment for just cause.

[35] Boisragon, Alan *The Benin Massacre* p. 67 London 1897

At any rate, even if Jack's only offence was adultery with Nana's wife, Itsekiri law sometimes allowed the death penalty to be inflicted on a man who committed adultery with the wife of an important chief.[36] Nana did not therefore engage in any indiscriminate barbarities as Tonwe seemed to imply.

Tonwe went on to narrate how on a number of occasions Nana had been inclined to see the Acting Consul-General but had been restrained by the other chiefs. He recalled how he had assured Nana of his safety in the hands of the British authorities and how he had tried to persuade Nana to accept the safe-conduct offered by the British. On 1 August, continued Tonwe, Nana had sent him and Thompson to Lagos to seek the advice of the Governor. On their return Nana was again inclined to accept the advice of the Lagos Deputy-Governor to the effect that he should seek a settlement with the British administration. But Thompson and Jackson warned him that it was dangerous to go to the Vice-Consulate without a lawyer to protect his interests. It was part of Nana's plan that Thompson and Tonwe should find him a lawyer while they were in Lagos. But no lawyer was retained largely as a result of a quarrel between Tonwe and Thompson over the former's refusal to hand over the money for retaining the lawyer to the latter. Tonwe claimed that on their return Thompson reported the quarrel to Nana and that as a result he was locked up. But under cross-examination by Nana, Tonwe shifted his ground. Nana did not actually lock him up; rather he had shut himself up out of fear. This was a clear instance of perjury—for Tonwe was testifying under oath—but it called forth no comments from the court.

Tonwe's evidence might have been designed to damn Nana, but some of his statements were a vindication of Nana's stand as he was soon to state it in his defence. Tonwe testified that after the burning of Oteghele Nana gave orders to his men not to allow anyone to go up the Ebrohimi creek. That was not all. Nana's orders were that his people should only open fire if the British troops went up the creek and fired at them. This was Nana's case throughout: that he only fired in self defence.

The last witness for the prosecution was Jackson, Nana's clerk.

[36] Omoneukarin p. 36

His evidence was mainly concerned with how Nana had dis-
tributed arms to his men in the month of August and how the
stockade was built during the same period, the work being completed about 4 August. He remembered that Jack had been nailed
to a tree on the orders of Nana but stated, 'Jack was killed for the
murder of Patapa'. Jackson also testified as to the instructions
given by Nana to the men in the stockade: 'the orders given by
Nana to the people in the stockade were that if they saw any
war launch coming into the creek they were to be fired at'.

Question by the Prisoner: Did you at any time go to the stockade
yourself?
Answer: No.
Question by Prisoner: How do you know I gave orders concerning what people in the stockade were to
do?
Answer: Some of the people that came from the
stockade told me.

In other words, Jackson's evidence in this particular respect was
based on hearsay. Yet neither did he give that impression when
he made his categorical statement, nor did the court make any
comments on this point after Nana's cross-examination.

The prosecution closed its case after Jackson's evidence, and
Nana was called upon to make his statement of defence. Incidentally, there were no witnesses for the defence. It is not known
whether this was because Nana refused to call any witnesses or
whether the peculiarities of the consular court forbade such witnesses being called. In the despatch in which Macdonald reported
the preparations for the trial, he gave the impression that arrangements were being made to get witnesses for the prosecution as
well as for the defence.

Reference has been made to Nana's defence at various points
in this work. Here only some interesting disclaimers and explanations will be considered. Nana began:

This palaver is not mine, it had been brought upon me by being
head of the house, no whiteman had a palaver with me, had the
question being one between myself and the Government there
would have been no row at all, the present troubles are due to a
standing feud between my father and Dore's father. Dore told

Towey to tell me that 'he was not chief Harrison that if he, Dore, did anything he will do it to the end'. Dore behaved very badly to me and told a lot of lies about me.

Nana was making a decidedly exaggerated claim when he asserted that he had had no 'palaver' with any 'whiteman'. The events of the years from 1891 to 1894 in particular make it quite clear that the 'whiteman'—trader and administrator alike—did have a quarrel with Nana. But Nana made two important points when he claimed that the 'palaver' had been brought on him by virtue of his position as 'head of the house'. This point was made in an earlier chapter,[37] and the evidence of the messengers and Tonwe gave some indication of how Nana had always to take into consideration the views of the people over whom he was 'head'. The other important point was the claim that the real explanation for the events of 1894 was the standing feud between the Olomu and Numa families. This feud has been discussed earlier and nothing more needs be said except that it is again significant that the court did not desire to have any more details of the feud to which Nana referred.

Nana disclaimed responsibility for the stoppage of trade at Abraka. On the issue of the stoppage of trade in 1886 to which Moor had drawn attention he stated that the other traders refused to accept the price of oil which had fallen from 100 pieces of cloth to 60 pieces per puncheon. There was no way by which he could coerce the traders to accept the lower price. It was only when he showed the traders the letter from the Consul, Hewett, that they consented to reopen trade and accept the reduced price.

On the issue of the refusal of Chiefs Dear and Erigbe to report to the Vice-Consulate, Nana made the obvious point that as his town was under blockade and he himself unable to leave Ebrohimi it was hardly fair to hold him responsible for the activities of the two chiefs.

Nana did not attempt to deny the fact that he possessed slaves, but he challenged the assertion that he raided the Urhobo country.

With regard to Mr Moor's statement that I and my headmen raided the slaves in the Sobo District to the number of 200 a year I deny

---

[37] See chapter III

this. It is a custom with the Sobos when they take trust to give one of their children as security, in this way numbers of Sobos may have been in Brohimie. I never raided the Sobos; nine years ago I had a fight with the Abraka but the natives all ran into the bush I only captured one old man who was subsequently ransomed, the cause of fight was the seizure of my canoes by the Abrakas and the killing of one of my men. I reported the matter to the consul. I am related to the Sobos, Abraka is the only country I am not related to.

Nana was again overstating his case, for there were occasional raids, though some of these arose out of disputes over trade. It has already been explained why it was that Nana's relations with the Abraka tended to be more hostile than relations with other Urhobo people.[38]

The building of the stockade, explained Nana, was undertaken as a defensive measure after it had become abundantly clear that the intentions of the British were hostile. Evidence of this hostility was the seizure of canoes carrying food to Ebrohimi, the burning of Oteghele without sufficient cause shown, and the continued shelling of Ebrohimi. Nana ended his statement of defence by describing the hardships of his last days in Ebrohimi, his escape and his eventual surrender to the Governor of Lagos.

The court found Nana guilty on all counts. To quote from the court's findings:

> Thereupon the court taking into consideration that the said Nana Alluma does not appear from the evidence to have been on all occasions a free agent in the action taken, sentences the said Nana Alluma for his said offences to be deported forthwith from the Benin District Niger Coast Protectorate for the term of his natural life to reside in such part of the Niger Coast Protectorate as may be from time to time directed by the court.

The court also confirmed the last paragraph of Moor's proclamation dated 25 September 1894 which declared 'all the goods and chattels, real and personal property, of the said chief Nana Alluma and his people . . . forfeited to the Government'.

Seven others—Bizani, Ololu, Oko, Eddu, Mamagu, Nafomi and Nisama—were tried with Nana. The charges against them were

[38] See chapter II

the same as those preferred against Nana. These men were convicted or freed mainly on the evidence of Tonwe. According to Tonwe, Bizani and Mamagu gave Nana 'bad advice'. Eddu did not speak at the meeting held to decide what was to be done. Nisama was away to Abraka at the relevant time. Ololu's views were always overridden by the others. Oko advised Nana not to fight against the British. The court acquitted Eddu, Nafomi and Nisama. Ololu and Oko were found 'guilty with extenuating circumstances' and sentenced to deportation from the Benin district for a period of two years, as well as to forfeiture of all goods. Bizani and Mamagu were found guilty and sentenced to forfeiture of goods and penal servitude for life.

Nana's trial was peculiar. Indeed the trial appeared to be more of a formality designed to satisfy any who might raise the cry of 'British justice' than a conscientious effort to see justice done. Long before the trial, Ralph Moor had made it clear that only Nana's deportation would meet the requirements of the British administration of the Niger Coast Protectorate. The trial seemed to have been designed to secure this end. Ralph Moor himself was the star prosecution witness. The evidence called merely related the events of May to October 1894, or else depicted acts of cruelty allegedly performed by Nana. Apart from Moor's frantic effort to relate part of his evidence to the charges, there was little such correlation. Nana was accused of having made war against 'Her Majesty the Queen in the Niger Coast Protectorate'. Yet no convincing effort was made by the prosecution to demonstrate that Nana was responsible for the commencement of hostilities. For if, as Nana claimed, he went to war in self-defence the charge could scarcely be regarded as fair. As a matter of fact the question of who should take responsibility for the outbreak of war is a difficult one. The first physical sanctions, such as the prevention of Nana's people from using the waterways of the district, were applied by Moor. Surely this could be regarded as an act of aggression. On the other hand it can be argued that Moor was forced to apply that physical sanction because of the disturbed situation allegedly created by the activities of Nana's men. As for who fired the first shot, the truth will never be known since each party to the dispute accused the other of beginning armed aggression. In view of all this one wonders whether the first charge as it was construed was a fair charge. There was no doubt that Nana had waged a war against the British. It was not even necessary to go to court to prove that fact. What had to be demonstrated beyond reasonable doubt was that Nana was guilty of having made war inevitable. This fact was clearly not proven at the trial. Yet Nana was pronounced guilty. Such are the ethics of war. The vanquished are invariably the aggressors. They pay the war indemnities. So it was with Nana.

According to the court proceedings, the first charge was levied in accordance with Article 48 of the Africa Order in Council 1893. This article laid it down that 'if any British subject' levied war against any power, including Her Majesty the Queen, without the sanction of the British Government, he would be liable on conviction to imprisonment for a term not exceeding two years with or without hard labour and with or without a fine of £1,000, or a fine of £1,000 without imprisonment. The Article continued: 'In addition to such punishment, every such conviction shall of itself, and without further proceedings, make the person convicted liable to deportation.'[39] The question which arises from this article, apart from the generous provision for deportation, is whether Nana was in law a 'British subject'. Legally it would appear that Nana was a 'British protected person', rather than a 'British subject' and that therefore Article 48 could not be invoked against him. Admittedly there tended to be little difference in practice in the concept of a 'British subject' and a 'British protected person' but this was a trial and this point was clearly arguable.

If Article 48 could not be invoked against Nana the only other article that could was Article 102(1) which stated:

'Where a person is convicted before a court of any crime or offence, the court may in addition to or in lieu of any other sentence order him to give security to the satisfaction of the court, by recognizance, deposit or money, or otherwise, for future good behaviour, and in

---

[39] The Africa Order in Council 1889 (also 1893) can be found as Appendix I in Hodges, F. E. *Consular Jurisdiction in Her Majesty's Protectorate of the Niger Coast* Stevens 1895

default of such security may order him to be deported forthwith, or after undergoing any other sentence passed upon him . . .

Granted therefore that Nana was in fact guilty of the charges against him, he could, according to Article 102(1) of the Order in Council (and Macdonald in his covering despatch stated that he was invoking this Article), be sentenced to deportation but only in default of security for future good behaviour being given. A minute by an official of the Foreign Office on Macdonald's despatch made it quite clear that the view stated above was likely to be the one to be upheld 'were the matter to come before the Privy Council'. But from the 'practical point of view' the official was inclined 'to let things slide and to take no official notice of the despatch'.[40] Another official on reading the above minute commented: 'A Sierra Leone lawyer who belongs to a class found everywhere on the coast might raise the point but we may wait till he does.[41]' 'I agree,' minuted K(imberley).

From the Foreign Office minutes it is evident that there was doubt as to the validity of the sentence passed on Nana by Macdonald. It is unfortunate that the Foreign Office did not see fit to correct the misconstruction and so vindicate British justice. Yet one can appreciate the difficulty in which the Foreign Office found itself. Moor had on two occasions before the trial pressed for the removal of Nana and his advisers from the Benin River district, and British policy was wont to respect the views of 'the man on the spot'. On the day Nana's trial opened at Old Calabar, the Foreign Office had sent a despatch to Macdonald in which it expressed 'cordial approval' and appreciation of Moor's action against Nana. Macdonald's despatch about Nana's trial was not written till two weeks after the Foreign Office despatch referred to above. In the circumstances a reversal of Macdonald's judgment would have amounted to an indictment of Moor's action which had already received 'cordial approval', at the same time as it would have constituted an unusual affront on 'the man on the spot'. In order, therefore, to save the faces of Moor and Mac-

---

[40] F.O. 2/64 Minute on Macdonald's despatch No. 49, 13 Dec. 1894 initialled W.E.W. and dated 18/6/95
[41] *Ibid* minute by another official dated 19/6/95

donald, the latter having obviously misconstrued the provisions of the Order in Council, Nana was allowed to be sentenced to life deportation. Little wonder Macdonald had no desire to have a lawyer plead the cause of Nana.

Little needs be said about the other charges, all of which were framed in such broad terms that it was easy to secure conviction. It was not stated, for instance, which provisions of the treaty of 1884 Nana had failed to carry out. While the punishment prescribed for the offence that constituted the third charge was deportation such a penalty was made conditional on failure to provide adequate security for future good conduct. One is naturally tempted to make comparisons between Nana's trial and those of Jaja of Opobo and Oba Ovonramwen of Benin. None of the three trials was in fact a fair one. Anene has described Jaja's trial as 'illegal' as Jaja, not being a British subject, was not 'amenable to the jurisdiction of a British court'.[42] The trial of the Oba of Benin, conducted by none other than Ralph Moor himself, was allegedly under 'Native Law and custom'. But the final verdict was not based on any Benin law. Rather it was based on Ralph Moor's declared belief: 'Now this is the white man's country. There is only one king in the country and that is the white man'.[43] Like Nana, Ovonramwen had become an anachronism from Ralph Moor's point of view.

The penalty imposed on Nana was undoubtedly severe, involving as it did life-long exile and loss of all property. Perhaps after all that had taken place this was no surprise. The trial might be open to various criticisms and the grounds for Macdonald's verdict questioned. But there can be no doubt that Nana represented an obstacle to the establishment of British rule in the Itsekiri and Urhobo areas, not so much in the sense that he prevented penetration of the hinterland or actively hindered the work of the consular officials as in the sense that his power, his wealth, his influence constituted an alternative source of authority against which the new British administration had to contend. His removal left the British alone in the field. Even when all that has

[42] Anene p. 90
[43] For details of the trial of the Oba of Benin, see C.S.O. 1/13/7— enclosures in Mokr to F.O. 18 Oct. 1897

M

been said, one still tends to agree with the views of a Lagos newspaper:

> We do not see why such undue severity should be exercised in the case of the unfortunate chief of Benin [River], who, whatever may have been his offence, was certainly the object of the envy, jealousy and hate of rival chiefs, who would have no compunction in charging him with the most heinous crimes. This fact we think should have had some consideration in determining the sentence passed upon him, particularly as the trouble between him and the British authorities appears to have been brought about in some most precipitate and yet unaccountable manner through the machinations of these very chiefs.[44]

[44] *Lagos Weekly Record* 16 Feb. 1895

CHAPTER VI

Exile, Return, Death

NANA'S FIRST home in exile was somewhere in the Upper Cross River probably at Old Calabar. A house was provided for him, one wife and his eldest son. The protectorate government granted him a monthly allowance of £10 a month.[1] The richest Itsekiri man of his day was thus reduced to a beggarly £120 a year. It might appear at first sight a generous gesture that the government decided to make the grant. As a matter of fact, the government was not thereby immediately incurring any additional expenditure. For despite the fact that on the fall of Ebrohimi a fire destroyed considerable stores, and despite the destruction of over 700 cases of gin,[2] the sale of Nana's effects realised a total of £6,686. 12s. 9d. Of this sum £2,300 was used to liquidate Nana's outstanding debts in the Benin district. The entire cost of the operations against Nana estimated at £3,258. 12s. 2d. was paid from the same source. In the Warri district £186. 9s. 7d. was paid out as part settlement of Nana's debts.[3] There thus remained over £900 which was credited to the protectorate government. The figures alone are an impressive testimony of the affluence of one of West Africa's wealthiest traders of the nineteenth century. At the rate of £10 a month, the government could maintain Nana in exile for a period of seven years without spending a penny from its reserves. There was, in the circumstances, nothing particularly generous about the £10 monthly grant to Nana. If anything the allowance was inadequate for the upkeep of Nana, his wife and son.

Not a great deal is known about Nana's life in exile. He remained in the Cross River for about two years. In April 1896 Nana addressed a petition to the Governor of the Lagos colony praying him to plead with the Niger Coast Protectorate authorities and so help secure his release from exile. Like the head of his

[1] F.O. 2/64 Macdonald to F.O. No. 49, 13 Dec. 1894
[2] F.O. 2/64 Moore to F.O. No. 28, 5 Oct. 1894
[3] F.O. 2/101 Moore to F.O. No. 40, 13 May 1896

people that he was, Nana did not forget to include in his petition the others who had been condemned with him to exile and imprisonment.[4]

Accompanying Nana's petition was another from Seidu Olowu also addressed to the Governor of Lagos. It is easy to misunderstand some of the statements contained in Olowu's petition. In typical African style Olowu began by showering praises on the Governor whom he described as 'exceptional among the roll of Governors ever assuming the office'. Nana, he wrote, was 'suffering through his own indiscretions'. He regretted that Nana had not consulted him before he 'rushed' into the 'unbridled licentiousness' which had earned him deportation. Then he craved 'His Excellency's intercession' for the release of Nana whom he prayed should be allowed to settle in Lagos if it was not possible to let him return to the Benin River.[5] Olowu's references to Nana's 'indiscretions' and 'licentiousness' should be seen strictly in their context. His obvious preoccupation was with the release of his friend from exile, not the rights and wrongs of the events which led to Nana's fall. To secure this release he was prepared to admit that his friend was in the wrong. This is not an unusual attitude for a suppliant to adopt.

In June 1896 Moor wrote to the Governor of Lagos who had forwarded these two petititions to him. Moor could not see his way to recommending the petitions for the favourable consideration of the British Secretary of State. He noted that attempts were being made to open up a regular waterway between Lagos and the Benin River. It was, in these conditions, Moor's view that the presence of Nana in Lagos would cause uneasiness in the Benin River district and the Urhobo country.[6]

In the covering despatch with which Moor forwarded the petitions to the Foreign Office, he again stated his unwillingness to recommend them for favourable consideration, 'on any grounds whether of justice, clemency or good of the country generally'.

[4] F.O. 2/101 Nana's petition—enclosure in Gallwey to F.O. No. 47, 11 June 1896

[5] *Ibid* Seidu Olowu's petition is an enclosure in the same despatch.

[6] Cal. Prov. 6/1 Vol. III Moor to Governor Lagos No. 29, 11 June 1896

While Moor protested the needlessness of entering into the details of the causes of the expedition of 1894, he nevertheless seized the opportunity to continue building up the case against the exiled chief. He wrote:

> I am convinced that it was for long the intention of this chief to resist the authority of the Government by force of arms. His act was long premeditated and carefully planned and his failure and punishment have served as a good lesson to many others throughout the Protectorate.[7]

Indeed Moor's animosity towards Nana seemed to have become personal. If the evidence of Tonwe and Jackson—two witnesses deliberately chosen by the prosecution—proved anything, it was that Nana did not really begin full-scale war preparations until August 1894, by which time the British had already mounted a blockade against Ebrohimi.[8] Yet Moor continued his claim that Nana had been preparing for war a long time before 1894. He recommended to the Foreign Office that Nana should never be allowed to return to the Benin River district. In order to ensure this he suggested that Nana should be removed altogether from the Niger Coast Protectorate. Moor argued:

> It would in my view be a good thing to let it be clearly understood among the semi-civilised chiefs of the immediate coast region that any chief taking up arms against the Government, would as the least punishment for such offence be removed altogether from the Protectorate.[9]

It was peculiar morality and justice which thus by implication made pronouncements about how African chiefs were to react to the appropriation of their rights and resources by the British imperial power.

The Foreign Office apparently approved Moor's suggestion that Nana be deported to the Gold Coast for, in November 1896, Acting Consul-General Phillips wrote to inform that office that Nana 'with four attendants' had been deported to the Gold Coast where he was installed in Christiansbourg Castle. Phillips reported that they were being given an allowance of 10s. a day.

[7] F.O. 2/101 Moor to F.O. No 47 11 June 1896
[8] See chapter IV [9] See note 7

However, in a letter to the Governor of the Gold Coast, Gallwey stated that Nana, his wife and son were to be paid an allowance of 5*s*. a day.[10] The Gold Coast Governor was asked to inform the Niger Coast Protectorate authorities whether this sum was regarded as sufficient for the maintenance of Nana and his family. The allowance was subsequently increased to 12*s* 6*d*. a day.[11]

Seidu Olowu's efforts to secure the release of Nana[12] were stoutly resisted by Moor who maintained his attitude that Nana should not be allowed to 'return for many years to come, if at all'.[13] At the same time a more powerful organisation took the protectorate government to task over Nana's exile. In 1897 the Aborigines Protection Society, through the Foreign Office, took up the question of the 1894 operations. It claimed that the 1894 operations as well as the Akassa disturbances in the early part of 1895 were 'mainly due to efforts on the part of the British authorities to induce the natives to carry on trade with Europeans under conditions prescribed by the latter'.[14] Moor denied the charge and sought to restate the case against Nana. Nana's offences were, according to Moor, that he established a monopoly of trade, and that he excluded other Itsekiri traders from areas 'to which he had under native custom and law' no more right than the other Itsekiri; that he fixed arbitrary prices for palm produce such that 'the producers gained little or nothing by their labour'; and that he indulged in the slave trade.[15] There was nothing new in the charges, except that they were not exactly those for which Nana had been tried and exiled. A few comments might be passed on them. The assertion that Nana had no special right by 'native custom and law' to the areas over which he established a monopoly merely shows how little Moor understood the society which he governed. For the issue at stake was not that of legal rights but rather what European diplomacy would

[10] See F.O. 2/102 Phillips to F.O. No. 110 28 Nov. 1896 and Cal. Prov. 6/1 Vol. III Gallwey to Governor, Gold Coast 19 Oct. 1896

[11] Cal. Prov. 6/1 Vol. IV Governor Gold Coast to Consul General, Niger Coast Protectorate No. 359/99, 17 April 1899

[12] Cal. Prov. 6/1 Vol. III Seidu Olowu to Governor Lagos 2 April 1897

[13] See for instance F.O. 2/121 Moor to F.O. No. 48, 3 May 1897

[14] F.O. 2/121 Moor to F.O. No. 49, 6 May 1897

[15] *Ibid*

have described as 'effective occupation'. British statesmen and administrators were doubtless familiar with the doctrine of 'effective occupation'—a doctrine which was not based on strict law, for the implication was clearly that even if a European power had signed a treaty with an African chief but failed to occupy effectively the chief's territory, another European power could move into that territory. In a similar way, the situation in this part of the Niger Coast Protectorate was such that usage allowed whoever opened up the trade of a particular area to possess, as it were, rights of effective occupation. Nana did no more. His only offence was that of being so powerful, resourceful and industrious that he carved for himself more 'spheres of influence' than did the other Itsekiri traders.

The fixing of prices for produce during this period was nearly always arbitrary, though there can be no arguing over the fact that the absence of competition in Nana's preserves did lead to low prices. But this was exactly the problem that existed between the Itsekiri and the British traders; the Itsekiri felt that the foreigners were fixing arbitrary prices for palm produce for their own benefit. It required time and greater understanding of world markets for the question of prices to be satisfactorily adjusted.

In defence of the operations of 1894 Moor made an interesting comment: 'The claim was that of the Jekri chiefs to equal right with chief Nana to trade in the markets where he wished to enforce a monopoly and this claim was justly supported by Her Majesty's Government.'[16] It thus appears that the Ebrohimi Expedition was the outcome of the dissatisfaction of the other Itsekiri chiefs. There is a sense in which this was true. Yet not once in the despatches of 1894 did Moor advance this claim. It is intriguing what efforts were made to avoid stating the real reason for which Nana was deported. Each time the issue was raised, some new reason or explanation seemed to emerge to justify the British action.

Despite the obvious disabilities of a life in exile, Nana would seem to have spent a fairly profitable time in the Gold Coast. As already mentioned he was allowed to take two of his sons with him. In 1899 five children were allowed to join him there, and in

[16] *Ibid*

1900 yet another five. By 1902 two more children had been born.[17] Indeed by this time the question of more of his children joining him in exile had become a problem to the Southern Nigeria government. Moor had to write to the Governor of the Gold Coast to inform him that no more of Nana's children or other relations were to be allowed to join him.[18] The reason why Nana kept asking for his children to be sent to him in Accra was that he seemed to have found the means to give these children some education or training in various crafts. In 1906 when he left Accra, he had a son in the Accra Grammar School and five sons at the Government Primary School—two in standard six and three in standard seven.[19] Nana himself was an accomplished carpenter and he seems to have passed on his skill to some of his relations. While in the Gold Coast he was converted, together with his household, to the Christian faith. His father had refused to allow Christianity to be propagated among his people and Nana had in 1884 forbidden Christian missionaries to practise in Itsekiriland. After his conversion and eventual return from exile the missionaries were to appeal to him to use his good offices in the interest of the Christian faith.[20] On the whole, apart from the obvious disadvantages of exile in itself, the British administration treated Nana with consideration. One particular gesture which must have given the exiled chief considerable satisfaction and joy was the permission granted to his sister, Beji, to visit him in Accra in 1902. Beji was an old woman and she had expressed a desire to see her brother before she died. Moor, rising above the hard feelings which he always seemed to bear towards Nana, not only allowed the ageing Beji to travel to Accra to see her brother, but paid the expenses of her journey to and from Accra from government funds.[21] It was a most humane gesture.

Whatever the advantages accruing to him in exile, Nana naturally continued to petition for leave to return to his home. In

[17] C.S.O. 12/25 Governor, Gold Coast to C.O. No. 97, 6 March 1902
[18] Cal. Prov. 9/2 Vol. 1 Moor to Governor, Gold Coast No. 44, 13 March 1902
[19] C.S.O. 12/25 File 4061/1906 Acting Governor, Gold Coast to Governor S. Nigeria No. 15, 15 Aug. 1906
[20] See pp. 180–1
[21] C.S.O. 12/25 Moor to C.O. No. 194, 28 April 1902

1898, 1902 and 1905 Nana addressed petitions to the appropriate British Secretary of State praying that he be allowed to return to his own country.[22] Gallwey and Moor until 1902, did not relent in their stand that Nana should be left to die in exile. It is food for thought for those who are inclined to argue that had Gallwey been in the protectorate in 1894 the hostilities might have been averted to dwell on the fact that in 1898 Gallwey had an opportunity of showing mercy to the exiled chief by recommending his repatriation to the British Secretary of State for Foreign Affairs. Not only did he fail to do so, but pleaded that Nana should never be allowed to return to the protectorate.[23]

In 1902 Moor gave two reasons for not desiring Nana's return. One of these was that the administration had just passed the Slave Dealing Ordinance and was only just beginning to take effective steps to deal with the whole issue of slavery. As Nana was one of the greatest slave dealers of his time, Moor feared that Nana's return to the Benin River or Warri district might create unrest and lead to difficulties for his former slaves who were only beginning to settle down to their new life as independent citizens.[24] By 1902 the conditions of the protectorate had changed so much that it is doubtful whether had he been allowed to return at that time Nana would have been able to continue successfully in the slave trade. Besides Nana's power, both as a trader and as an individual, had been so broken as a result of the war of 1894 that the basis of his prosperity even as a slave owner had been irreparably shattered. Even when that had been said one can still sympathise with Moor's view in 1902. He had cause to fear what the redoubtable ex-Governor could do if set free once again.

From the point of view of the British administration, the second reason was equally weighty. 'At the present time,' wrote Moor, 'there is no place in this country for a man of ex-Chief

---

[22] These petitions are to be found as enclosures in F.O. 2/179, Gallwey to F.O. No. 110, 9 July 1898; Cal. Prov. 9/1 Vol. II Governor, Gold Coast to High Commissioner S. Nigeria 19 Feb. 1902 and C.S.O. 12/25 Governor Gold Goast to High Commissioner S. Nigeria 3 Jan. 1905

[23] F.O. 2/179 Gallwey to F.O. No. 110, 9 July 1898

[24] C.S.O. 12/25 Moor to C.O. No. 194, 28 April 1902

Nana's position.' The government, argued Moor, was beginning
to consolidate its hold over the Urhobo people of the hinterland.
These were the very people over whom Nana had previously
exercised great influence. Moor did not consider that Nana's return in 1902 would facilitate British penetration of the Urhobo
hinterland. It was also Moor's view that Nana himself would be
a little embarrassed by the situation as it then existed. Therefore,
although he conceded that it was hard not to allow Nana to
return after some eight years in exile, Moor was of the opinion
that it would be to the advantage of the protectorate and better
for chief Nana himself for him to spend the rest of his life in
exile.[25] One might disagree with Moor's opinion, but at least one
must admire the honesty with which he now faced the issue:
Nana was too influential a personage to be allowed in the protectorate. This was, in fact, why he had been removed in the
first instance, though Moor was then unwilling to accept this
fact. By 1902, however, British imperial interests had attained
such dimensions and had become so obvious that little purpose
could have been served by seeking to hide them beneath the kind
of facade which Moor had tried to build up in 1894.

Nana's last petition was written in April 1906.[26] It was lucky
for him that by this time both Moor and Gallwey had left the
services of the protectorate. The new Governor of Southern
Nigeria, Sir Walter Egerton, had not been involved in the Nana
episode and so could take a more detached view of Nana's request.
Himself unfamiliar with the Benin River and Warri districts, he
decided to seek advice from those who had actually worked
there.[27] Accordingly, he addressed letters to W. Fosbery, a former
Provincial Commissioner, and F. S. James, then Provincial Commissioner, Central Provinces, for the Benin River and Warri
districts were in the Central Provinces. Fosbery confessed that he
had no knowledge about what the feelings of the people of the
area were about Nana's return from exile. However, he recalled Moor's despatch of 1902 and expressed doubts as to

[25] C.S.O. 12/25 Moor to C.O. No. 194, 28 April 1902
[26] The petition can be found in C.S.O. 12/25 File 197/06. See Appendix VII.
[27] C.O. 520/35 Egerton to C.O. No. 124, 12 May 1906

'whether Nana would be content to settle down as an ordinary
individual in a neighbourhood where formerly he exercised such
sway'. He reminded the Governor that Oba Ovonramwen (Overami) was in exile at Old Calabar and argued that if Nana were
allowed to return from exile the Bini people would agitate for the
return of their Oba. As a compromise solution Fosbery suggested
that Nana be brought back to Old Calabar and be kept there for
the rest of his life. At Old Calabar, argued Fosbery, Nana would
be more readily accessible to all relations who desired to see
him.[28]

F. S. James' advice was radically different from Fosbery's and
was perhaps largely responsible for Egerton's decision to recommend the repatriation of Nana. James did not consider that the
reasons advanced by Moor in 1902 were tenable in 1906. Members of Nana's original household, argued James, were widely
dispersed and it was unlikely that they would return to Nana if
the latter were allowed to come back to the district. He reported
that he had discussed the matter with Chief Dogho, by this time
the leading figure in Itsekiriland, and Chief Ogbe, an influential
Warri trader; both these men were of the view that 'Nana's
return or non-return would have no political effect on this part
of the Protectorate'. James did not think that Nana and Oba
Ovonramwen should be considered on the same plane. He argued
that the Oba's main offence was that he used his 'juju' to terrorise
the locality. The Government had removed the Oba and put
itself in his place. If the Oba were allowed to return, argued
James, the adherents of his 'juju' would think that the 'juju' had
overpowered the government and such an attitude of mind would
lead to certain unrest. On the other hand:

> Nana' removal was on all fours with the removal of Jaja of Opobo,
> entirely on account of the great power in trade to which they both
> attained owing to their own individuality, and which power on
> account of the jealousies existing at the time amongst themselves
> and the leading firms in the Protectorate, it was considered advis-
> able should be broken down, but which but for this same jealousy

---

[28] Minute by Mr W. Fosbery 19 April 1906 enclosed in the above
despatch.

might well under careful supervision have been utilised for the benefit of the country in those early days of the Administration.[29]

Although James did not specifically request that Nana be allowed to return, the implications of his arguments were clear enough. If the Governor saw fit to allow Nana to return, James suggested that Nana be allowed to settle in the town of 'America' near Koko where his brother was staying at the time. 'It may be', he went on, 'that with Nana's abilities an impetus may be given to the trade round and about Koko.'[30]

On the strength of the views expressed by James, Egerton wrote to the Colonial Office seeking approval of his plan to let Nana return from exile and settle at 'America'. Egerton proposed paying to Nana a monthly allowance of £10 for a period of two years to enable him settle down well enough to look after himself.[31] The Colonial Office approved Egerton's proposals[32] and Nana left Accra on 4 August 1906.[33]

This is the place to put on record the contributions of one of Nana's greatest friends, George W. Neville, a London merchant who knew Nana personally. He exerted himself unceasingly to secure his release. It would appear that he even took the trouble to write to Sir Claude Macdonald who had left the services of the protectorate to secure the latter's support in his fight for Nana's release. Macdonald was reported to have stated that he favoured the proposal to have Nana return to his country, and to have promised to lend all the help he could.[34] In February 1906, Neville wrote to Liverpool Chamber of Commerce urging the Committee of the African Trade Section of that body to adopt a resolution calling for the release of Nana. On 28 February, following the adoption of such a resolution, the Chamber addressed a request to the Colonial Office praying for Nana's release. The Colonial Office replied to the effect that the matter was being

[29] Minute by Mr F. S. James 3 May 1906 enclosed in the same despatch.   [30] *Ibid*

[31] C.O. 520/35 Egerton to C.O. No. 124, 12 May 1906

[32] C.S.O. 12/25, File No. 197/06 C.O. to Officer Administering the Government of S. Nigeria No. 259, 6 July 1906

[33] C.S.O. 12/25 File 4061/906 Acting Governor, Gold Coast to Governor, S. Nigeria No. 15, 15 Aug. 1906

[34] *Lagos Weekly Record* April 7 1906

referred to the protectorate authorities.[35] The *Lagos Weekly Record* continued its interest in the Nana episode by giving publicity to Neville's efforts and adding its own plea for the return of the exiled chief. The paper condemned the policy of deportation and argued that the removal of enterprising traders like Nana was detrimental to the development of trade as the African traders were bound to lose interest in any large-scale commercial enterprise in the face of the fate of men like Jaja and Nana.[36] These various pleas must have had some effect both on the protectorate authorities and the Colonial Office. When Nana was eventually released, the *Weekly Record* lauded the action of the Colonial Secretary and Sir Walter Egerton was singled out for special praise.[37]

Nana left Accra with a wife, ten children and a cook. He left behind his six children then at school in Accra. Nana specially requested that these children be allowed to finish their respective courses and obtain the necessary certificates. The Gold Coast Governor kindly consented to let the children continue their schooling career so long as Nana continued to pay for their upkeep. After ten years in Accra Nana could at last go back to his home. He left Accra with at least some satisfaction: he had given education to a number of his children. Incidentally, the Gold Coast Director of Education reported that Nana's sons were 'extremely intelligent'. Not only did they learn quickly, but were reported to be 'particularly good at work of a technical nature'.[38]

Nana arrived at Forcados on 6 August 1906 and was transferred into the government launch *Vixen* which took him to 'America' on 8 August. Reporting the arrival of Nana, the Provincial Commissioner expressed the hope that Nana's abilities would give a much needed fillip to the trade of Koko.[39] He was not to be disappointed.

[35] Holt Papers Box 23 Report of the Committee of the African Trade Section Liverpool Chamber of Commerce 1907

[36] *Lagos Weekly Record* April 7 1906

[37] 'The Repatriation of Chief Nana' *Lagos Weekly Record* 21 July 1906

[38] C.S.O. 12/25, File 4061/1906 Acting Governor, Gold Coast to Governor S. Nigeria No. 15, 15 Aug. 1906

[39] C.S.O. 12/25 Provincial Commissioner, Central Province to Acting Governor, Lagos No. 45/555/6, 8 Aug. 1906

It is impossible to say exactly how Nana felt about his homecoming. It must have been a different kind of life to which he returned. He was no longer Itsekiriland's richest and most powerful man. Indeed he was worse off than many of those who must have laboured for him in his days of glory. It was not long before the British administrative officers of the Sapele district began reminding Nana of his new and lowly status. According to Nana, twelve days after he arrived at 'America' the District Commissioner from Sapele and his assistant paid a visit to Koko. They sent for Nana to come on board their launch. When Nana did go on board, the District Commissioner proceeded to give him a number of injunctions: Nana was not to seek to take back any of his wives or 'boys'; he was not to attempt to collect any outstanding debts; he was to remember that he was no more a chief and was therefore to order his life as became an ordinary citizen; the eyes of the administration would be on him and any misdemeanours would be promptly reported to Lagos. The District Commissioner, according to Nana, informed him of the £10 monthly allowance which the government had decided to grant him. The District Commissioner insisted that at the end of every month Nana was to travel to Sapele to sign the necessary vouchers and draw the allowance. When Nana requested that he be allowed to give his son, Johnson, the authority to sign and draw the allowance on his behalf, the District Commissioner refused to grant the request. If Nana did not personally report to the Treasury the allowance would not be paid.[40] If Nana's account is correct, the District Commissioner was heavily emphasising that Nana was no more the powerful and respected man he used to be. But Nana had not altogether lost his dignity and although he admitted that 'he who has been stung by a serpent is afraid of rope,' he clearly resented the District Commissioner's attitude and sent what amounted to a letter of protest to the Provincial Commissioner.[41] The old fighting spirit was not altogether dead.

A letter from the Acting Provincial Commissioner, Central Provinces, to the District Commissioner, Sapele, demonstrated

[40] C.S.O. 12/25 Nana to Provincial Commissioner Warri 25 Aug. 1906
[41] *Ibid*

that the attitude of the government was not that represented by the District Commissioner. The Provincial Commissioner informed his district lieutenant that the Governor was anxious that Nana be well treated. He warned against the police, interpreters and other government servants making it unnecessarily obvious that the times had changed. Nana was to be allowed to authorise any of his sons to draw his allowance. While Nana could not 'claim' his wives and former 'boys' any such wives and 'boys' who desired to go back to him were not to be hindered from so doing. As a further token of the government's goodwill the Provincial Commissioner directed that, as a present from the government, £10 worth of corrugated iron be sent to Nana for use on the dwelling house he was then building.[42] The government seemed as anxious to be friendly as they had been to find fault in 1894.

Nana's homecoming was greeted with jubilation by some of the Itsekiri, and with even more by the Urhobo people with whom he had had connections. Canoe-loads of people from Ovwia, Aladja and other places in Udu clan, Mogba and Ukan in Agbarho clan, and Okpara in Agbon clan went to 'America' with presents to rejoice with Nana on his return. Gifts of cows and bulls came from Mogba, Ukan and Okpara. To this day cows and bulls are to be seen feeding around 'Nana's palace' in Nana's Town, near Koko. Whatever Moor's views about Nana's tyranny and cruelty, the people, who knew him more intimately than Moor ever could, accorded him a rousing welcome of the kind that could only be accorded to a friend and not to a fallen enemy. Constant visits by private individuals continued for a long time after his return, and many of those who had been 'freed' by the British expedition of 1894 voluntarily went back to work for their returned master.[43] These manifestations of loyalty and affection were so genuine and obvious that they excited the envy of Chief

[42] C.S.O. 12/25, Acting Provincial Commissioner, Warri to District Commissioner, Sapele 10 Sept. 1906.

[43] The account here given of the people's reaction to Nana's return is based on information collected from the field. See Ikime chapter III and Appendix I and also Dogho's interview with Governor Egerton an account of which is given below on pages 178–9.

Dogho, who was by this time a British Political Agent. According to one source, Nana was accorded such honour by all the people round about that even Dogho had to treat him with deference; when his canoe met that of Nana on the river, he would draw aside until Nana had passed.[44] No greater tribute could have been paid to Nana than his reception by the people on his return from exile.

The one man who was disturbed by Nana's return was Dogho. Although by 1906 there was no question of Nana ousting him from the strong position in which he had been entrenched since 1894, Dogho felt uneasy at the tremendous goodwill which Nana still enjoyed. Dogho therefore seized the first opportunity that came his way to obtain some assurance from the government that Nana would not be allowed to become the powerful chief he had once been. It was only two months since Nana's return. Governor Egerton was visiting the Benin area in connection with the unrest in the Benin City Territories. As Dogho was the Political Agent in charge of this part of the protectorate, the Governor granted him an interview on board his boat, the *Ivy*. The interview was meant to discuss the unrest in Benin and for some time this was the subject of discussion. But it was easy to switch the discussion on to Nana, especially as Nana's return had given some hope to the Bini that their Oba too would be allowed to return. The discussion which took place between the Governor and Chief Dogho is quoted in full:

> *Chief:*   There are also false rumours about Nana's coming back.
> *Governor:* Tell me a few of the rumours about Nana's coming back.
> *Chief:*   When he came back all the people here said that he has come and the Government has given him as much power as he had before and the Government gives him more facilities. It is a surprise to them how a man who has fought with the Government had been deported should be brought back and given such full power.
> *Governor:* But they have forgotten all the other men who have not come back.
> *Chief:*   They now hope that all the rest would come back. Since Nana came back a rumour went through all the Sobo and

---

[44] Burns, A. C. *Colonial Civil Servant* p. 38 London 1949

Jekri towns and all the trading markets that he has been given, the highest position a chief could obtain from the Government and the Sobos and Jekris all passing down to see him.

Governor: They go to see him but he has not even got a boy to pull a canoe.

Chief: They assist him.

Governor: He was here before the Government took over control and then he fought with the Government and lost his position and was turned out. Several times he asked to come back and this last time I consulted Mr. Fosbery and Mr James and they both said that he had been away for a sufficiently long time but he might come back. So I agreed with them and let him come back. I told him that he must not open any old palavers—he had been away for a long time and he has lost all his power and money. So now he is given £12 a month for 2 years in order that he may be able to establish himself again, and be able to gain an honest living, but he is not the powerful chief he used to be. I think he is a clever and able man and I hope he will establish himself properly but he has been clearly told that he must not interfere with anybody else. I pressed that upon him. I want him to be friendly with all the other chiefs. All that has taken place is past and finished—now we ought to be all friends together—he is a free man. Mr James has explained to me before that if he comes back this will be the position. I hope some of his boys will go back to him. I cannot force them to go.

Chief: Lots of his boys use to go there and compliment him.[45]

From this interview it would appear that Dogho had not lived down the enmity which existed between him and Nana in 1894. When consulted earlier in the same year about Nana's return, he did not oppose it. Two months after Nana's release he sought definite reassurance about the security of his own position. He got that reassurance, but he also must have realised that the

[45] C.O. 520/37—enclosure 4 in Egerton to C.O., confidential, 31 Oct. 1906. All the other accounts claim that Nana was given an allowance of £10 a month after his return from exile. Here the allowance is said to be £12. This is probably a reporter's mistake.

N

government was not inclined in 1906 to be as anti-Nana as it had been in 1894. The government could afford to be charitable. Its influence and authority were fairly well established by 1906.

Mr Fosbery's fears as to whether Nana would be able to settle down as a private individual after his release were soon dispelled as with characteristic vigour and application the ex-Governor soon organised his new life. In 'America' he built a new village on the model of Ebrohimi. From all accounts this village, now known as Nana's Town, Koko, was in his time as much a model of cleanliness and good planning as Ebrohimi had been. 'Nana's palace', so his house is still fondly called, might not look palatial today, but it impressed all visitors to the town. Lugard described if as 'a really wonderful piece of Native design and construction'.[46] The house was designed and built by Nana and his sons. The town itself was laid out with wide streets, which were all kept scrupulously clean.[47] He quickly fulfilled the hopes entertained about him, for as a consequence of his activities it was reported in 1909 that the Koko area was acquiring a new importance economically and politically.[48] Nana was also sufficiently enterprising to have 'taken up a considerable amount of Government work'[49] probably as a government contractor.

When in 1907 Bishop James Johnson undertook a missionary tour of the Sapele and Warri areas, he visited Nana. Bishop Johnson was aware of Nana's conversion to the Christian faith and had actually confirmed one of Nana's sons at Accra. He now sought to use Nana's town as a base for the spread of Christianity in the neighbourhood of Koko. Nana and his sons agreed to arrange weekly services in the town and do their best to spread the faith. Unfortunately no other records have come to light

[46] Perham, Margery *Lugard: The years of Authority, 1894–1945* pp. 512–3 London 1960

[47] Burns p. 37. Burns was immensely impressed by Nana. He wrote, 'Nana was one of the most interesting Africans I ever met, a man of strong character and good manners.'

[48] C.O. 592/7, Annual Report, Central Provinces, 1909

[49] Supplement to S.N. Government Gazette No. 60, 19 Aug. 1902 Quarterly Report, Central Provinces, 31 March 1908

about the progress of Nana's town from the missionary point of view. Bishop Johnson had this to say to Nana:

> The chief is somewhat tall and spare and is evidently a man of will, purpose and courage. His very long imprisonment, isolation and comparative loneliness and the disappointment connected with these have not deprived him of these. He submits as a Christian to all the loss he has sustained and appears to care more now for the things of heaven than for those on earth.[50]

It was just as well for Nana to begin to dwell on things heavenly, for he had not very long to continue his sojourn here on earth.

Late in 1914, seven years after Bishop Johnson's visit, Nana became ill. He was taken to the Sapele General Hospital where Dr Adams, then in charge of the hospital, looked after him. He recovered from the illness and returned to Koko. But early in 1916 his health broke down again and this time he was admitted into the General Hospital, Warri, to which hospital the same Dr Adams had been transferred. Eight of his children accompanied him to Warri where they found accommodation in order to be near their ailing father. With them were some of Nana's wives. Nana responded once again to Dr Adams's treatment and was well enough to be discharged from hospital in May. Apparently, however, Nana's sturdy constitution had broken down, what with the tremendous activity of his life and the comparative gloom of twelve years in exile. Early in June he suffered a relapse from which he could not recover. He died in his 'palace' on 3 July 1916.[51]

Nana's death at the age of about sixty-four came as a shock not only to his family but also to many Itsekiri and Urhobo people who had thought that the celebrated ex-Governor had more years left to him. In life Nana was a great and respected man. In death he was accorded all the honour that his illustrious life deserved. Messages of condolence to the family came from the Government itself, from his great friend George W. Neville, from John Holt, and from the Liverpool Chamber of Commerce

---

[50] G. 3. A3/011 (C.M.S. Archives, London), Report (by Bishop Johnson) of Work in the Benin District

[51] C.S.O. 14/18 Telegram from Resident, Warri, to Secretary, Southern Provinces 4 July 1916

which at the instance of Neville had prayed the Colonial Office
to release Nana from exile in 1906. The town of Koko itself was
full of visitors mainly from Itsekiriland and Urhoboland who
had come to pay their last respects to Nana. Although at the
time there was no Olu in Itsekiriland, the royal family was
officially represented at Nana's burial by Prince Ikere, son of
Olu Akengbuwa I. The Ologbotsere family was also duly represented. Although Dogho himself could not rise above the feud between Numa and Olomu to pay his personal respects to one who
was at least a worthy foe, he nevertheless delegated some of his
closest relatives—Omatsola, Ikpogho and Dabo—to represent the
Numa family at the burial. Every part of Itsekiriland was ade-
quately represented. As for the Urhobo country, contingents of
mourners came from Abraka, Agbarho, Agbon, Ogharefe, Udu
and Evhro (Effurun), home town of Nana's mother. Nana was
buried in the 'palace' itself. The traditional funeral rites which
were performed in January 1917 lasted for nine full days and
provided an opportunity for the display of the colourful dances
for which the Itsekiri and Urhobo are noted. Today Nana's family
recalls with pride and satisfaction the great honour done to the
memory of their father on this occasion.[52] It was a fitting end to
the life of one of the most compelling personalities in Itsekiri and,
indeed, Nigerian history.

Nana was survived by a large number of wives and children.
Most of these children were born into circumstances very different from those which had conditioned the life of their father.
Neither in the economic nor political sphere could they hope to
have the same scope for action as their father had had. Living
as they did in 1916 in British Nigeria, they had to fashion their
lives along new paths. Many of these children had to leave Koko
to other parts of the country to earn their living. But even in the
changed circumstances the Nana family has continued to play a
notable role in the affairs of Itsekiriland. Mention might be made
of two of Nana's sons who have featured prominently in the
politics of Itsekiriland.

[52] I owe this account of Nana's illness, death and burial to his son,
Chief Newton Celleone Nana, to whom I am also indebted for the brief
sketch of the careers of Nana's children which follows.

Johnson, Nana's eldest son, who succeeded to the headship of the Nana house in 1916 was born in the 1870's. Johnson was very close to his father. In the crisis of 1894 he stayed with him till the last. He accompanied his father in the flight to Okotobo and the escape to Lagos. He went with his father to Old Calabar for the trial and accompanied him on exile to Accra. Educated while in the Gold Coast, he returned to Koko with Nana in 1906, and played his part in the task of resettlement. Like his father he became a government transport contractor. He owned a large rubber plantation which he worked with hired labour. In the native court system operating at the time, he was appointed a warrant chief and sat on the Sapele Native Court. In 1927 Johnson Nana was one of those reported to have spearheaded the anti-tax agitation in Itsekiriland.[53] Dogho then 'paramount chief' of Itsekiriland, was known to have given his consent to the introduction of taxation. Was Johnson Nana's opposition to direct taxation determined by Dogho's approval of it, and was this the old Numa–Olomu feud manifesting itself in new forms? That is a question which must remain open. The introduction of direct taxation was followed by the setting up of Native Administrations. In his new system Johnson became a member of the Itsekiri Council, a body which was the supreme Native Authority for Itsekiriland. At the time of his death in 1952, Johnson Nana was the President of the Koko Native Court. Johnson Nana left behind a reputation for courage and uprightness and was without question one of the most well known and popular figures in Itsekiriland in the forties of this century.

Johnson was succeeded by Newton Celleone Nana who is now well in his seventies. Like Johnson he was educated in the Gold Coast and returned with his father in 1906. Like Johnson he combined private business with public service. He owns a rubber plantation as well as an area of 'palm bush'. In 1924 he worked as a government road-building contractor in which capacity he undertook the building of a number of roads in Warri Township as well as the road which links Warri to Ovwia in Udu clan. In 1949 he was elected chairman of the Itsekiri Divisional Council on the death of the then Olu, Ginuwa I. He held that office until a new

[53] C.S.O. 26/2 File Vol. V Annual Report, Warri Province 1927

Olu was installed in 1950 whereupon he gave it up to the Olu but remained a member of the Divisional council. In the days before the commencement of party politics, Newton's appointment as chairman of Itsekiriland's supreme governing body must be seen as evidence of the popularity he enjoyed and the confidence reposed in him by the ruling class. Since 1950 Newton has continued to be prominent in Itsekiri politics, taking part in the strife and rivalry of party politics. A member of the N.C.N.C., he did enjoy a fair amount of party patronage. In 1961 under very different conditions from those of 1949, he became chairman of the Itsekiri Divisional Council once more. At the same time he was appointed President of the Grade C Customary Court at Koko and held that office until he retired from public life in 1965 for health reasons. In the recent split in the Itsekiri country which saw the deportation of the Olu Erejuwa II, Newton took sides with the anti-Olu faction to which faction belonged the influential and powerful late Chief Festus Okotie-Eboh, Minister of Finance in the Federal Cabinet of Nigeria's First Republic. Indeed having joined the Okotie-Eboh faction in securing the deposition and deportation of the Olu Erejuwa II, Newton was one of the four people appointed as Regents over Itsekiriland until the present Olu was installed late in 1965. It may be stretching the point to argue that in the 1960's the old feud between the 'royal line' and that of Ologbotsere was still on. But it certainly is interesting that Newton Nana was in the anti-Olu group. The military regime has since brought back Erejuwa II to his throne. The politically appointed Olu, who styled himself Akengbuwa II, has been removed by the same regime.

At the time of writing, Newton lives a quiet life in retirement running his private business. As landlord over the land of Koko at a time when it looks as if Koko is set on the road to economic prosperity, Newton is assured of a sufficient annual income from land rental to enable him to run the affairs of the Nana family. At the moment there is some anxiety about Nana's health since that illness in 1965 which forced him to retire from public life. But Newton can face death with the satisfaction that he has led a full life and played his part in the affairs of his country. The kind of life which both Johnson and Newton have lived has been different in many respects from their father's. Nevertheless they have held aloft the name of Nana before the Itsekiri people. Compelled to act within a much smaller compass they have ensured by their respective careers that the name Nana should never be forgotten in the annals of Itsekiriland. So the memory of the illustrious Governor of the River continues to be very much alive.

To return to Nana Olomu himself. He was without question a great man. This greatness did not derive only, or even mainly, from his struggle against the British, but rather from his personal achievements—the achievements which brought about the clash with the British. All who met him both before and after 1891 were impressed by his intelligence, energy and drive, and strength of character. These were the the attributes which enabled him to build up a trading empire of considerable extent and organisation. In the age in which Nana lived, it required great energy and skill to secure that monopoly which was to be his ruin. From all accounts a large number of slaves and free men worked for him. He might not have known them all, but they seemed to owe him such instinctive loyalty that some were even prepared to face death in his service.[54] The ability to call forth such loyalty is not given to every man. He was generally acknowledged to be the most powerful man in terms of armaments in the Niger Coast Protectorate and in perhaps the whole of West Africa.[55] Despite his great wealth and power, however, he is not remembered as having been overbearing or unduly cruel. On the contrary, despite his occasional excesses, the opinion of him that has survived is that of an upright man who stood for justice and good neighbourliness. Like Kosoko of Lagos, Jaja of Opobo and other leading Nigerians of the nineteenth century, Nana's life was an eloquent testimony to the capabilities of Africans for organisation in the political and commercial spheres at a time when Africans were still regarded by many people from Europe as virtually sub-human.

Nana was no less illustrious as typifying African resistance to

[54] See Chapter IV, p. 113
[55] See for example Alan Burns, *History of Nigeria*, p. 174 and F.O. 2/64, Moore to F.O. No. 28, 5 Oct. 1894

foreign rule. He ranks high among those who put up a stout resistance to British encroachments in this part of West Africa. His undoubted influence in Itsekiriland as well as part of the Urhobo country constituted a source of irritation and frustration to the British in their determination to penetrate into the hinterland and so to undermine the power and position of the middlemen. Constantly aware of his own position and influence he refused despite the British presence to abdicate what he conceived to be his rights and prerogatives. This attitude brought him into conflict with British imperial power and earned for him humiliation and exile. Far from derogating from his importance and reputation the humiliation and exile which he suffered have served to further enhance his prestige in the eyes of his countrymen and to win for him a worthy place in the history of his country.

Epilogue

THE DEPOSITION and deportation of Nana filled the British administration with sanguine hopes of a general improvement in the commercial prospects of the Benin River district. Moor wrote to the Foreign Office anticipating a 'considerable increase in trade and general prosperity'.[1] A later commentator argued that by the removal of 'this turbulent spirit immense benefits accrued to the trade of the district, the merchants being enabled to deal direct with the producers, who in their turn gained the advantage of receiving a fairer price for their palm oil'.[2] As a matter of fact these benefits did not immediately accrue. While the value of exports for the year from August 1893 to July 1894 was £110,411 16s., the value of exports for the year 1895 (January–December) was only £52,649.[3] This was no doubt because of the dislocation caused to trade as a result of the events of 1894. But the next two years showed only little progress. Indeed in 1897 there was a marked slackening of trade as a result of the Benin expedition of that year. Continued infiltration by the Royal Niger Company into certain parts of the Urhobo country also had an adverse effect on the trade of the Benin River district. When all that has been said, there remains the fact that the deportation of Nana had removed Itsekiriland's greatest trader. No comparable figure arose to take his place. The decline in trade must partly be attributed to Nana's fall from power.

Mockler-Ferryman's other claim that the British merchants were enabled, as a consequence of Nana's deportation, to trade directly with the producers deserves comment. As late as 1905 the administrative staff of this part of the Protectorate of Southern Nigeria still complained of the unwillingess of the British merchants to establish permanent depots in the hinter-

[1] F.O. 2/64 Moor to F.O. No. 28, 5 Oct. 1894
[2] Mockler-Ferryman, A. F. *British Nigeria* p. 100 London, 1902
[3] See Cal. Prov. 8/2 Vol. 1. Quarterly Reports on the Benin District for the year 1895 and 1896 and Cal. Prov. 8/2 Vol. II for similar reports for the year 1897

land. It was not till 1907 that the firm of John Holt began to
take steps to set up stations in the Urhobo hinterland; and it was
not till after 1914 that these steps began to yield any real divi-
dends. Other firms moved into the hinterland at an even later
date. The Niger Company's first inland depot was not established
till 1908. The African and Eastern Trading Corporation and, a
German firm, the Dekage Trading Company, did not join the
hinterland trade until the 1920's.[4] There was thus no immediate
rush into the hinterland as a consequence of Nana's deportation.
The middlemen traders continued to be utilised by the European
merchants, though as the hinterland was opened up so more and
more of the producers took their produce direct to the European
agents. But this was a development of the period after 1914.
There was good reason for the reluctance of the merchants to
move into the hinterland. In addition to the point already made
that it was cheaper to utilise the services of the middlemen, there
was also the fact that the merchants feared—whether justifiably
or not is immaterial—to penetrate the hinterland before government outposts were established there to safeguard their property.
In other words, economic penetration had to wait for the political
penetration of the hinterland; and the political penetration of this
part of Southern Nigeria was not accomplished until about 1914.[5]

A major factor responsible for the fall of Nana was the imperial
ambitions of the British. Nana was obnoxious to the British partly
because they thought he stood in the way of their penetration of
the hinterland and partly because he refused to yield his own
position and authority within his community. The fall of Nana
was therefore followed by a determined effort to establish British
authority in this part of Southern Nigeria. The Itsekiri offered no
further resistance after the fall of Nana—they were witnesses of
the deadly efficiency of the British Navy and British-trained and
British-led troops. At any rate the fact that Dogho, the leading
Itsekiri man after Nana's disgrace, was a British agent undermined whatever resistance the Itsekiri might have been inclined
to put up.

With the Urhobo and Kwale to the hinterland, however, the

[4] Ikime, *Itsekiri–Urhobo Relations* &c pp. 221–3 and 379–80
[5] Ikime, *Itsekiri–Urhobo Relations* &c

situation was very different. Away from the coast, where the navy could be easily called in, these peoples put up, what must have been to the British, an unexpected resistance. This resistance was not the less irritating because it was more passive than active. When the Vice-Consul, Gallwey, made his first exploratory trip to the hinterland, he reported how eagerly the Urhobo looked forward to being placed under British 'protection'.[6] When, however, the actual penetration got under way and the people began to realise what British 'protection' entailed, their attitude changed radically. The British political officers found that it was not enough to pay occasional visits to these people and to explain to them various aspects of British policy. Military and police patrols were necessary for the effective 'pacification' of the Urhobo and Kwale hinterland.[7] It was this 'pacification' and the establishment of British authority which eventually brought about changes in the conduct of the commercial relations between the hinterland producers and the coastal middlemen. In 1905, for instance, the old question of prices came up again. The Urhobo and Kwale complained that the Itsekiri to whom they sold their palm oil and kernels were not paying them a fair price. The reaction to such a situation in the era of Nana would have been for the Urhobo to hold back supplies in the hope of forcing up prices. In the new circumstances of the area being under British control, the Native Council of Sapele which had been established in 1901, met and fixed minimum prices for both oil and kernels. These prices were to be subject to monthly revisions to meet local and foreign price fluctuations.[8] New sanctions were being brought to bear on old issues.

In dealing with Nana the British had found it necessary to cloak the real motive for their actions with plausible excuses. There was no need to engage in similar subtleties with the Kwale and Urhobo. The reports of political officers who laboured in the hinterland were plainly different from those of Ralph Moor. After

[6] F.O. 84/2111, Gallwey's report on his 'visit to the Oil markets of the Sobo and Abraka districts'—enclosure in Macdonald to F.O. No. 30, 12 Dec. 1891

[7] Ikime *Itsekiri–Urhobo Relations* Chapter IV

[8] C.O. 520/31 Egerton to C.O. No. 258, 22 June 1905

a visit to the Ethiope, the District Commissioner at Sapele wrote in blunt terms to the effect that little 'permanent good' would result from visiting the country around Okpara, Ukhuokori and Orogun 'unless the officer visiting [was] . . . in a position to enforce his wishes if not carried out otherwise'.[9] An 1896 report complained that during the last quarter of that year, 'the chiefs of Sobo towns of Jeremy and Obodo . . . became too independent' and so had to be visited by a miliary patrol. As a result of the independent attitude of those towns, one of their chiefs was removed.[10] There were other instances when people described as 'chiefs' of their respective communities lost their position because it was held that they were by inclination anti-government. As Moor reported, some of the Urhobo were doubtless glad at the fall of Nana. They too were soon to witness the deportation, by the British, of their own people for refusing to preside over the dissolution of their inheritance.

The one area in Urhoboland where Nana found it extremely difficult to maintain constant friendly relations was that comprising the Abraka and Agbon clans. It was against these clans that his wars in Urhoboland were fought. In 1893 Gallwey complained of the disturbed situation of the Agbon clan[11] (Okpara and Eku) while the immediate prelude to the showdown of 1894 had to do with a stoppage of trade in the Abraka area. The British records tend to give the impression that the unsettled state of affairs in this area was entirely brought about by the escapades of Nana and his 'boys'. It was little realised that the Urhobo people concerned were extremely difficult to control until, having deported Nana, they themselves attempted to 'pacify' this area. Despite the fact that this area was the first to be visited by British officers, it was among the last to be brought under effective control. In 1904 a District Commissioner reported how this part of Urhoboland 'always resolutely pursued its own course' and retained 'its native habits and customs in spite of the many

[9] Cal. Prov. 10/3 Vol. III Report on visit to Okpara, Kokori and Owe, April 1902
[10] Cal. Prov. 8/2 Vol. I, Warri District, Quarterly Report for Quarter ending 31 Dec. 1896
[11] See p. 91 ff

warnings received at frequent intervals' from British political officers.[12] If the British, with the extra prestige conferred on them by their power and their recent success against Nana, found things difficult in this area, it is unlikely that Nana found things any easier.

One of the ostensible reasons for the offensive against Nana was that he engaged in the slave trade. Yet the British administration in the Niger Coast Protectorate (later Southern Nigeria) did not pass any law against the trade in slaves or the institution of slavery itself immediately after Nana's fall. In this situation there is no reason to believe that the Nigerian peoples did not continue to indulge in the trade, though as the British established their control over larger tracts of the country so it became increasingly difficult to engage profitably in the slave trade without running the risk of detection. It was not, in fact, until 1901 that the British legislated against the slave trade and slavery. That it took this long before slavery and the slave trade were abolished by law was a token of the realization by the British of the vital role slavery played in the economic and social life of the delta peoples. Although the legal status of slavery was abolished in 1901, there was still in practice a slave class in the delta states. The Native House Rule Proclamation (later Ordinance) of 1901 was, in some ways, an attempt to fill the void that was created by the formal abolition of slavery. But the ordinance was castigated as setting up a system which was 'very close to legalised slavery'. Protests against it came from the Aborigines Protection Society, missionaries, the Lagos Press and members of the British Parliament. Despite these protests the British administration in the Protectorate of Southern Nigeria remained for a long time unwilling to repeal the ordinance. Their unwillingness stemmed not from a blindness to the evils and abuses of the ordinance, but from an awareness of the utility of slaves or a similar class as an inexpensive labour corps which could be employed not only for trade purposes but also for such works of public utility as porterage, building of roads and bridges and the like. When in 1911 the various coastal people were consulted about abolishing the 'House' sys-

[12] C.O. 520/25, Political Report on the Kwale Expedition—enclosure in despatch No. 260, 3 June 1904

tem, the Itsekiri chiefs, led by Dogho, the man who had done so much to encompass the fall of Nana, protested against abolition 'before another seven or ten years'. Other coastal peoples sent in similar protests. Therefore in 1912 the ordinance was not repealed but amended to remove some of the abuses. It was not till 1914 that Lugard finally swept away the system.[13] It thus required two decades after the fall of Nana to solve the question of slave trade and slavery. If the British found it so difficult to do away with slavery in the circumstances of the time, one can readily understand how it was that in the age in which Nana lived he should have seen the need for slaves and have proceeded to acquire some through the accepted channels of the time.

There were two sides to the Nana episode—a British side and an Itsekiri side. Throughout this work attention has been drawn to the role played by the anti-Nana group among the Itsekiri. The leader of this anti-Nana group, Dogho, quickly rose on the ashes of Ebrohimi. He was appointed British Political Agent for the Benin River District in 1896, and gradually he extended his field of operations all over the Warri district as well. When after 1914 the Lugardian system of administration was extended to the south, it was Dogho who in 1917 was appointed Paramount chief of the Warri district—a district which at the time included not only the Itsekiri but the Urhobo, the Ijo, and the Kwale peoples.

The details of Dogho's career as Paramount chief cannot be fully discussed here, but a few observations may be made. Dogho grew to become easily the most powerful man in the then Warri (now Delta) Province. Not only was he Paramount chief; he was also President of the Benin River Native Court and President of the Warri Native Court of Appeal—a court which served all the peoples of the Warri (now Delta) Province. In his capacity as Paramount chief he was entitled to be consulted by the Resident of the Province about the appointment of members of the native courts in Itsekiri, Urhobo and Ijo lands. He thus acquired an influence over the local administration of most of Warri Province, an influence which he did not scruple to use for personal gain.

[13] For a full discussion of the subject of slavery and the House system, see Tamuno (Ph.D. Thesis pp. 326–41) to whose work I am indebted for this summary.

The kind of power and influence exercised by Dogho as a consequence of his multiple appointments was different from the power and influence for which Nana is remembered. Nana acquired his power and influence as a result of the labour and organisation and drive of the Olomu family. Dogho's position was largely dependent on the goodwill of the British. Nana's connections with the neighbouring peoples, like the Urhobo and Ijo, were mainly economic and social; Dogho's connections were largely political because the power he wielded was political power delegated to him by the British.

Dogho's position and authority did not go unquestioned. The other peoples of the province, notably the Urhobo, consistently protested against the 'arbitrary paramountcy' granted over them to Dogho. They protested over having to take their appeal cases to a court presided over by a stranger, in the person of Dogho, and made up of a majority of Itsekiri men. Even in Itsekiriland itself his position came in for bitter questioning. He was known to have appropriated to himself the subsidies, a compensation paid by the government to all those elders of the coastal principalities who used to receive a share of the traditional comey, which ought to have gone to other Itsekiri men. The descendants of the Olu Akengbuwa were incensed at the arrogation to himself of various royal prerogatives, notably that which had to do with the collection of rents on public lands. In the twenties various court actions were taken out against Dogho by these descendants. Dogho did not lose a single one of the suits taken out against him by the Itsekiri and the Urhobo. The courts upheld the prerogatives conferred by the British on their protegé. Even when the issue of the subsidies came before the Resident and ultimately the Governor, these officers did not see fit to put right what was clearly an irregularity. Dogho was allowed to go on receiving the subsidies due to other men on the grounds that he had been doing so for many years. In 1894 administrative officers seemed to have listened avidly to tales of Nana's misuse of his power and position. In the 1920's and 1930's the British administration shut their eyes to glaring instances of abuse of power by Dogho. Well they might. Nana was an African nationalist who refused to yield to British imperialist ambitions and so had to be broken. Dogho was a British lackey whose position and authority had to be upheld at all costs. Hence, despite mounting attacks against Dogho, the British failed to review his position till he was removed by death in 1932.[14]

For the Itsekiri people as a whole, the fall of Nana marked the end of an epoch. Until that time the Itsekiri had played a vital role as the middlemen of the trade between the hinterland producers and the European merchants at the coast. But with the fall of Nana, followed as it was by the British penetration of the hinterland, the Itsekiri gradually began to lose their position as middlemen traders, and to face the competition of the hinterland peoples in the commercial field. This development, which took place from the second decade of the present century onwards, posed new problems and led to a new relationship between the Itsekiri and the hinterland peoples.

[14] The Career of Chief Dogho is discussed in full by the present writer in 'Chief Dogho: The Lugardian System in Warri, 1917–1932' *J.H.S.N.* Vol. 3 No. 2, Dec. 1965 pp. 313–33

Agreement between Consul John Beecroft
and Diare ('Governor') and other Itsekiri Chiefs
4 April 1851*

At a conference held this day, the 4th of April 1851, on board Her
Majesty's Steamer 'Jackal', present John Beecroft Esqr Her Britannic
Majesty's consul for the Bights of Benin and Biafra, Lieut. Commander
Bedinfeld, Her Majesty's Steamer, 'Jackal', Lieutenant Lombard . . .
Mr. Pendlebery, Agent for Messrs Horsfall & Sons, W. Day, Harrison &
Co., W. Stowe, Reuben Hemminway Esqr, and Mr. Briden Demean
Bibb, Jerry of Jacqua, the chief duly elected, with Jubaffaa and the
principals of their town, Odessa of Yellow Town, Offalicoo of Fish Town
and Tomah of Ullibah, the following laws and regulations were made
and enacted.

Article 1st

That the Chief of the River Benin with the chiefs and people of the above
mentioned Towns, pledge themselves that no British subject from this
date shall be detained on shore or molested in any way under any
pretence whatever, and if they (the chiefs and people as above mentioned) do so they will incur the displeasure of Her Majesty, the Queen
of England, and be declared enemies of Great Britain, and on such a
complaint being made a Man of War will immediately come to Benin
River and protect British subjects and Property.

Article 2nd

That in case of any misunderstanding between the Resident Agents
Supercargoes and Masters of any of the vessels and the chief and people
of the River Benin all and every such Resident, Agent, Supercargoes and
Masters of the British Vessel shall be at full liberty to go on shore free of
molestation, and will with the chief and Gentlemen of the River Benin
peacefully settle any dispute between the Parties.

Article 3rd

That upon the arrival of any British merchant vessel off or in this River
for the purpose of trading therein, the Agent or Supercargoes of such
vessels shall upon the sending of five Pawns per register tonnage to the
Chief or person authorised to receive such custom, or comey, be allowed
the privilege of trading without further molestation, the comey or
custom to consist of a fair assortment of the goods usually brought out

* Taken from Cal. Prov. 5/7 Vol. 1

for Trade viz Guns, Powder, Cloth, Cowries, Rum, Tobacco, Salt, Beads, Caps, Knives, Iron Bars, Earthenware, etc.

Article 4th

The Comey or Custom, to be tendered on the ship's arrival, or as soon as convenient, and if not accepted by the Chief such vessel shall be at liberty to commence trade. This however does not exempt such ships from paying the usual custom or comey if subsequently demanded.

Article 5th

That if at any time any Agents or Supercargoes of any ship or vessel (after having paid or tendered the usual comey or customs for the Privileges of Trading) can prove that the trade of his ship has been stopped whether directly or indirectly upon any pretence whatever the Chief is to be held responsible for such stoppage and pay one Puncheon of Saleable Palm Oil per diem per 100 tons Register to said ship as compensation for the loss incurred, the said oil to be paid within 7 days, after such stoppage shall have been made and continue to pay the same as long as the trade of any such ship is stopped.

Article 6th

That after the custom or comey has been paid, or tendered, to the Chief every Trader shall be allowed to trade in his own name, and neither the Chief or any other trader is entitled to exact other customs, comey or pay whatever.

Article 7th

That the Chief shall not, nor shall he permit any of his principals or chiefs or rather Tribes of the different towns or villages to demand or enforce any trust from any of the Resident Agents or Supercargoes of any ship or ships upon any pretence whatever.

Article 8th

Whereas several boats have been plundered, and lives sacrificed, it is deemed just and right, that all such aggressions, and depredations, committed upon British Subjects and Property crossing the Bar or otherwise within the limits of the Chief of the River Benin dominions shall be satisfactorily adjusted by the said Chief.

Article 9th

And further be it enacted that any breach of any article of this Treaty shall be punished by the party or parties being guilty of the same, paying ten puncheons of saleable Palm Oil.

Article 10th

Should any person take any trust from any Resident Agent or Supercargo of any vessel and be unable to pay his debts his house and property to be forfeited and sold by orders of the Chief of the River Benin. The proceeds of the sale to go to the liquidation of the debt and that he be no longer allowed to trade. The Agent or Supercargo of any vessel trading with him after his name has been published by the Crier to be liable to the penalty of Five Puncheons of Palm Oil. After the debtor has paid his debt he shall again be allowed to trade.

Given under our hands on board HM Steamer 'Jackal' River Benin 4th day of April, 1851.

(Signed) John Beecroft, Her Britannic Majesty's
Consul of Bights of Benin & Biafra

Lt. Commander Bedinfeld, HM Steamer 'Jackal'
Mr Pendlebery, Agent for Messrs Horsfalls & Sons

[There followed the marks of:
Jerry Idiare, Moodawaa, Jubuffaa (Idibofun), Ane, Alluma (Olomu), Adeliwa, Abomay, Odessa, Bogie, Obeadee, Ephia, Allya, Ogre, Chichee, Achelo, Juatao, Amma, Nunezwaree, Abasshamunee, Amatiama, Abejokoo, Fomma, Geggie, Affaliwo, Tomah, Captain Black, Datchee, Epioha, Margoogamee, Munaawaree, Unao, Liverpool, Ogoriee, Mahamaa.]

APPENDIX II

*Treaty with Chiefs of Itsekiriland, 1884**

Her Majesty the Queen of the United Kingdom of Great Britain and Ireland, Empress of India, &c., and the Chiefs of Jakri being desirous of maintaining and strengthening the relations of peace and friendship which have for so long existed between them;

* F.O. 93/6/10

Her Britannic Majesty has named and appointed E. H. Hewett, Esq., Her Consul for the Bights of Benin and Biafra, to conclude a Treaty for this purpose.

The said E. H. Hewett, Esq. and the said Chiefs of Jakri have agreed upon and concluded the following Articles:—

Article I

Her Majesty the Queen of Great Britain and Ireland, &C, in compliance with the request of the Chiefs, and people of Jakri, hereby undertakes to extend to them, and to the territory under their authority and jurisdiction, Her gracious favour and protection.

Article II

The Chiefs of Jakri agree and promise to refrain from entering into any correspondence, Agreement, or Treaty with any foreign nation or Power, except with the knowledge and sanction of Her Britannic Majesty's Government.

Article III

It is agreed that full and exclusive jurisdiction, civil and criminal, over British subjects and their property in the territory of Jakri is reserved to Her Britannic Majesty, to be exercised by such Consular or other officers as Her Majesty shall appoint for that purpose.

The same jurisdiction is likewise reserved to Her Majesty in the said territory of Jakri over foreign subjects enjoying British protection, who shall be deemed to be included in the expression 'British Subject' throughout this Treaty.

Article IV

All disputes between the Chiefs of Jakri, or between them and British or foreign traders, or between the aforesaid Kings and Chiefs and neighbouring tribes, which cannot be settled amicably between the two parties, shall be submitted to the British Consular or other officers appointed by Her Britannic Majesty to exercise jurisdiction in Jakri territories for arbitration and decision, or for arrangement.

Article V

The Chiefs of Jakri hereby engage to assist the British Consular or other officers in the execution of such duties as may be assigned to them; and, further, to act upon their advice in matters relating to the administration of justice, the development of the resources of the country, the interests of commerce, or in any other matter in relation to peace, order, and good government, and the general progress of civilization.

Article VI

The subjects and citizens of all countries may freely carry on trade in every part of the territories of the Kings and Chiefs parties hereto, and may have houses and factories therein.

Article VII

All ministers of the Christian religion shall be permitted to reside and exercise their calling within the territories of the aforesaid Kings and Chiefs, who hereby guarantee to them full protection.

All forms of religious worship and religious ordinances may be exercised within the territories of the aforesaid Kings and Chiefs, and no hindrance shall be offered thereto.

Article VIII

If any vessels should be wrecked within the Jakri territories, the Chiefs will give them all the assistance in their power, will secure them from plunder, and also recover and deliver to the owners or agents all the property which can be saved.

If there are no such owners or agents on the spot, then the said property shall be delivered to the British Consular or other officer.

The Chiefs further engage to do all in their power to protect the persons and property of the officers, crew, and others on board such wrecked vessels.

All claims for salvage dues in such cases shall, if disputed, be referred to the British Consular or other officer for arbitration and decision.

Article IX

This Treaty shall come into operation, so far as may be practicable, from the date of its signature, except as regards Articles VI and VII which are to be left for negotiation on a future occasion.

Done in duplicate on board H.B.M.S. 'Flirt' anchored in Benin River this sixteenth day of July, 1884.

(Signed) Edward Hyde Hewett.

[There followed the marks of:
Nana (Governor), Chanomie (Tsanomi), Dudu, Numa, Ogree, Fragonie, Nafomie, Etchie, Mudwa, Brigby, Awalla, Peggy.]

Witness to above signatures:

(Signed) Theo. Hilliard
Chairman of Court of Equity.

*General Memorandum on the Ebrohimi War**

The Admiral will, acting with the Consul-General, exercise general supervision and direction of the movements.

2. *Right Attack:* Captain Powell will, on landing, immediately advance to the end of the road, and from there endeavour to get in the rear of the guns, and then make this way to the solid ground about Nana's house.

3. The Admiral and his staff will be with the column along the road.

4. *Left and Centre Attack:* Captain Campbell will establish his guns, and c., in the best position for harassing the enemy, but will not open fire unless they do, or in compliance with orders. He is to be prepared to advance up the main creek as opportunity offers. If possible, definite orders for him to advance will be sent, but in default of these he must act to the best of his judgment.

5. The stockade is the base, and the wounded are to be sent there. A reserve of water, and ammunition will be stored there.

6. As soon as the creek is open all communications between the two bodies to be by it.

7. The greatest caution is to be exercised when the town is gained to avoid casualties by explosion of small stores of powder which may be scattered about.

8. Any spirits found lying about to be immediately destroyed. Sentries to be placed on any store-houses.

9. The men are to be kept carefully in hand, and houses, &c., are not to be set on fire except by order.

The landing will be effected by 5.30 a.m. at the stockade.

The Niger Coast Protectorate troops and cutters to land outside the stockade below creek.

Right Attack: Force to advance along the road in the following order: Skirmishers:

50 Niger Coast Protectorate troops . .) Captain Evanson
17 ditto, with Maxim gun . . . .) and Mr. Roupell
40 road cutters . . . . Mr. Leckie and Mr. Campbell
Rocket party . . . . . Lieutenant Heugh and Sub. Lieutenant Harvey.
18 men, Maxim gun Mr Staddon, gunner, Her Majesty's ship, 'Phoebe'.
37 marines . . . . . . Sergeant of 'Phoebe' in charge.
'Philomel' . . . . 2 N.C.O.'s and 14 privates
'Phoebe' . . . . 2 N.C.O.'s, 14 privates, and 1 bugler
'Widgeon' . . . . 1 N.C.O. and 5 privates.

* F.O. 2/64, Enclosure 1 in Moor to F.O. No. 28, 5 Oct. 1894

50 seamen 'Phoebe' Lieutenant Hickley and Lieutenant Parks.
Ambulance . . . . . . Lieutenant-Surgeon Brown and
         Dr Roth, Niger Coast Protectorate.
35 Seamen 'Widgeon' Lieutenant Grant-Dalton and
         Mr Herlihy, gunner, 'Widgeon'
To remain at bend of the road until ordered to advance.
Left and Centre Attack: Landing party from 'Philomel', with
Maxim gun . . . . . . Lieutenant Gore Browne
         Lieutenant Clarke
7-pr. gun . . . . Sub-Lieutenant Tomlin
3-pr. gun . . . . Gunner Jennings
Rockets . . . . Boatswain Tubb
Explosive party . . . . Surgeon Maitland
         Engineer Richardson will establish
themselves in the stockade and advance when possible.

Lieutenant Marston, of 'Widgeon,' assisted by Mr Atkins, Assistant Engineer, 'Philomel,' to be in charge of base at stockade under the orders of Captain Campbell, fifty carriers will be available to forward reserve stores to front.

The Surgeons of 'Widgeon' and 'Alecto' will remain to receive wounded at the stockade.

Staff Commander Maclean will be in charge of ships and will be responsible for the firing.

The men are to wear blue and hats; they are to take one day's provisions and 100 rounds of ammunition.

Portable bridges for crossing small creeks to be provided by 'Phoebe.'

Distinguishing signals: 'Philomel', three G's before and after bugle calls. 'Widgeon', two G's before and after bugle calls.

Details of arrangements to be made by officers in command of columns.

     (Signed) FRED. G. D. BEDFORD
       Rear-Admiral, Commander-in-Chief
'Philomel', at Benin, September 24, 1894
The respective captains and Officers
commanding Her Majesty's ships, &c., Benin River

APPENDIX IV

List of Munitions of War captured on the fall of Ebrohimi*

Arms

1. 106 cannon, from 3-prs to 32-prs.
2. 445 heavy swivel blunder-busses, about half of them brass.
3. 640 long Dane guns.
4. 1,151 short flint-lock and cap guns.
5. 17 cases of short swords.
6. 5 large swivel mountings for small cannon.
7. 10 Revolvers, various calibres.

Ammunition

1. 1,640 kegs of powder, over 14 tons.
2. 500 zinc cylinder case-shot, filled.
3. 500 bamboos cylinder case-shot, filled.
4. 1,000 or more, bamboo cylinders, ready for fillings, of all calibres, to suit the cannon.
5. 14 kegs small round shot.
6. 540-gallon iron pots of balls of various sizes.
7. 2 cases Snider ammunition, about 1,600 rounds.
8. 5 cases machine gun ammunition, containing 36 feeders filled ready with 43 rounds in each—1,548 rounds.
9. 1 case, containing 5 empty feeders for machine-gun.
10. 2,500 rounds solid-drawn machine-gun- ammunition.
11. 300 rounds Eley revolver cartridges, various calibres.

Captured since overleaf list was made.
1. 1 machine gun.
2. 78 kegs gunpowder, about 2/3 ton.

Author's note:
  Specimens of items 2, 3, 4, and 6 under 'Ammunition' were sent to the British Foreign Office.

---

* F.O. 2/64, Enclosure 3 in Moor to F.O. No. 28, 5 Oct., 1894

APPENDIX V (a)

*Exhibit I at Nana's Trial**

H.B.M's Vice Consulate
Benin.
9th August, 1892.

Sir,

The Warri Vice-Consul has written to tell me that many of the smaller Native traders tell him that they are still frightened to trade at Warri because no proper message has come up to Warri yet from you and some of the other Benin chiefs. I am very surprised at this for *you* promised Captain Gallwey you would send up a proper message and tell them that *any man* can trade at any place he likes with his own money.

I want to know if you have kept your promise—*truly*—and if so *why* the Africans are afraid to trade at Warri and Sapele.

I want your answer tomorrow morning so I can send back answer to Warri consul tomorrow afternoon and so that he and I can write good accounts to Consul-General.

(Signed) H. Haly Hutton
Acting Vice-Consul, Benin River.

Chief Nana,
    Brohimie.

APPENDIX V(b)

*Exhibit J at Nana's Trial**

H.B.M.'s Vice Consulate
Benin.
1st December, 1893.

Chief Nana,

I was up at Okpara last week and am very dissatisfied with the state of affairs up there—and you will have to give me a very clear explanation of your conduct or abide the consequences.

You have *pretended* to be a friend of the Government before my face, *whereas behind my back* you do all you can to go against the government and put the Sobos against it.

---

* F.O. 2/64, Exhibits at Nana's trial

P

Your boys spend their time in spreading lies about the Government —and I only wish to catch one man doing so and I will make a lasting example of him for the benefit of you, your boys and your Sobo friends.

Your Headman Eddu (at Okpara) refused to come and see me on my launch—saying you would be angry if you knew of your boys speaking to the consul.

I sent for him 3 times. There was no palaver—I told him so, and I simply wanted to show him I took an interest in the markets. Ubari Mude's brother would not allow his people to sell me fowls: saying he and the consul didn't agree; and that Nana was his master.

You ought to be very proud having such brave and big men on your side as Mude and Ubari. *I* look upon them as small boys, and will treat them so when the time comes.

Had my soldiers been with me I would have made prisoners of Ubari and Eddu—and probably burnt Ubari's houses.

As it is I may find it necessary to always keep soldiers at Okpara— unless a very great change comes.

You are a fine example of a loyal chief drawing £200 a year from the Government because you are 'true'.

You will either remove Eddu and Ubari from Okpara or punish them. If not I must do so when my soldiers arrive.

I am going to report the matter very strongly to the Consul-General. In the meantime I will stop your subsidy.

I have always been your friend and reported very well on you to Sir Claude Macdonald and even paid you the subsidy which Mr Hutton had cut. I now see that probably Mr. Hutton was quite right in stopping the money and I was wrong to believe you and pay it. However, before taking further action, I want your explanation. If you wish to try your strength against the Government, *well and good*. I will know exactly what to do in that case.

I fully believe you are injuring trade to the best of your ability and should I find you out you must expect full punishment and you cannot say I have not warned you in time.

Your underhand dealing has disgusted me.

(Signed) H. L. Gallwey.

P.S.

I have seen Mr. Harrison, and he is of the same opinion as I am that you are damaging trade both *here* and at *Warri*.

If I am right in my surmise, things must go very badly with you. If you are not loyal (true) yourself you have no right to injure other people by putting them against the Government, as they must suffer when the time comes.

(Initialled) H. L. G.

Chief Nana.

Nana's Trial: Comments by Foreign Office Officials

'This makes a long story, which it is perhaps unnecessary to print unless questions are asked.'

*

'I should think it is not now probable that questions will be asked.'

'These people were tried in our Consular Court and under the provisions of the Africa Order in Council and they can only be punished in such manner as is by that Order in Council provided so far of course as this trial is concerned.'

'Nana's chief offence appears to have been an offence against article 48 of the O in C for which he was liable on conviction to be imprisoned for any term not exceeding two years with or without hard labour and with or without further proceedings make him liable to deportation.'

But I think such deportation means deportation under Art. 102 of the Order in Council which provides that

(1) Where a person is convicted before a court of *any* crime or offence the court may in addition to or in lieu of any other sentence order him to give security to the satisfaction of the court . . . for future good behaviour *and in default* of such security, may order him to be deported.

The calling on him to find security is not a further proceeding (Art. 48) and though the conviction of itself makes him liable to deportation it is only to such deportation as is contemplated by the Order in Council (Art. 102) viz. deportation on failure to find security for good behaviour.

Had any other deportation been meant I think Art. 48 would have said so in terms.

Though I think this is the better interpretation—the matter is certainly arguable the other way viz that the deportation specified in Art. 48 is a special kind of deportation not subject to the condition precedent of a failure to find sufficient security, when called upon, of good behaviour as specified in Part XIII of the Order which deals with the subject of 'Deportation and Removal' (See Articles 102 & 103).

On the whole though I do not personally agree with the latter view and think that the former view which I have indicated would probably be upheld were the matter to come before the Privy Council.

I should be inclined from the practical standpoint to let things slide and to take no official notice of the despatch.

(Initialled) WEW
18/6/95.

*

A Sierra Leone Lawyer, who belongs to a class found everywhere on the Coast, might raise the point but we may wait till he does.

(Initialled) HPA (?)

June 19/95

*

I agree.

(Initialled) K.

*

[*Author's Note:* The comments quoted above can be found as Foreign Office minutes in F.O. 2/64, Macdonald to F.O. No. 49 13 Dec.1894. The proceedings of Nana's trial were enclosed with the despatch.]

APPENDIX VII

*Nana's Last Petition**

Christiansborg, Accra,

Gold Coast Colony,

West Africa,

2nd April, 1906.

The humble petition of Nana, Ex chief of Benin River West Coast Africa showeth:

1. That your Lordship's petitioner encloses here in two petitions marked A & B respectively forwarded in years past, which in my humble opinion may suffice Your Lordship in a way after perusal as touching the grounds of my deportation to this country and other parts for the past twelve years.

2. That Your Lordship's petitioner does not intend to say a word on the subject matter but simply to convey to Your Lordship his solemn and utmost regret of the matter in question.

3. That Your Lordship's petitioner thinks it necessary to place once more the whole circumstances before Your Lordship as embodied in the petitions marked as above but not waste your valuable moments.

4. That Your Lordship's petitioner doth cry with sincerity of heart, and crave through Your Lordship for pardon, and forgiveness from His

---

* C.S.O. 12/25, File 197/06

most Excellent Majesty King Edward VII of the United Kingdom of Britain and Ireland.

5. That Your Lordship's petitioner repents of the evil which brought about his present misfortune, and therefore begs most reverently and most sincerely to be pardoned and forgiven as you have hitherto done for others who repented of their evils.

6. That Your Lordship's petitioner sees and even words fail him to be able to express his ignorance and folly of the wrongs already committed and repents of them even now and therefore begs to be forgiven which is divine and casting all his faults away whatever they may be, and as in duty bound Your Lordship's petitioner will ever pray.

To The Right Honourable
The Secretary of State for the Colonies.

A Note on the Sources

As indicated in the preface, I have made use of material collected in the
field. It is scarcely necessary here to emphasise the importance of this
kind of material, whose value is increasingly being recognised. Chapter
II of this work gives some indication of how useful oral evidence can be.

Apart from oral evidence most of the material for this work has come
from administrative records. I have used both the Public Records Office,
London, and the Nigerian National Archives, Ibadan. The sources are
therefore shown under these two heads.

PUBLIC RECORDS OFFICE LONDON

F.O. 84. *Slave Trade:* This class of documents consists of despatches
from the British Consuls to the Foreign Office and constitutes an important source of information for this study. The footnotes indicate
which particular volumes have been consulted.

F.O. 2. *Africa Consular:* Like the previous class, this one, which
begins with the appointment of consuls for the Bights of Benin and
Biafra, has useful information. Volume 64 is largely devoted to the
affairs of Nana as is evident from the footnotes in chapters II–VI.

Other Public Record Office material consulted was F.O. 93/6/10
(Treaties) and F.O. 403 volumes 31, 76, 171, 178 and 216. The F.O. 403
series are printed papers embodying some of the material in the F.O. 84
and F.O. 2 series.

NIGERIAN NATIONAL ARCHIVES, IBADAN

Cal. Prov. Papers: These are records of the Oil Rivers and later Niger
Coast Protectorate and contain some material which can be found in the
F.O. 84 and F.O. 2 series at the Public Records Office. The particular
papers used in this study include Cal. Prov. 2/2 vol. 5; Cal. Prov. 5/7
vol. I; Cal. Prov. 6/1 vols. III and IV; Cal. Prov. 8/2 vol. I and Cal.
Prov. 9/2 vol. II.

C.S.O. Papers: These papers have been collected from what used to be
office of the Chief Secretary to the Government Nigeria. Only a few
volumes have been consulted for the purpose of this work: C.S.O. 7/13
vol. 4; C.S.O. 12/25 and C.S.O. 14/18.

The Jaja papers (Jaja 1/3 and Jaja 3) have been consulted for purposes
of comparison between Nana and Jaja.

SECONDARY SOURCES

The books listed below do not deal specially with Nana. They are mostly
books on Nigerian history which discuss Nana in a few pages or para-
graphs. A few of the books, like Flint and Hodges, have been included

because they discuss aspects of British policy which are relevant to this study.

ADAMS, CAPTAIN JOHN   *Remarks on the Country Extending from Cape Palmas to the Congo* London 1823

ANENE, J. C.   *Southern Nigeria in Transition, 1885–1906* Cambridge University Press 1966

BINDLOSS, H.   *In the Niger Country* Edinburgh 1898

BURNS, A. C.   *Colonial Civil Servant* London 1949
History of Nigeria London 1955

CROWDER, M.   *The Story of Nigeria* London 1962

DIKE, K. O.   *Trade and Politics in the Niger Delta* London 1956

FLINT, J. E.   *Sir George Goldie and the Making of Nigeria* London 1960

GEARY, W. N. M.   *Nigeria Under British Rule* London 1927

HODGES, F. E.   *Consular Jurisdiction in Her Majesty's Protectorate of the Niger Coast* Stevens & Sons 1895

JOHNSTON, SIR H.   *The Story of My Life* New York 1923

MOCKLER-FERRYMAN, A. F.   *British Nigeria* London 1902
Up the Niger London 1892

MOORE, W.   *History of Itsekiri* Stockwell 1936

OMONEUKARIN, C. O.   *Itsekiri Law and Custom* Lagos 1942

PERHAM, M. & MARY BULL   *The Diaries of Lord Lugard* Vol. IV London 1963

PINNOCK, J.   *Benin: Concerning the country, Inhabitants and Trade* Liverpool 1897

UNPUBLISHED THESES

IKIME, O.   *Itsekiri–Urhobo Relations and the Establishment of British Rule, 1884–1936* Ph.D. Ibadan 1965

TAMUNO, S. M. (now T. N.)   *The Development of British Administrative Control of Southern Nigeria, 1900–1912* Ph.D. London 1962

ARTICLES

HICKLEY, LIEUT. J. D.   'An Account of the operations on the Benin River in August and September, 1894' *Royal United Services Institution Journal* Vol. 39

LLOYD, P. C.   'The Itsekiri in the Nineteenth Century' *Journal of African History* Vol. IV No. 2 1963
'Nana Olomu, Governor of the River' *West Africa* 29 June 1957

NEVILLE, G. W.   'Nana Oloma of Benin' *Journal of the Royal African Society* Vol. XIV 1915

TAMUNO, T. N.   'Some Aspects of Nigerian Reaction To The Imposition of British Rule' *Journal of the Historical Society of Nigeria* Vol. III No. 2 1965

NEWSPAPERS

Journal of Commerce Liverpool 20 & 21 August 1894
Lagos Weekly Record (8 September 1894)
          3 November 1894
          16 February 1895
          7 April 1906
          21 July 1906
Liverpool Review 1 January 1887

Index

Abejioye, Olu, 27, 27n.
Aborigines Protection Society, 168, 191
Abraka, district, 29, 32, 43, 44, 90, 97, 100, 129, 148, 150, 158, 182, 190; — people, 31, 40–2, 47, 90, 98, 190
Accra, 170, 175, 183
Adams, J., *Remarks on the country extending from Cape Palmas to the Congo*, London, 1823, 4
Aderibigbe, A. B., 'The Ijebu Expedition, 1892', *Historians in Tropical Africa*, Salisbury, 1962, 131, 132n.
Africa Order in Council, 1893, 161, 162, 163
African and Eastern Trading Company, 188
African Association, 65
Agbarho clan, 29, 34, 42, 177, 182
Agbemeta, 42
Agbon clan, 29, 177, 182, 190
Agreements and Treaties, vii, 18, 19, 23, 62, 63, 69, 197–9
Akassa area, 60–1, 168
Akengbuwa I, Olu, 8–9, 10, 12, 13, 33, 34, 35, 36, 182, 193
Akengbuwa II, Olu, 184
Akiabodo, 80
Aladja, 74, 177
Alecto, H.M.S., 103, 104, 107, 112, 123, 132, 149
'America', 174, 175, 176, 180
Amukpe, 32
Anene, J. C. *Southern Nigeria in*

Transition Cambridge, 1966, 6, 34n
Aro Expedition, 74
Aruea, 95
Asantehene, 132–3
Ashanti, 132; — Expedition, 1896, 133
Asorokun, 27

Baba, 48
Bai Bureh, 132
balance of trade, Itsekiri, 58, 59
Batere, 12, 13, 36
Bedford, Rear-Admiral, F. G., 121–3
Beecroft, John, 14–18 *passim*, 28, 195–7
Benin, City Territories, 19, 178; — district, 20, 28, 55, 59, 60, 61, 72, 73, 78–80, 84–6, 95, 105, 106, 108, 109, 120, 121, 127, 133, 135, 151, 153, 159, 162, 167, 171, 187, 192; — Expedition, 1897, 187; — River, 1, 2, 12–15 *passim*, 21–2, 23, 24, 27, 31, 36, 37, 41, 65, 73, 76, 78, 81, 84, 94, 97, 98, 101, 104, 112, 116, 121, 130, 144, 145, 166; — River Native Court 192. *See* Oba of Benin
Berlin West African Conference, 1885, 65
Bindloss H., *In the Niger Country*, Edinburgh, 1898, 44, 59n., 85, 110
Bini, 1, 9, 173, 178
Bizani, 139, 154–5, 159, 160

211